'Dr Diesen's book is a rare specimen of intelle[...] also very well researched and a pleasure to re[...] ideologized subject, the author is able to stay analytical. One of the best works in political philosophy written in recent years. A must-read for those trying to understand where the world is moving.' – *Sergei A. Karaganov – Higher School of Economics, Moscow*

'In this exciting and original work, Diesen challenges much of the accepted thinking about global order and the dynamics of international politics today. Diesen provides a powerful critique of post-Cold War liberalism and explains how the rise of populism challenges dominant discourses. In this battle Russia appears to side with the insurgency, but the depth of Russia's commitment to global change is unclear. This book is essential reading in helping us understand the vital issues in this debate.' – *Richard Sakwa - University of Kent*

'The two main questions of our time are whether the liberal West survives and whether it learns to coexist with Russia. In this timely book, Glenn Diesen analyzes the West's ability to recover from the rise of populism and offers a sharp critique of the Western tendency to scapegoat Russia.' – *Andrei P. Tsygankov, San Francisco State University*

'Diesen's *The Decay of Western Civilization* is civilizational analysis on the scale of Spengler or Sorokin. One need not accept Diesen's thesis of decline to appreciate the grandeur of his vision.' – *Salvatore Babones, University of Sydney*

'A very unorthodox, controversial and thought-provoking book. A valuable source helping to understand complex dynamics of political and economic megatrends in the modern world.' – *Andrey Kortunov, Director General of the Russian International Affairs Council*

'In the 20th century, Russia was the model society for the world's communists, but for centuries before that, Russia was the go-to country for Europe's radical conservatives. We are now coming full circle. Diesen's book is of key interest as perhaps the best example of this to date.' – *Iver B. Neumann, Norwegian Institute of International Affairs*

The Decay of Western Civilisation and Resurgence of Russia

What explains the rise of populist movements across the West and their affinity towards Russia? UKIP's Brexit victory, Trump's triumph, and the successive elections and referendums in Europe were united by a repudiation of the liberal international order. These new political forces envision the struggle to reproduce and advance Western civilisation to be fought along a patriotism–cosmopolitanism or nationalism–globalism battlefield, in which Russia becomes a partner rather than an adversary. Armed with neomodernism and geoeconomics, Russia has inadvertently taken on a central role in the decay of Western civilisation.

This book explores the cooperation and competition between Western and Russian civilisation and the rise of anti-establishment political forces both contesting the international liberal order and expressing the desire for closer relations with Russia. Diesen proposes that Western civilisation has reached a critical juncture as modern society (gesellschaft) has overwhelmed and exhausted the traditional community (gemeinschaft) and shows the causes for the decay of Western civilisation and the subsequent impact on cooperation and conflict with Russia. The author also considers whether Russia's international conservativism is authentic and can negate the West's decadence, or if it is merely a shrewd strategy by a rival civilisation also in decay.

This volume will be of interest to scholars of international relations, political science, security studies, international political economy, and Russian studies.

Dr Glenn Diesen is Visiting Scholar at the Higher School of Economics in Moscow and Adjunct Research Fellow at Western Sydney University. Dr Diesen specialises in Russia's approach to European and Eurasian integration, and the dynamics between the two. This includes central topics such as ideology, energy and geoeconomics. He is the author of *EU and NATO Relations with Russia* (Routledge, 2015) and *Russia's Geoeconomic Strategy for a Greater Eurasia* (Routledge, 2017).

Rethinking Asia and International Relations
Series Editor – Emilian Kavalski,
Li Dak Sum Chair Professor in China–Eurasia Relations and
International Studies, University of Nottingham, Ningbo, China

This series seeks to provide thoughtful consideration both of the growing prominence of Asian actors on the global stage and the changes in the study and practice of world affairs that they provoke. It intends to offer a comprehensive parallel assessment of the full spectrum of Asian states, organisations, and regions and their impact on the dynamics of global politics.

The series seeks to encourage conversation on:

- what rules, norms, and strategic cultures are likely to dominate international life in the 'Asian Century';
- how will global problems be reframed and addressed by a 'rising Asia';
- which institutions, actors, and states are likely to provide leadership during such 'shifts to the East';
- whether there is something distinctly 'Asian' about the emerging patterns of global politics.

Such comprehensive engagement not only aims to offer a critical assessment of the actual and prospective roles of Asian actors, but also seeks to rethink the concepts, practices, and frameworks of analysis of world politics.

This series invites proposals for interdisciplinary research monographs undertaking comparative studies of Asian actors and their impact on the current patterns and likely future trajectories of international relations. Furthermore, it offers a platform for pioneering explorations of the ongoing transformations in global politics as a result of Asia's increasing centrality to the patterns and practices of world affairs.

For more information about this series, please visit: https://www.routledge.com/Rethinking-Asia-and-International-Relations/book-series/ASHSER1384

Recent titles

The Decay of Western Civilisation and Resurgence of Russia
Between Gemeinschaft and Gesellschaft
Glenn Diesen

External Powers and the Gulf Monarchies
Edited by Li-Chen Sim and Jonathan Fulton

China's Relations with the Gulf Monarchies
Jonathan Fulton

The Decay of Western Civilisation and Resurgence of Russia

Between Gemeinschaft and Gesellschaft

Glenn Diesen

gdiesen@gmail.com
g.diesen@hse.ru
Prof. Higher School of Economics

Routledge
Taylor & Francis Group

LONDON AND NEW YORK

First published 2019
by Routledge
2 Park Square, Milton Park, Abingdon, Oxon OX14 4RN

and by Routledge
52 Vanderbilt Avenue, New York, NY 10017

First issued in paperback 2020

Routledge is an imprint of the Taylor & Francis Group, an informa business

British Library Cataloguing-in-Publication Data
A catalogue record for this book is available from the British Library

Library of Congress Cataloging-in-Publication Data
Names: Diesen, Glenn, author.
Title: The decay of western civilisation & resurgence of Russia : between Gemeinschaft and Gesellschaft / Glenn Diesen.
Description: Abingdon, Oxon ; New York, NY : Routledge, 2018. | Series: Rethinking asia and international relations | Includes bibliographical references and index.
Identifiers: LCCN 2018006461| ISBN 9781138500327 (hardback) | ISBN 9781351012638 (e-book)
Subjects: LCSH: Western countries—Foreign relations—Russia (Federation) | Russia (Federation)—Foreign relations—Western countries. | Political culture—Western countries. | Civilization, Western. | LIberalism. | Populism.
Classification: LCC D2025.5.R8 D54 2018 | DDC 327.470182/1—dc23LC record available at https://lccn.loc.gov/2018006461

ISBN 13: 978-0-367-58738-3 (pbk)
ISBN 13: 978-1-138-50032-7 (hbk)

Typeset in Times New Roman
by RefineCatch Limited, Bungay, Suffolk

To my wife Elena, and our children – Konstantin, Andre, and Maria

Man, to the degree that he tries to shape his behaviour to the requirements of civilisation, is unquestionably a cracked vessel. His nature is the scene of a never-ending and never quite resolvable conflict between two very profound impulses.

George Kennan (1993: 17)

Contents

Introduction

In recent times, almost all elections and referendums in the West have become a vote on preserving liberalism. Following Brexit and the triumph of Trump, the elections in Netherlands, France, Austria, Germany, Czech Republic, and across the continent became unprecedented challenges to the so-called international liberal order that Western civilisation is purportedly built upon. The potential impact is profound as liberalism has become the foundation for internal cohesion in a shared Western civilisation, and the external demarcation by excluding Russia and subsequently perpetuating the ideological binary divide of the Cold War. While the political establishment and media across the West oppose the new movements by attempting to limit the scope of acceptable political opposition, their efforts can at best only postpone the new trend by combatting the symptoms rather than the disease. It is the internal contradictions within liberal democracy and laissez-faire capitalism that shake the foundation of Western civilisation and create a demand for illiberal alternatives.

Liberalism, the positioning of political and economic freedoms of the individual at the centre, is the greatest achievement and a cornerstone of Western civilisation. The people of the West heightened the intrinsic value of the individual, while incrementally attaining the right to live as they want in terms of their democratic and economic freedoms. The West has developed stable, civil, and dynamic societies. The perpetual need for change and rebirth to avoid stagnation is organised cordially through democratic structures and a dynamic economy. Yet, success has a tendency of producing hubris and a virtue taken to the extreme becomes a vice. All political and economic systems require development and rejuvenation, thus the conviction of having transcended history can condemn the West to live in an eternal present. Increasingly rational societies have toppled unelected and arbitrary feudal and religious structures. Albeit, they are replaced with a secular bureaucracy that does not account for the imperishable and irrational instincts embedded in human nature. Liberal democracy has incrementally mutated society into a hedonistic and nihilistic postmodernist construct that repudiates traditions, norms, societal structures, and the particularities of a civilisation as remnants of a bygone totalitarian past. Economic liberalism relentlessly enhances efficiency to the extent that public regulations, trade unions, cultural particularities, local communities, national identities, kinship, and even the family unit are assessed by their declining rational utility in complex society. Unconstrained economic competition undercuts traditional social structures that facilitate indispensable human relationships at a rate that civilisation cannot withstand. As history demonstrates, all civilisations eventually outgrow the culture and systems that supported their existence.

The purported rise of 'populism' on both the Left and the Right represents a growing disillusionment within Western societies at the grassroots level that has been harnessed by a variety of political forces. The relatively prosperous, tolerant, civilised, and peaceful West has accumulated unsustainable debt, become fervently divided, disengaged, and never runs out of enemies to bomb. The home of the Statue of Liberty incarcerates more people than any other nation, while technology-fuelled interconnectedness and personal wealth correlates with alarming rates of solitude and suicide. Unhinged individualism, disintegrating families, and the demise of Christianity have hollowed out spirituality, creative life, and the need for inter-personal connectivity in smaller communities. The seven deadly sins in Christianity: lust, gluttony, greed, sloth, wrath, envy, and pride, are now largely glorified and promoted as an idyllic lifestyle by embracing immediate desires and gratification. The populace is destined to either search for meaning in a society that celebrates violence, dysfunctions, and anti-social behaviour, or distract themselves with drugs, alcohol, anti-depressants, vulgar entertainment, and an obsession with sex, shopping, and consumption. Historically, when a civilisation has been incapable or unwilling to defend and reproduce itself, the people attempt to revive the remnants of the community and even look towards competing civilisations at the periphery for assistance. The self-indulgence and excesses in the final years of Rome were similarly deceptive by giving the impression that the Roman Empire was at its height at a time when its culture was being decimated and subsequently dooming its civilisation to fail.

While the alternative philosophies and policies proposed by the rising political movements across the West may be inconsistent and flawed, their commonality is to represent Hegel's pendulum swing as a reaction to the excesses and intrinsic flaws in liberal democracy and free-market capitalism. With the demise of fascism and communism, only liberalism remained as an ideology of modernity. Francis Fukuyama (1992) argued in *The End of History and the Last Man* that liberal democracy and free-market capitalism remained as the sole ideological alternative. Yet, the victory of liberalism would produce its downfall by being embraced to its fullest extent. The hubris that swept the West after 'winning' the Cold War temporarily brushed over signs of decadence and strengthened ideological convictions about the existence of a single and universal model for political, social, and economic development. Liberal democracy and free-market capitalism are celebrated as dual pillars of the Western political philosophy that has subsequently become the foundation for the contemporary structures of globalisation. The West's embrace of Fukuyama's thesis is indicative of pernicious absolutism as liberalism transitioned from an ideology to an unchallenged truth. Ideology has subsequently become a burden by obstructing insight into the contradictions in human nature.

Recognised since the time of the ancient Greek philosophers, liberalism is characteristically a temporary political system that eventually turns against itself. Plato, Socrates, and Aristotle warned that democracy has a temporary and transitionary inclination. The longer a democracy exists, the freer it would become, and it would eventually liberate people from the traditions, laws, and institutions that hold together the community and society. Human beings have organised themselves in hierarchies throughout time, which evolutionary biology has embedded into the nervous system (Peterson 2018). Subsequently, the populace is liberated from the constraints of traditional hierarchies that also endowed life with meaning and order. Liberalism has failed because it functioned too well. Narcissism and nihilism are inescapable when individuals are freed from authority and institutions, as they are only defined by themselves (Deneen 2018). Eventually, democracy turns on itself, as the rule of the majority is construed as a form of totalitarianism that disregards and oppresses the minority. Our contemporary postmodernist era largely reflects these bleak predictions as Western civilisation is on the path to 'liberate' itself by deconstructing both community and society (gemeinschaft and gesellschaft).

Unfettered free-market capitalism consumes itself by its excesses. Much like the challenge with liberal democracy, civilisation is sustained and advanced when the state preserves a balance between the traditional/irrational and the modern/ rational. Under increasingly complex economic structures, people are dislodged from their traditional communities that sustained social capital. The reduced role of the state diminishes the ability to protect traditional structures from being deconstructed by excessive efficiency. Public ownership, protectionism, and regulation are no longer revered as guarantees for social stability, rather they are denounced for inefficiency or considered to be theft by corrupt bureaucrats. The Cold War dichotomy between capitalism and communism has polluted the discourse and prospects for middle-ground alternatives. States have traditionally risen to power on economic nationalism and geoeconomics, while the hegemon promoted free markets to integrate the world into an international system it controlled. Economic statecraft is an indispensable tool to preserve the traditional community that facilitates social needs and unity, while concurrently building competitiveness and power in international trade. Albeit, there is an inherent contradiction among these objectives that must be harmonised. The more advanced and complex an economic system becomes to ensure the state's survival in the international system, the more it will deconstruct the traditional community as the source of identity, spirituality, meaning, and solidarity. 'Creative destruction', the destruction of professions and industries that communities depend upon, is escalating as markets become increasingly global and new technologies are introduced with ever-greater frequency. This trend will further intensify as the world is entering a new industrial revolution centred on communication, automation, and robotics. At a time when the state retreats from markets, there is increasing need for state intervention to address the unprecedented extent of people being dislodged from their traditional lives, and the ever-fiercer geoeconomic rivalry with both allies and adversaries. As China and Russia have released themselves from the constraints of communism and skilfully master economic statecraft, their influence over strategic markets, transportation corridors, and mechanisms for financial cooperation is escalating the shift of geoeconomic power from the West to the East.

The traditional political Right and Left appear to be largely incapable of addressing the mounting challenges as they remain ideologically and intellectually constrained by the political framework inherited from the Cold War. In the current state of polarisation and dismay, systemic incentives mount for new political movements to fill the vacuum. With the demise of classical conservativism, the political and economic philosophy of the Right advocates the virtues of free trade and globalism, while berating the loss of traditional values in vain as the former causes the latter. The Left is similarly constrained by a political philosophy committed to redistribution of wealth to unproductive groups at the expense of competitiveness of society. Concurrently, the Left remains ideologically committed to detest the defining ethno-cultural particularities of society as hierarchical, exclusive, and totalitarian. As liberal democracy and laissez-faire capitalism are heralded as representing the core of Western civilisation, the ideological commitment to these principles undermines the capacity to address the philosophical and geoeconomic quandary of the contradiction between the community and society.

Globalisation, loss of social capital, disenchantment with moral relativism, and a culture of excess has incentivised the rediscovery of religion, ideology, national identities, and reaffirmation of traditional values that could be expressed in unpredictable manners. A paradoxical development is unfolding as states are pursuing regional integration to develop a larger society that enhances their collective influence in the international system. Simultaneously, the efforts to re-connect with identities closer to the individual are producing internal division within states, to the extent that secessionist movements are prevailing. Brussels exemplifies this contradiction by being the capital of the world's most successful integration project in terms of geoeconomic power and development of a shared 'European' identity more suitable to complex societies. Yet, concurrently there are secessionist pressures to split Belgium into two separate countries due to the different identities, languages, and traditions.

Cooperation and competition with Russia will inevitably be impacted by the West's decline. Pressure to restore internal solidarity within the West creates systemic incentives for the elites to reinvoke narratives of Russia as an imminent external threat. Moscow evidently has much to gain from discord to lessen the collective bargaining power of the West that is frequently used to marginalise Russia. Depicting Russia as the source of the West's systemic problems is politically expedient as the 'populists' challenging the status quo can be denounced as agents of the Kremlin. It is a very attractive and reasonable tactic as the new political movements across the Western political spectrum are indeed expressing much greater benevolence towards Russia. Portraying grassroots movement as an intricate ploy by the Kremlin to subvert Western democracy may be intellectually lazy and even blatant propaganda, but it has sway over the masses who have internalised anti-Russian imagery for over a century and are in desperate need for a meaningful frontier.

However, using Russia as an instrument to augment internal solidarity is problematic as the large neighbour in the east embodies the philosophy of the populists that divides the West. The benevolence towards Russia by 'populists' is symptomatic of the West's democratic–authoritarian binary divide of the world being replaced by a patriotism–cosmopolitanism or nationalism–globalism divide, which converts Moscow into an ally to preserve community and civilisation. Russia's appeal to the 'populists' is the bold and unapologetic commitment to preserve traditions, national culture, Christian heritage, national identity, and the family structure. The growing dismay in the West over a self-serving financial elite incites empathy for Russia's geoeconomic strategy for state intervention to develop strategic industries, transportation corridors, and mechanisms for cooperation with new international financial institutions to obtain autonomy from the Western-centric economic architecture.

Armed with a neomodernist political philosophy and geoeconomic strategy, Russia has inadvertently attained significant soft power by offering an alternative to the ailing international liberal order. The endurance of Russia's new magnetism in the West will however be contingent on the extent to which it can develop a relatable international conservative movement and remain a nation with an economy rather than become an economy with a nation. In other words, Russia is an important and divisive variable in the West by representing the intent to rejuvenate gemeinschaft (traditional community) that is under siege by excessive gesellschaft (complex society). The political vacuum produced by the West's growing impotence invites rival powers at the periphery. While Russia was denied a seat at the table following the Cold War, it is becoming increasingly aware of the opportunity to bring its own chair and restructure the order.

The purpose of this book is to examine the decay of Western civilisation and the impact on relations with Russia. The puzzle to be explored is that once the challenges of the ideological struggles of the 20th century were seemingly concluded, and the end of history celebrated, the foundations of a shared Western civilisation began to unravel. The West has become overextended, overly rational, and excessively universal, which impede the ability to reproduce the distinctive, irrational, and traditional. Without any external frontiers as remedy for rising nihilism, the West has discovered its own irredeemable flaws and began to follow the path of previous declining civilisations by no longer being willing to defend and reproduce itself.

From the early 1990s Russia was prematurely dismissed as a declining power with nothing to offer the world in terms of political philosophy and economic development. Defined as a non-relevant entity in international affairs and its domestic instability being the main source of security concern to the West, Russia was demoted to a peripheral object of security in a Western-centric world. Russia's role in international security was demoted to making domestic reforms to become more like the West. Liberal democracy and relative economic strength ruled supreme and Russia was not equipped with sufficient competitiveness and had no alternatives. Russia's recovery and renewed assertiveness has prompted Western leaders to assure their population that Russia has nothing to offer the world in terms of values and ways to organise society. President Obama argued: 'their economy doesn't produce anything that anybody wants to buy except oil and gas and arms' (Conway 2016).

In recent years, Moscow has gradually begun to embrace an ideological alternative by ostensibly focusing on balancing two mutually contradictory necessities: the reproduction of the 'irrational' traditional community, and the development of 'rational' complex society based on efficiency and geoeconomic principles. Unlike the former Soviet revolutionary effort to challenge and radically alter the foundations of Western civilisation, Russia is positioning itself as the defender and champion of traditional European civilisation. Russia represents Toynbee's (1946: 30) 'external proletariat' that allies itself with the 'internal proletariat' in the West against what are scorned as revisionist postmodern elites detached from traditional community.

Western civilisation is in decline due to the inability of the unrestrained liberal order to preserve a balance between the traditional and modern to accommodate the rational and irrational in human nature. The contemporary contradictory gravitational pull towards tribalism and globalism epitomises the eternal civilisational struggle between community and society (gemeinschaft and gesellschaft). The science, economic structures, and natural laws introduced by the Enlightenment and Renaissance advanced humanity towards the modern. Yet, modernity came at the expense of the traditional, which caused a pendulum swing back manifested as the Counter-Enlightenment movement and Romanticism of the 19th and 20th centuries. The mounting conflict that reached its pinnacle with the Second World War, incentivised Western civilisation to incrementally abandon ethno-cultural particularities of civilisation and instead embrace universality civic ideals of liberal democracy and free-market capitalism. Yet, an internal crisis becomes evident due to the inherent faults in the absolutism of liberal democracy and free-market capitalism. A new pendulum swing towards the innate and irrational that has been neglected and deconstructed under excessively rational liberalism is waiting.

This book builds heavily on the philosophy developing throughout the 19th century that was eventually embraced by German and Italian fascists. Recognising that the philosophy of Heidegger and Nietzsche inspired the policies of Hitler does not imply endorsement of the latter. Instead, the study of Heidegger offers insight into the imperishable contradictions within humanity and civilisation, and the hazards it produces. Building on the philosophy of the 19th century is a response to the liberal authoritarianism that characterises and constrains contemporary intellectual debates in the West. The admirable pursuit of greater truths has degraded to absolutism, which is used with political expediency by equating recognition of fallible paradoxes within the human conditions with endorsement. Liberal authoritarianism subsequently narrows the scope of intellectual debate into the paradoxes and contradictions of Man. The uncompromising liberal insistence on rights at the heart of citizenship has produced a neglect of responsibilities. The traditional is dismissed as outdated as there are no alternatives to modernisation. The need for liberal economics and complex economic structures encourages neglect of traditional culture and family values. The benefits of secularism are construed as invalidation of religion, which is imperative for meaning and can function as a moral compass. The emancipation of women imperils demographic reproduction and weakens the family unit. Tolerance for other cultures often results in cultural relativism and reduced willingness to defend one's own culture and civilisation. Critiquing liberalism and excessive rationality for eroding the shared meaning and purpose of civilisation can coexist with recognising the virtues and necessity of liberal principles. Last, arguing that Heidegger provides the antidote to nihilism as the prevalent challenge to Western civilisation does not equate to an endorsement of fascism.

Research design

A deductive approach is taken to answer the research question of *how to explain the causes for the decay of Western civilisation and the subsequent impact on cooperation and conflict with Russia?* The strengths and weaknesses of civilisations are argued here to be contingent on their ability to balance and harmonise gemeinschaft (community) and gesellschaft (society). Community represents the traditional, spiritual, irrational, and inter-personal organisation of human interactions, which contradicts the development of rational, efficient, contractual-based human interfaces found in large-scale industrial society. As argued by Huntington (1993a), civilisations base their internal cohesion on an internal cultural make-up and community as the foundation for organising large civilisations as meta-strategic power entities. In the era of geoeconomics, rational and calculative international rivalry is increasingly pursued with economic statecraft. This tends to lead to economic determinism as efficiency becomes the sole objective, while the preservation of culture and traditions is neglected and belittled as obsolete ideas from a bygone era. Civilisation thus consumes itself as the decay of community also erodes the foundation for society.

To answer the research question, the first two chapters conceptualise civilisations, theorise the sources of their ascendance and decline, and interactions with other civilisations such as Russia at the periphery. Second, the following four chapters are devoted to exploring the rise and decline of Western civilisation based on the theoretical framework from the first two chapters. Last, the final three chapters assess Russia as the West's 'other' that emerges as a neomodernist and geoeconomic challenger. The book assesses the extent to which Moscow is acting in accordance with the systemic incentives to assert its civilizational influence in the West with neomodernism and geoeconomics.

Chapter 1 conceptualises civilisations through the prism of the gemeinschaft/ gesellschaft (community/society) dichotomy. A neoclassical realist theoretical framework is outlined to survey the strengths and the weaknesses of civilisations based on the balance between community and society. It will be argued that the challenges of civilisations are defined by the internal struggle of Man, who gravitates in opposite directions between the rational and irrational. Over thousands of years, primitive Man developed instincts to survive in nature, which manifested themselves in dependence on the community for security and a sense of meaning. The community represents the irrational – smaller, distinctive, and homogenous groups based on shared kinship, spirituality, and inter-personal ties. The relatively recent emergence of rational Man enabled the pursuit of greater efficiency and thus the construction of a larger and more complex society, which is based on more diverse, universal, and impersonal contract-based interactions. Civilisation gravitates in opposing directions: towards complex society for the advancement of the humanity and to compete against rival civilisation, and towards the innate and spiritual that provides meaning and a sense of belonging. Liberalism is argued to be paradoxical by peacefully organising renewal, while also undermining civilisation when there is excessive focus on rights, rationality, and efficiency as it hollows out the community.

Chapter 2 outlines a theory on the cyclical rise and fall of civilisations through the prism of gemeinschaft and gesellschaft. The theme of recurring birth, rise, decline, and death of civilisations remerges in most religions and folklores relating to genesis. These patterns are also reiterated in the empirical study of civilisations by most of the leading scholars on this topic. Based on this material, a four-stage seasonal civilisational theory is outlined. Spring/adolesce denotes the initial simplistic state of civilisation, with community and culture not being corrupted by society. Summer/maturity signifies civilisational advancement as society develops, yet the balance between community and society is harmonised. A large and consolidated community sets the necessary foundation for the construction of complex economic structures of society. Autumn/decay indicates the progression of society at the peril of the community. Yet, expansionism and frontiers can function as a temporary remedy to growing nihilism by providing meaning and expectations of a better future. Winter/death suggests the demise or invasion of civilisation, which is followed by rebirth. Civilisation is unwilling or incapable to defend its culture. A split subsequently develops between a cosmopolitan elite who is detached from community and benefits from complex society, and an internal proletariat seeking to replenish the community as they suffer most from the demise of the traditional and gain less from complex society. The latter looks outwards to civilisations at the peripheral in search for allies against the elite, and as an agent for the rebirth of the community.

Chapter 3 surveys modern Western civilisation as an amalgam of political liberalism and nationhood. The rise and greatness of Western civilisation derives from its political pluralism, which facilitated the balance between political structures founded on traditional structures based on the community, and the liberal and rational ideals of liberating Man from the arbitrary authority. Modern Western civilisation reappeared through the construction of the nation-state as a process of ethno-cultural homogenisation that allowed the state to harness and embody the shared particularities of the community. A strong balance developed between responsibilities towards the community and the elevation of the rights of the individual, which laid the foundations for the development of increasingly complex societies. The weakness of modern Western civilisation is the tendency to construe ever-increasing liberalism and rationality as advancement, which eventually imperils the arbitrary authority embedded in its culture and existence. The artificial dichotomy between ethno-cultural and civic nationalism represented the initial loss of balance, setting the stage for excessive civic nationalism and a pending counter-reaction.

Chapter 4 analyses the postmodernist graveyard of Western civilisation. Postmodernism depicts narratives, truths, institutions, and hierarchies that sustains civilisation as mere social constructions to attain oppressive power. Political postmodernism produces devastating nihilism by discarding traditional identities, cultures, nations, religions, the family units, genders, and civilisation itself as arbitrary and totalitarian social structures. Tolerance and equality as prominent virtues in Western civilisations degrade into vices. Tolerance is corrupted by being translated into an embrace of cultural and moral relativism, while the success and superiority of bourgeois cultural and moral practices is dismissed as oppression Similarly, equal opportunity is replaced with equal outcome as superior performance by some sub-groups in society is interpreted as evidence of systemic and institutional discrimination. Diversity and Aristotle's 'equality of unequals' converts the 'melting pot' into a 'salad bowl', and subsequently reverses the homogenisation of the state-building process. In its place emerges a factitious and divisive society divided into sub-groups that are defined by their privilege or victimhood. Identity politics incentivises competition for victimhood status as a political currency, while the rivalry between identity groups replicates the anarchy in the international system. The decline of identity and loyalty to the state in favour of responsibilities towards sub-groups undermines the rule of law, legitimacy of government, and democratic rule of the majority as perceived forms of totalitarianism.

Chapter 5 addresses the geoeconomic rise of Western society to global primacy for five centuries. While Western Europe and the US were initially prioritised preserving the community and culture, rivalry in the international system compelled the adoption of more complex societies to be competitive. Consistent with the economic nationalist policies of Friedrich List, leading Western powers were elevated to greatness with state intervention to assert control over strategic industries, maritime transportation corridors, and mechanisms for international financial cooperation. Fears about the erosion of community and rising nihilism was a dominant key topic in the 1800s, however, expansionism and establishment of frontiers and settler societies provided a temporary remedy. The Cold War confrontation mitigated political animosity from rival geoeconomic policies among Western powers as the US benefitted from and therefore allowed economic power to shift from the core to European and East Asian frontlines. Furthermore, the ideological undercurrents of the Cold War negated the social upheavals from growing 'creative destruction'.

Chapter 6 surveys the consequences of unconstrained economic liberalism on the community and society. Free-market capitalism has taken on a new radical

repetition

form since the controlled capitalism prior to the 1980s, while new technologies and complex value-chains in the global marketplace further diminish the role of the state. Traditional inter-personal organisations of human interactions are dismantled by 'creative destruction' as entire skillsets, trades, and industries vanish. The reliance on increased mobility of a global workforce that can sustain cultural identities with their original homeland culminates in extreme individualism as families are geographically dispersed and traditional society is dislocated. The loss of skilled work, growing wealth disparity, unsustainable public and private debt, loss of civility, and estrangement and polarisation of society is indicative of the failure of Western governments to respond to the structural economic changes. Responding with mass immigration to replace the dying population unwilling to reproduce itself is indicative of the West becoming an economy with a nation rather than vice versa. Simultaneously, Western societies are becoming less competitive. Former communist adversaries such as China and Russia are embracing economic statecraft, and the geoeconomic rivalry between Western powers, previously restrained by the Cold War, has resurfaced and upsets internal cohesion. The US and Europe drift apart, while the concentration of power in Germany and the geoeconomic decline of the EU is fragmenting the continent. Excessive protectionism and autarchy is unviable as relative economic power becomes increasingly important to determine the primacy or subordination of states. Yet, the ensuing structural economic changes necessitate more government intervention to preserve societal cohesion and international security. There is increasing pressure on governments to support manufacturing and innovations by actively re-educating and directing excess labour and capital into high-skilled and high-wage professions.

Chapter 7 assesses the strengths and weaknesses of Russian civilisation. Russia's geography greatly impacts its balance between gemeinschaft and gesellschaft, as a European identity embraces modernity and an Eastern/Slavophil identity gravitates towards the traditional and spiritual. The vast Eurasian geography makes Russia inclined to be a gemeinschaft-based civilisation. Yet, Russia's cooperation and conflict with the West throughout history has promoted rapid modernisation resulting in the destructive purging of the traditional. While the Eurasian geography can be a great source for balancing the mutually dependent traditional community and complex society, the swift and destructive pendulum shifts between the rational and irrational has been the principal problem for Russia in modern history. The historical preference for spiritual society above the morally corrupt European manufacturing societies was reversed following Russia's inadequate performance in the Crimean War. The radical and rapid economic modernisation from the early 1890s made Russia the fastest growing major economy, albeit at the expense of the spirituality and kinship of the community. The dramatic pendulum swing and shift to communism in 1917 was destined to fail as it crippled Russian economic statecraft, while the ethno-cultural and religious distinctiveness was purged in the attempt to transcend the past and establish a new Man.

Chapter 8 explores Russia's nascent Eurasian revival, which supports neomodernism and competitive geoeconomics. The postmodernist influence of the international system under Western stewardship is perceived to have weakened the modern rules-based system as legality is decoupled from legitimacy. With relative power shifting from the West to the East, both political and economic philosophy are undergoing change. Rising powers such as Russia, China, India, Brazil, and Iran display increased willingness and capability to challenge the existing geoeconomic architecture and political culture. Neomodernism responds to the failures of postmodernism, without returning to modernism. Russian Neomodernism, much like rising Chinese neo-Confucianism, embraces modernisation but rejects that modernisation is not a linear process by dismantling the traditional. Consistent with the European philosophies of the 19th century, it is believed that modernisation must be balanced by strengthened culture and traditions to address the innate and imperishable in human nature, and to maintain a distinctive identity in a globalising world. Eurasian geoeconomics remove Russia from the periphery of Europe, where Russia is vulnerable to the West's collective bargaining power that marginalises Russian autonomy and influence. Repositioned to the heart of Eurasia, Russia can skew the symmetry within economic interdependence by reducing its reliance on any one state or region, while concurrently increasing dependence by others on Russia.

Chapter 9 surveys the rise of 'populists' in the West and their affinity towards Russia. Russia is conceptualised as Toynbee's (1946) 'external proletariat' to the West. Russia's aspirations to be a gemeinshaft-based civilisation creates a tremendous attractiveness for the 'internal proletariat', who are undergoing an identity crisis and civilisational struggle. The West is increasingly divided between a cosmopolitan elite detached from the community that benefits from complex economic structures, and an 'internal proletariat' seeking to revive the traditional. The internal and external proletariat find common cause in opposing the excesses of the elites. The rise of Trump, the Brexit campaign under UKIP, Le Pen in France, Orban, in Hungary, Kaczyński in Poland, Babis in the Czech Republic, Kurz in Austria, the AfD in Germany, and numerous other right-wing conservative movements across the West share many commonalities. These movements unapologetically reject globalism to the extent it undermines nationhood and traditions, and most of these movements express a remarkable degree of empathy towards Russia and the belief that they have a common cause.

It will be concluded in this book that with ever-increasing efficiency at the expense of the traditional and spiritual, civilisations are burdened by their own greatness. The former mutual dependence and linkages between culture and economy have unravelled. Managing an increasingly complex society becomes even more convoluted when the values of society encourage unconstrained appetite for self-indulgence and neglects responsibility. The extraordinary historical resilience of the West, especially the US, should not be ignored. Yet, the current instabilities are different as the seemingly irreconcilable differences and tensions are stirring from within. Liberalism in the US was a founding principle rather than a partisan issue, and the crisis of liberalism can unravel the shared identity. While the internal cohesion in the West weakens, the geoeconomic rise of the East is reversing the foundations for the West's past 500 years of global primacy. Furthermore, the push for ending Western-centric globalisation is largely construed by Eurasian powers as defending their own culture from modernism and the West. The stakes are raised for all sides. Russia benefits from preserving its defining distinctiveness and may get the opportunity to finally reach a post-Cold War political settlement by eliminating the new dividing lines in Europe. Yet, with declining internal solidarity in the West, increasingly more chaotic and unpredictable behaviour will present formidable threats. The Western elites will only harden their positions as they conflate societal security with xenophobia, and common cause with Russia as the surrender of liberal democratic values. The greatest unpredictability may, however, emerge from the new populist political forces. As the instinctive, primordial, and irrational components of human nature are destined to remain ill articulated and obscure, unsavoury, and morally disreputable political forces may lead to the revival of distinctive culture, kinship, and traditions.

Part I
Theorising civilisations

1 Civilisations balanced between gemeinschaft and gesellschaft

Introduction

Plato argued 2,500 years ago that there are two orders that Man must balance, the internal order of the soul and the external order of the commonwealth. The instinctive within the soul and the calculative required to engage with the external environment necessitate two conflicting ways of organising human interactions. The principal challenge for civilisations is to balance and harmonise the opposing impulses gravitating towards the irrational and the rational. Man is a social creature who acts in groups, perpetually drawn between traditional communities (gemeinschaft) and larger complex societies (gesellschaft). Civilisations developed as a network of local communities and cities with robust and distinctive pre-urban ethno-cultural features, which became capable of forming advanced societies by organising large groups of people and complex economic structures. Smaller and distinctive communities based on inter-personal ties and kinship provide a sense of belonging and security, while the ambition for intellectual freedom, economic prosperity, and power in the competition between groups spurred the need to form larger and more complex societies based on contractual interactions, calculative and rational structures.

Civilisation is conceptualised here as a meta-strategic disposition of power, the highest organisation of human tribes that gratifies the innate and primordial need for traditional social groups, and organises people into rational, advanced, and competitive societies. Civilisations are thus destined to endure internal friction due to their mutually dependent and contradictory inward-looking and outward-looking utility. These two functions are interdependent as social capital in cohesive communities is a prerequisite to form and sustain advanced and complex societies. Similarly, a prosperous and competitive society is needed to safeguard the sacred particularities from external rivals. Yet, these two functions of civilisation are also mutually opposing by gravitating simultaneously towards the instinctive and the conscious. States are under systemic pressures to attain greater autonomy to preserve and reproduce one's own culture, and concurrently embrace regional integration for collective bargaining power against adversaries.

This chapter will first distinguish between community (gemeinschaft) and society (gesellschaft) with neoclassical realist theory on civilisations. The community represents the instinctive and irrational need for inter-personal ties in smaller communities founded on kinship and shared spirituality. The society denotes the calculative, rational, efficient, and competitive large-scale industrial society based on impersonal and contractual interactions. The ability of decision-makers to act in a rational and calculative way to maximise power and security in accordance with the neorealist balance of power logic largely depends on internal cohesion to perform as a unitary actor, which is contingent upon a sound understanding of the irrational and primordial nature of Man as recognised in classical realism. *but of Woman?*

Second, the tendency in human nature to swing from one extreme to another undermines the ability of civilisations to find a balance between community and society. The advancement and excesses of rationality during the Enlightenment and Renaissance produced the counter-Enlightenment movement and Romanticism as a reaction. The subsequent disastrous German experiment with National Socialism caused disenchantment in the West for the distinctive and irrational, and subsequently unleashed a radical push towards the universal and rational. The neglect of the distinctive causes a new imbalance with pending consequences.

Last, it will be argued that liberalism is especially vulnerable to neglect in the irrational component of Man and civilisation due to hostility towards arbitrary authority. Political liberalism tends to become increasing free by deconstructing the arbitrary but necessary authority of traditional social institutions. At its extreme, democracy turns on itself by denouncing the will of the majority as a form of totalitarianism over the minority. Economic liberalism similarly advances efficiency at the expense of the inefficient components of community. Economic determinism represents the extreme when all facets of civilisation are defined primarily by the economic utility, in which faith, the family, and tradition are set to lose their utility and attractiveness.

Community versus society

The evolution of human consciousness established the internal contradiction between the instinctive and rational that defines the human condition and civilisations. The flawed narrative of a linear evolution of rationality suggests that Man gradually developed his consciousness and has since the Enlightenment continued the path towards shedding his superstitions and irrational traits. The competing view is that the primordial instincts Man developed over tens of thousands of years to survive cannot be transcended. Instincts are biologically entrenched in the nervous system and the brain to reward the 'correct' and traditional behaviour with a sense of security and meaning, and to punish deviation from the instinctive with a sense of discomfort, insecurity, and nihilism. By comparison, if an animal became completely conscious it would be much like the human animal, torn by opposing impulses. A penguin suddenly equipped with consciousness to make rational decisions would likely not walk a hundred kilometres through perilous weather to mate at the ancestral breeding grounds, but instead seek a more convenient location or even reconsider the utility of mating. Such rational behaviour

No would have designed a dog-pulled sled or built a train →

would, however, contradict what his instincts demand for self-preservation and thus trigger great discomfort and a sense of emptiness. Likewise, primitive Man who only relatively recently emerged out of nature is torn between acting on his primordial impulses and simultaneously becoming a modern civilised Man.

The concept of community (gemeinschaft) and society (gesellschaft) was initially developed by Tönnies (1957[1887]). Human development was postulated to adhere to objective realities in accordance with the positivism in German sociological tradition. Community embodied the purity of youth, and society signified the necessary but decaying process of adulthood. Tönnies may have based this concept on Thomas Hobbes' distinction between 'concord' and 'union', with the former being the consensus-based ruled found at a local level and the latter representing the control required by the state (Hont 2015: 6). Max Weber (1924a) also deliberated on the human struggle between smaller community and larger society over prolonged periods of time and recognised the imperative of finding a balance between the two.

what?

Community or gemeinschaft is the natural habitat for human beings. Man developed the instinct to seek refuge in close-knit communities with high social capital where kinship is the foundation for solidarity (Tönnies 1957[1887]). Communities are defined by inter-personal ties and interactions within small, rural, and traditional groups. United by blood, place, spirit, and common fate, the sense of community is typically defined by shared ethno-cultural and religious ties. The community is the foundation for belonging, morality, trust, and even a sense of immorality by reproducing its distinct character. Families are the strongest community in terms of providing meaning, common understanding, mutual sympathy, belonging, and shared security. In simple economic systems with more autonomy, such as agricultural societies, personal ties are maintained and serve an important function for local and recurrent commercial interaction. Social interactions within the community appeal to affinity and tradition as a key objective. The appreciation for personal ties within communities strengthens cooperative social organisation and cohesion. Communities therefore generate morality, justice, order, and security based on concord, with emotional ties as the mechanisms to uphold shared responsibilities and rights. As opposed to citizenship by contract, the smaller and homogenous social groups nurture a sense of moral obligation based on emotional attachment and traditions. In the community, law becomes indistinguishable from morality. The community appeals to what Plato and Aristotle refers to as 'thumos' or spiritedness. The human soul consists of three components; the intellect (theoretical reason), appetite (physical desire), and thumos (passion/spiritedness). Thumos represents the emotional and irrational centre of the soul that instinctively seeks passionate affection. Communities are 'sacred', which is defined as what must be preserved since loss of the sacred creates moral panic and loss of the self. Genetic evolutionary restructuring to decouple from the individual from the family unit and community would require thousands of more years of evolution (Luttwak 1995: 80).

Society or gesellschaft denotes large-scale modern, industrial, cosmopolitan, and rational organisation of human interactions. Hegel posited that Man seeks

1st step toward "global warming" + melting of Arctic ice caps / glaciers?

complex societies to liberate people from the intellectual restraints of small communities. Adam Smith described the birth of civilisation as the process when backward towns were exposed to fine arts, manners, and scientific understanding. Society offers the prospect of greater economic prosperity and to become more competitive and capable of survival as it us guided by rationality and efficiency. Social interactions in society are more calculative and function as a means to an end. Societies rise with the development of technology and more intricate economic structures, yet society remains an artificial construct that becomes mechanic and spiritless by organising interactions with impersonal ties and contractual exchanges.

Man became 'civilised' and founded civilisations when various communities became interdependent and competition was organised with rules and justice to advance a common good. With different degrees of cultural heterogeneity, civilisations differ in terms of organising politics, the economy, culture, and social interactions. Civilisations are characterised by their material strength, culture, and ethics (Schweitzer 1949). Furthermore, civilisations define the relations between 'God and man, the individual and the group, the citizen and the state, parents and children, husband and wife, as well as differing rights and responsibilities, liberty and authority, equality and hierarchy' (Huntington 1993a: 25). The success of the nation-state is attributed to its ability to bridge the community and society. The community was recreated within a larger entity of power by constructing shared identity and citizenship, comprising legally enforced rights and responsibilities. Societies are also facilitated to maximise political and economic gains, which requires larger bureaucracies and organisational structures with complex division of labour. Increasingly multifaceted societies formed through region-building and globalisation are therefore less capable of facilitating the identity of the community.

Neoclassical realism on civilisations between gemeinschaft and gesellschaft

Neoclassical realism can bring together classical realism and neorealism to survey the strengths and weaknesses of civilisations. Employing neoclassical realism is ideal to explore the challenges of civilisations as it assesses both the rational and irrational aspects of Man. Classical realism surveys the preservation of the primordial and instinctive as the foundation for internal cohesion, which is required for states to act rationally and calculatedly as advocated by neorealism. Humans act in social groups, with the state as the highest sovereign social group and therefore the principal actor. While state-centrism is at the heart of realist theory, it is not an eternally fixed truth as authority overlapped in the past, and the highest sovereign evolved from city-states to empires. States pooling sovereignty in regional or civilisational configurations for collective bargaining power or the state fragmenting into smaller entities of power is therefore consistent with realist theory.

Classical realism explores objective laws of human nature that influence politics. While there are varying perspectives on human nature among classical

male nature

testosterone/thanatos-driven male half of Humanity!

male!

realists, they share a pessimism and view conflict as the natural state. The position taken here builds on the arguments of George Kennan that human nature is not inherently bad, rather the predisposition to conflict derives from the duality of Man and contradictory impulses. Kennan (1993), commonly known as the architect of the US containment policy against the Soviet Union, referred to Man as a 'cracked vessel' in conflict with his own contradictions and tensions with other human beings. The cracked vessel condition has its roots in contradictions between the instinctive, ancient, and simple nature of Man, and the drive for evolving and constructing greater civilisation (Kennan 1993: 27). While the natural creed of humanity is to drift towards close-knit social groups as a family, kinsmen, and local community, Kennan notes that Man's innate impulses also embodies a 'universal need for people to feel themselves a part of something larger than themselves, and larger than just the family' (Kennan, 1993: 74). Yet, while Man 'tries to shape his behaviour in accordance with the requirement of civilisation', he remains a deeply uncomfortable member of society due to his duality (Kennan 1993: 17).

Neorealism, or structural realism, as advocated by Kenneth Waltz (1979), employs a rational and calculative approach to international security. The international distribution of power is theorised to create systemic pressures or incentives for how states should act to survive. Peace can only exist when all states are balanced as states do not constrain themselves. Security is maximised by acting rationally in accordance with the balance of power logic by either band wagoning or balancing. Wars and other disruptions in the international system can disrupt the balance of power, yet the system will naturally move towards an equilibrium as states must constrain rival powers. The need to accumulate power provides great incentives for states to construct larger entities of power and increasingly complex societies to harness political, economic, and military power. Thus, the rational decision for states would be to become more efficient and integrate military power for collective strength in traditional geopolitics, or in the contemporary geoeconomic era pool economic strength for collective bargaining power.

Neorealism became the dominant political theory in the late stages of the Cold War when immense structural pressures had greater influence than human nature. Human nature was perceived to have less of an influence since the world was unequivocally divided into two diametrically opposite ideologies for two opposing centres of power. The hostility and clearly delineated 'us-them' ideational frontiers were a source for cohesion within states, regional blocs, and civilisations. After the Cold War, classical realism has returned as a pertinent analytical tool since human nature yet again became a cogent variable to assess impediments to the rational behaviour of states.

Neoclassical realism recognises the state must act as a unitary actor to mobilise both the material and political resources in accordance with the balance of power logic. Neoclassical realism bridges the gap in neorealism by assessing the rationality of the decision-makers as a human element. Neorealism is solely a theory on the systemic pressures created from the international distribution of power. Waltz was explicit that neorealism is not a foreign policy theory as decision-makers do not always act in accordance with the balance of power logic, which suggests that Waltz repudiated the rational actor assumption (Mearsheimer 2009: 242). Neoclassical realism extends upon neorealism by including the human element of classical realism as an intervening variable between the systemic pressures and foreign policy. Neoclassical realism suggests that identities, ideologies, institutions, and social cohesions produce 'rational' behaviour when they enable the state to maximise security by acting in accordance with the balance of power logic. In contrast, the state is 'irrational' when decision-makers are prevented from acting on the incentives outlined by neorealist theory. The state's ability to act rationally is therefore contingent on representing and balancing the community and society. Failing to sustain cohesive communities undermines the sustainability of society, while a weak society leaves the state vulnerable to external powers. Maintaining solidarity requires the state to homogenise the population with ethno-cultural and civic nationalism to harness the characteristics of the community. In contrast, excessive empowerment and political autonomy of communities and sub-groups can create rivals to the identity and loyalty of the state.

The Hegelian pendulum between the rational and irrational

The contradictory impulses towards community and society can only be resolved with a balance. Such a balance is undermined by Man's inclination to first swing ferociously from one extreme to another. The propensity in human nature to swing as a pendulum between extremes in the pursuit of greater truths is a common concept in philosophy and social science. Plato's *Symposium* posited that we use strong contrasts to express truths, which undermines the stable and balanced middle ground or 'metaxy'. The weakness of this human condition is that the imbalance from pursuing an extreme at one end will eventually cause a reaction pushing towards the other extreme. For example, unfettered capitalism at the expense of social equity increases the political attractiveness of socialism, while the inefficiencies in radical socialism spurs desire to embrace the ideology of free market forces. Propagating an absolute truth at one end will therefore reduce the feasibility of reaching the optimal middle as a compromise. Hegel's 'pendulum theory' similarly theorised that events in human history tend to swing from one extreme to another before eventually settling at the centre as a stable variable. Hegel viewed history as a lethal rivalry over interpretations of who we are, and how to resolve the ensuing conflicts. The middle-ground/metaxy is undermined by modernist ideologies propagating the idea that the inherent flaw of Man can be transcended. Through informed and honest political discourse, the pendulum can reduce its volatility and stabilise towards the centre.

The Hegelian pendulum increased its velocity when Western civilisation thrived under burgeoning rationality during the Enlightenment and the Renaissance. The Enlightenment was spurred by scientific advancements, which promoted philosophy and social ideas about intellectual advancement and rationality in human nature. The Enlightenment is appropriately revered as a domineering pillar of Western civilisation by permitting sophisticated and complex societies to emerge that culminated in powerful states and empires. Epitomised by the American and French revolutions, the Enlightenment advocated for reason and individual freedom to liberate man from the superstition and darkness of medieval and archaic organisation of society with arbitrary religious authority. The new social and economic models accepted the market as preferable to older systems where the rulers distributed public goods. The subsequent emergence of political modernisation and the social contract set the foundation for both liberal democracy and free-market capitalism as rational endeavours. Religion was increasingly secularised, and power transferred to the state. The subsequent shift to an evolutionist perspective on civilisation entailed a future-oriented focus on science, modernity, and universalism to advance human kind. However, the subsequent exuberant material success that lifted humanity to unprecedented levels of prosperity also began to strain civilisation by neglecting nature, culture and spirituality.

The absolutism of the Enlightenment and rationality neglected that Man is flawed by also acting on ancient instincts (Herder 1966[1800]). Western civilisation began to break from the traditional and religious as a source of bloodshed throughout the Middle Ages. Albeit, the medieval traditions and ideals with organic unity and spirituality were also weakened (Burckhardt 1959). In *The Civilisation of the Renaissance in Italy*, Burckhardt (2010[1878]) depicted the Renaissance and modernity as a pernicious and dark development. The rapid changes produced a disconnect with the past, individualism led to egotism and hedonism, and culture became a commodity. The dismissal of religion is devastating as shared faith is an important source for community by providing the required sense of identity, belonging, and immortality. In Marxists core-periphery analysis, the advanced and prosperous urban society at the core will use its relative power to extract the resources from the weaker community at the periphery. Once the community and culture is depleted, the society and civilisation also perish. Lindberg recognises that the primordial instincts become louder when ignored:

> More and more, as civilisation develops we find the primitive to be essential to us. We root into the primitive as a tree roots into the earth. If we cut off the roots, we lose the sap without which we can't progress or even survive. I don't believe our civilisation can continue very long out of contact with the primitive.
>
> (Whitman 1969)

US President Herbert Hoover (1963: 17) similarly posited:

> The human animal original came from out-of-doors. When spring begins to move in his bones, he just must get out again. Moreover, as civilisation, cement pavements, office buildings, radios have overwhelmed us, the need for regeneration has increased, and the impulses are even stronger.

Civilisations are built on the past and promise of future inheritance and experiences, with moral unity established within political and religious institutions (Guizot 2013[1828]). While Nietzsche was an atheist and advocated rational thinking, he challenged the intellectual presumptions of the Enlightenment that rejected the irrational. Recognising the contradictions of human nature, Nietzsche deplored the decline of religion and the 'death of God' as he argued that Christianity provides the foundation for ethics in the West. Man would no longer be willing to die for religion, albeit he would also have less to live for and therefore become empty, nihilistic, materialistic, and self-absorbed. Irrespective of whether national identities are imagined or if God really exists, they remain imperative as the foundation for morality and altruism. Ethics is not a rational given, rather the ethics underpinning the moral foundation of Western civilisation is predicated on the existence of a God. Human nature does not display evidence of altruism. The willingness of animals, much like humans, to assist each other, is contingent on genetic links and kinship to reproduce their own kind, which suggests that altruism is really self-interest in disguise (Harman 2010). Absence of the kinship and religion would therefore not produce a moral and egalitarian society, but a society where the worst floats to the top. Solzhenitsyn (1986) cautioned the West that replacing morality with law was a path to totalitarianism, as people become susceptible to accept anything that is legislated.

Nihilism and the absence of altruism is not a disorder in the rational world, rather it represents a logical destination. Rational and self-conscious human beings seek to gradually dismantle and abolish the irrational components of their past to remove restraints and obtain greater control over the future. Yet, in the absence of a spiritual society and neglect of the past, the future has less meaning. The nihilist rejects all traditional institutions and forms of authority at the peril of social order. Mikhail Katkov, a 19th-century conservative Russian journalist with significant political influence, expected the moral decay of nihilism to eventually produce revolution. Tradition, unalienable land property, and honouring the past are powerful tools to develop 'homogenous, enduring characters for long generations' in society (Nietzsche 1967: 65). Nietzsche therefore expressed concern that technology and complex economic structures were undermining the ability to preserve traditions:

> Now the breaking up of landed property belongs to the opposite tendency: newspapers (in place of daily prayers), railway, telegraph. Centralisation of a tremendous number of different interests in a single soul, which for that reason must be very strong and protean.

Nietzsche (1967: 3) expected nihilism to corrode the sense of a shared purpose and fate as a civilisation, and ultimately leave Man isolated, self-absorbed, and confrontational:

> What I relate is the history of the next two centuries. I describe what is coming, what can no longer come differently: *the advent of nihilism* . . . For

some time now our whole European culture has been moving as toward a catastrophe, with a tortured tension that is growing from decade to decade: restlessly, violently, headlong, like a river that wants to reach the end, that no longer reflects, that is afraid to reflect.

Dostoyevsky was similarly preoccupied with moral decline in the absence of religion. In *Crime and Punishment*, Dostoyevsky depicted the state of mind of a rational Man contemplating murder. The rational/calculative assessment favoured murdering an old lady as she inflicted harm on those around her, while stealing and redistributing her possessions would improve the life of others and make the world a better place. Without constraints by a higher divine force, nihilism prevailed due to the moral relativism within a cost/benefit analysis. Man acts on instincts, then rationalises it, and delude himself to believe ethics and morality was contingent solely on rationality. The sociopath and psychopath are extremely rational as their actions are based purely on self-interest without consideration of others that make up a collective group belonging to the self.

The discipline of psychology also recognises the rivalry between the rational and irrational aspects of Man. Sigmund Freud (2015[1930]) noted that within humanity there is a perpetual friction between immutable instincts and conformity in civilisation. Society cannot evolve beyond and transcend the community by becoming immune to the irrational. Freud (1963: 119) posited that 'the primitive mind is, in the fullest sense of the word, imperishable'. Neglecting non-rational aspect of life as tradition, arts, and spirituality lead to disillusionment and moral panic. Eliminating the irrational aspect of Man eradicates both hate and love, which deprives Man of meaning and fuels violence. Carl Jung (1973: 227) similarly recognised that inherited instinctive impulses constrain rationality, arguing that 'free will only exists within the limits of consciousness. Beyond those limits there is mere compulsion.' Jung theorised that archetypes, imagery inherited from our early ancestors and moulded through our evolution, remain present in the collective consciousness. These images are interpreted and transmitted consciously through tradition and culture as a bastion of meaning and order. The erosion of culture, traditions, and spirituality therefore inhibits the capacity of human beings to interpret and pass on the archetypes. This argument in psychology is to some extent supported by neuro-biology as the brain distinguishing between the 'natural' and 'civilisation' since the biological categories and social interactions are distinct from man-made entities associated with civilisation (Yong 2012).

The struggle between rational and irrational is also popularised in literature. The notion of Man being pulled between nature and civilisation was depicted in the *Strange Case of Dr Jekyll and Mr Hyde* (Stevenson 2004[1886]), and the more recent *The Double* (Saramago 2005). Stevenson (2004[1886]) argued that 'the curse of mankind' was to have primitive man and modern man in perpetual struggle. Developing civilisation by suppressing rather than nurturing the animal within that seeks the innate would result in the pendulum eventually swinging fiercely in the opposite direction. The priest or politician, who ignores his primitive instincts by behaving too 'civilised', is more vulnerable to chaotic behaviour as the pendulum swings towards nature. In the masterpiece, *Heart of Darkness,* Conrad (1996[1899]) depicted European society as hollow at the core and its people similarly empty inside, which could easily culminate in destruction. Man must develop the aptitude to exercise internal control over dark impulses such as greed and the temptation for dominance. Conrad suggested that European civilisation had become excessively reliant on external forces to constrain these dark impulses, primarily by the fear of the law and being reprimanded in public. Thoroughly convinced of being civilised, the European Man was unprepared to constrain nefarious impulses when they emerge. Subsequently, Conrad posited that once the authority of the state and the law rescind, European peoples would be unleashed and predisposed to commit horrific acts as they become consumed by their untamed desires.

The Enlightenment sparked the self-professed counter-Enlightenment movement and Romanticism, which unapologetically embraced the irrational as an unassailable component of Man. Identity founded solely on the society and civics provide less meaning and depth to the people (Herder 2002[1772]). The tilt towards universal values and norms commonly results in resistance and an eventual radical pendulum swing back to the distinctive. In the later stages of the 18th century, Romanticism rose and revived medievalism by emphasising emotion and admiration for nature and the past. The romantic period, especially profound in Germany, aimed to resuscitate community and culture. The proliferation of French culture had invigorated German cultural impulses to balance by asserting cultural autonomy. The focus on distinctive national culture in the 19th century was instrumental for German unification, which contrasted with France's more universalistic ideas of civilisation. Albeit, from 1870 France also embraced national culture as the indicator of civilisation, that further intensified after the bloodshed in the First World War (Al-Azmeh 2012). Europe was largely a cultural concept with a variety of 'others'. The English inclinations to define civilisation as culture further compounded the national distinctiveness, yet with porous borders as the cultures were not completely secluded.

Romantic nationalism did not seek to eliminate the modern but harmonise it with the traditional. Gadamer (1976) scorned Enlightenment prejudices against the incommensurable of culture and civilisation. Klages (1981[1929]) likewise defined this battle to be between the soul and the intellect. Industrial society degraded the soul by disconnecting Man from the environment he had relied upon since he came into existence. The world was split between the natural emotional/ spiritual connections and the rational material world. Heidegger (2010[1927]) depicted modern industrial society as a tyrannical element by obstructing engagement with the purity of nature. Heidegger argued that Plato's ideas in terms of what it means *to be,* the distinctive *being* or 'dasein', had been forgotten at the peril of civilisation. Building on the ideas of Nietzsche, Heidegger (2014[1953]) posited that by neglecting and not reproducing the cultural and spiritual traditions, Man succumbs to nihilism and enters an era of intellectual and cultural crisis.

The subsequent embrace of organic ethno-cultural distinctiveness was central among German counter-Enlightenment thinkers throughout the 1800s and into the 1900s. The radical advocacy of returning to pagan roots to protect the sacred connection between Man and nature neglected the rational and therefore undermined the harmonisation of the primitive nature of Man with reason and truth. When a political counter-movement emerged to celebrate tradition, culture, and the natural emerged, Heidegger and several of his contemporaries were immediately pulled towards the ideology. For Heidegger and others, this meant joining the Nazi party. The impact of rapid economic structural changes on communities was a key focus of German philosophers and scholars. The political economy of fascism accurately recognised the need for greater state control over strategic industries and that a powerful industrial economy had to be balanced by replenishing gemeinschaft through the celebration of culture and traditions instead of materialism. The national socialists expected that national rebirth with cultural and spiritual restoration would in return immediately produce prosperity (Welk 1938: 38–39). A social hierarchy consisting of distinctive and cooperative classes was expected to instil order as opposed to advocating the equality of unequals.

The palpable weakness of 20th-century fascism was the malicious and reprehensible xenophobia, violence, and unhinged dictatorial powers. In Germany, the divide between community/soul and society/intellect adopted a ferocious racial component. The Jewish population, a people expelled from their ancient homeland, had less attachment to the land and agricultural society, and were commonly represented as affluent merchants without the shared spiritual roots of the Germans. The Jews were depicted as epitomising the excessive advancement of society that was tearing away at German Volk culture and the soul of the community. Paul de Lagarde, an ardent anti-Semite, portrayed the Jews as a foreign element corrupting the spirituality of the German people. Simplifying the complex perpetual struggle between the traditional and modern within the human consciousness as a mere corruption by an ethnic minority is intellectually lazy but effective for the discontent masses. It is seductive to establish a new frontier with achievable objectives to overcome what is an imperishable struggle. Optimism proliferates as the contemporary decay is believed to be reversible towards a glorious future, and in the process the duality of Man is nourished as the population can engage in barbarity against the inferior to advance civilisation. While Adolf Hitler's *Mein Kampf* lacked the intellectual depth of his contemporaries, his argument similarly blamed industrial capitalism as the source of declining culture and eventual collapse of civilisation.

The rise of excessively rational Western society

In post-war Germany and the West, the philosophy, political theory, and debate on the delicate dilemma between gemeinschaft and gesellschaft disappeared partly due to the disastrous experimentation with National Socialism to harmonise culture with power. Reflecting the prevailing sentiments of the new Germany, Habermas (1998) initially contested the utility of identities in complex societies and then later argued in favour of a shallow 'constitutional patriotism' as pride to be part of a democracy. Latent emotions associated with the traditional are rediscovered and mobilised for confrontation when they are perceived to be under assault. Rather than transcending the community, the efforts to create a post-national federalised Europe Union is setting the conditions in place for a reaction that swings the pendulum back towards the defence of radical nationalism to preserve ties to the past.

As modern industrial capitalism took hold after the Second World War, the dilemma between community and society became more prevalent. The sociology of the 1950s was preoccupied with the notion that the individual became alienated in mass society. Modern industrial society converted the primordial need for inter-personal relationships in communities into an instrument to serve complex economic systems in advanced society. Mills (1951: 182), an American sociologist, addressed how the loss of community affected the individual:

> In a society of employees dominated by the marketing mentality, it is inevitable that a personality market should arise. For in the great shift from manual skills to the art of 'handling', selling and servicing people, personal or even intimate traits of employees are drawn into the sphere of exchange and become commodities in the labor market.

Modern society prostitutes the cognitive and emotional. As the inter-personal ties of a community is commodified and replaced with manipulative rational/ commercial interactions, people become alienated from each other and from themselves: 'Men are estranged from one another as each secretly tries to make an instrument of the other, and in time a full circle is made: one makes an instrument of himself and is estranged from it also' (Mills 1951: 188).

Islamic fundamentalism has its roots in the protection of the traditional and sacred. Sayyid Qutb, commonly recognised as the father of modern Islamic fundamentalism, developed his radical views as a student in Colorado in 1949. Qutb was initially captivated by the affluence, modernity, and glamour of American life, before being appalled by the vanity and emptiness lurking beneath. The attraction of modern life and affluence was represented by the pristine front yards in American suburbs, yet people were more preoccupied with maintaining appearances than engaging in meaningful interactions. Industrial capitalism was believed to erode even the most sacred and intimate part of the human spirit, as even the churches were seen to imitate culture. The reference to gemeinshaft and gesellschaft were implicit in Qutb's writings:

> The majority of people in the most affluent and materially advanced countries, such as the United States of America or Sweden, lead the most miserable lives. Anxiety, depression and boredom are eating into people's lives who despite their affluence and energy, are driven to a culture of fads and mental and sexual perversion, and all kinds of anti-social escapist behaviour that allows them no peace or security. The fundamental cause of this pervasive

unhappiness is the spiritual wilderness in which Western societies are living today. For, in spite of the prosperity and material well-being they enjoy, these societies lack the spiritual reassurance and faith that can only come with belief in God and placing our full trust in Him.

(Nolan 2016: 199–200)

The exceptional American mathematician turned terrorist, Theodore Kaczynski (1995), expressed similar motivations. Kaczynski (1995) mailed his long essay to the media, *Industrial Society & Its Future*, as he terrorised the US with bombs. The advanced society following the industrial revolution was argued to be a disaster for humanity as people had been 'oversocialised' to 'behave in ways that are increasingly remote from the natural pattern of human behavior' (Kaczynski 1995: 2). Modern society profits from decadence rather than providing solutions. When society makes people sick and unhappy, the symptoms are pacified with drugs and vulgar entertainment. Americans were living the lives of jaded aristocrats, they were 'bored, hedonistic, and demoralised' (Kaczynski 1995: 5). Efforts to advance society while preserving community were dismissed as futile:

They whine about the decay of traditional values, yet they enthusiastically support technological progress and economic growth. Apparently it never occurs to them that you can't make rapid, drastic changes in the technology and the economy of a society without causing rapid changes in all other aspects of society as well, and that such rapid changes inevitably break down traditional values.

(Kaczynski 1995: 7)

As Man decouples from community, there is inevitably a crisis of consciousness, resulting in irrational behaviour as community is sought to be recreated. Former US presidential candidate Al Gore (2013: 367) expressed concerns about a 'collective identity crisis' as we seek to rediscover 'who we are'. The rational is then contested as 'we begin to value powerful images instead of tested truths':

The resurgence of fundamentalism in every world religion, from Islam to Judaism to Hinduism to Christianity; the proliferation of new spiritual movements, ideologies, and cults of all shapes and descriptions; the popularity of New Age Doctrines and the current fascination with explanatory myths and stories from cultures the world over – all serve as evidence for the conclusion that there is indeed a spiritual crisis in modern civilisation that seems to be based on an emptiness at its center and the absence of a larger spiritual purpose.

(Gore 2013: 367)

In modern literature, Nowicki (2013) explores in *Lost Violent Souls* how the hollowness of the modern world, deprived of the traditional and spiritedness of community, produces political violence due to angry and violent men who are in a despairing search for meaning. The answer for our current dismay is to find a balance between 'love for the natural world and love for our wondrous civilisation' (Gore 2013: 367). Remarkably, Gore recognised that his own preoccupation with environmental activism had developed when he sought to understand the meaning of his own life (Gore 2013: 367). Dugin (2012) argues that the ideology of liberalism was succumbing to the same fate as fascism and communism due to the embrace of modernity and utopianism, which implied the pernicious neglect and rejection of the pre-modern and spiritual.

Liberalism's excessive rationality and efficiency

Liberalism, deriving from the Latin word *liber*, translates to 'free' or freedom. Freedoms can be enjoyed by citizens when rights and responsibilities are balanced and preserved. Liberal citizenship tends to disproportionately emphasise rights of the individual at the expense of responsibilities towards the shared community. As individuals are rational utility-maximisers, they eschew obligations to the state. The rejection of responsibilities is ultimately harmful to the individual, as responsibilities bestow function to human beings and thus a sense of meaning. The Lockean understanding of human nature as good and rational is at the heart of the flaws within liberal thought. The intrusive role of the state advocating morality for stability is deemed redundant if it is assumed that human nature is inherently good. The conflicts of humanity are instead believed to be overcome by externalising the internal goodness and altruism of Man with democracy, institutions, law, interdependence, transparency, and understanding. Entrenched in the philosophy of John Locke, liberalism does not deem the community as imperative for stability, socialisation, morality, and meaning. Liberalism presumes that conflict derives from impediments to equality and autonomy. The egalitarian impulse of liberalism therefore places rationality, human freedom, and prosperity at the centre, which is not to be constrained by communitarian or republican virtues.

The balance between rights and responsibilities in liberal citizenship is gradually dismantled with the advancement of liberalism. The ability to exercise the rights of the autonomous individual is contingent on upholding a firm and functioning community (Kymlicka 2002: 212). The strength and internal cohesion of the community is contingent on shared responsibility to assimilate by gravitating minority cultures towards an ethno-cultural core. Advancing liberty by challenging arbitrary authorities in society and government is a contradiction as it also diminishes the dominant culture. Any functioning community requires a delineation and discrimination between insiders and outsiders by preserving defining particularities to make membership meaningful and valuable. The responsibilities towards the community therefore entails adapting to and reproducing the majority culture as an overarching umbrella identity, as opposed to embracing a multicultural concept that segregates the primary identity. With reduced focus on shared ethno-cultural identity, there is less internal compulsion of the individual to live up to the responsibilities towards the community. Hegel critiqued Locke's assumption of universal norms and morality as ethos is predicated on the cultural particularities and social context of distinct communities. Kukathas and Pettit (1990: 95) similarly posit:

> Morality is something which is rooted in practice – in the particular practices of actual communities. So the idea of looking to uncover abstract principles of morality by which to evaluate or redesign society is an implausible one. There are no universal principles of morality or justice discoverable by reason.

Political liberalism augments the agency of the individual, who innately aspires to become increasingly free from constraints and rules. The longer a democracy exists, the freer it will become. The archaic societal structures based on constraints, virtue, and spiritual principles are replaced with social efficiency that embraces materialistic self-indulgence, anti-social behaviour, and excesses. Thus, liberalism tends to denigrate towards freedom from the past, traditions, rules, and authority, while advocating freedom for alcohol consumption, gambling, abortion, and other anti-social behaviour. Plato's *The Republic* exemplified Greek philosophers' early caution against excessive liberalism, individualism, and democracy. When freedom is pursued in the extreme, the pendulum will eventually swing in the opposing direction. Unconstrained liberalism is pernicious by growing more extreme and eventually turning on itself. Plato and Socrates famously expressed pessimistic expectations about the durability of democracy. Plato (2016: 51) recognised that:

> The great charm [of democracy] is, that you may do as you like; you may govern if you like, let it alone if you like; go to war and make peace if you feel disposed, and all quite irrespective of anybody else.

Yet, unrestrained freedom generates extravagance and immoral self-indulgence, plunging 'into the freedom and libertinism of useless and unnecessary pleasures' (Plato 2016: 215). The duality of man was recognised by Socrates, who argued that structures ensuring order were required for peace, as opposed to unlimited freedom and democracy given that 'in all of us, even in good men, there is a lawless wild-beast nature' (Plato 2016: 57). The fabric of society eventually unravels when the masses endeavour to liberate the individual from all compulsions and constraints imposed by the authority of traditional social institutions such as government and family. Eventually, all expressions of authority are equated to unwarranted control and totalitarianism. Plato (2016: 216) concluded that democracy would inherently be a temporary and transitory form of government as the ensuing chaos would eventually result in inviting a tyrant to re-establish order:

> Can liberty have any limit? Certainly not . . . By degrees the anarchy finds a way into private houses . . . The son is on a level with his father, he having no respect or reverence for either of his parents; and this is his freedom . . .

> Citizens chafe impatiently at the least touch of authority . . . they will have no one over them . . . Such is the fair and glorious beginning out of which springs tyranny . . . Liberty overmasters democracy . . . the excessive increase of anything often causes a reaction in the opposite direction . . . The excess of liberty, whether in states or individuals, seems only to pass into excess of slavery . . . And so tyranny naturally arises out of democracy, and the most aggravated form of tyranny and slavery out of the most extreme form of liberty.

Alexis de Tocqueville famously made comparable observations on his examination of the US, postulating that unchecked individualism and materialism would undermine democracy itself. The self-absorbed individualism and materialism inherent in a democracy, where affluence is the principal motivation of the people, weakens the community and produces a superficial happiness contingent on ignorance and distraction. Henry Adams (1919: vii–viii) criticised the belief that democracy paves the way for perfection as it 'ignore[s] certain fundamental facts which are stronger than democratic theories', primarily that 'the strongest of human passions are fear and greed'. John Adams (1814), the Second US President, similarly posited:

> Remember Democracy never lasts long. It soon wastes exhausts and murders itself. There never was a Democracy yet, that did not commit suicide. It is in vain to Say that Democracy is less vain, less proud, less selfish, less ambitious or less avaricious than Aristocracy or Monarchy. It is not true in Fact and nowhere appears in history.

Economic liberalism perpetually enhances efficiency by shedding inefficient and non-material achievements such as religion, family, traditions, and smaller communities. Public ownership, regulations, trade unions, cultural particularities, national identities, kinship, and personal ties have an abating function in complex societies. In the absence of classical conservativism, economic determinism ensues as economic interests dictate cultural, social, political, intellectual, and technological facets of a civilisation. Individualism and materialism benefit from the construction of a complex society with a growing division of labour, labour mobility, population size, market expanse, technological advancement, and concentration of power in a bureaucratic and oligarchic elite to manage society.

Pre-modern society and Man had limited exposure to market forces. Polanyi's (1957) *The Great Transformation* explored the devastating impact on social order and human nature as England transitioned initially towards a market economy. Polanyi (1957) depicted protectionism as the natural human response to creative destruction and social disturbances resulting from free trade, and expected Man to eventually confront ever-increasing efficiency to restore his natural pre-modern environment. The commodification of everything sacred to Man in a liberal market economy inevitably creates a dialectical process where new ideologies emerge that advocate protectionism (Polanyi 1957). Likewise, Bell (1976) defines economising as:

> efficiency, least cost, greatest return, maximization, optimization, and similar measures of judgment about the employment and mix of resources . . . There is a simple measure of value, namely utility. And there is a simple principle of change, namely the ability to substitute products or processes because they are more efficient and yield higher return at lesser cost, the principle of productivity. The social structure is a reified world because it is a structure of roles, not persons, and this is laid out in the organizational charts that specify the relationships of hierarchy and function.

The Protestant capitalist ethics of a moral system and reward has diminished under the growing bureaucracy that is instrumental for progress, which alienates and traps Man in Weber's 'iron cage'. Rational calculation 'reduces every worker to a cog in this [bureaucratic] machine and, seeing himself in this light, he will merely ask how to transform himself from a little to a somewhat bigger cog' that eventually 'drives us to despair' (Weber 1924b: 413–414). The objectives of rational society will to a lesser and lesser extent coincide with the preservation of culture and the community. Morality is defined as augmenting the local traditions that are sacred to the population to obtain popular support for rational economic policies that enhances the economic competitiveness of the state. An economic system must inspire capitalist competition to advance society, while concurrently containing hedonistic actions where they harm the collective (Davidson and Davidson 1988).

State intervention has always been required to redistribute the excess labour and capital to strategic industries and minimise creative destruction. As new technologies and the international market place produce increasingly complex economic structures with a more mobile global workforce, people will inevitably be estranged from their traditional communities. Schumpeter's 'creative destruction' refers to the profound changes in economic structures that eliminate former skills, trades, and industries (Luttwak 1993a). Economic liberalism advocates a more modest role for the state at a time when there is greater necessity for intervention to mitigate the adverse effects of creative destruction on the community and to strengthen society. The inherent flaw in economic liberalism is the assumption that excess capital and labour is directed by the hidden hand of the market into new productive areas of the economy. This assumption rests on the empirical evidence from the industrial revolution when enhanced efficiency within agriculture liberated excess labour from rural communities, and market forces directed the people to manufacturing in urban centres. However, in the absence of an industrial and innovative industry capable of employing the large labour force from increasing creative destruction, the labour and capital may be directed towards low-skilled and low-paid professions. Furthermore, the strains on the community were severe due to the rapid shift in human habitat as people were dislodged from their communities where they had relied on stronger inter-personal ties and enjoyed greater economic autonomy. In the cities, the inter-personal ties diminish and economic autonomy reduces, resulting in new power relationships between the elites and the working class.

Conclusion

It has been argued here that the philosophy of the duality of Man, which had much sway in the 19th century, should be re-examined and analysed through contemporary political theories. The rational and calculative neorealist political theory prevalent during the Cold War was dominant as the duality of Man was supressed and internal cohesion ensured by the binary divide in terms of both ideology and power. The subsequent misperception that Man is completely conscious and rational resulted in the neglect of classical realism. Subsequently, international relations have drawn less upon the literature on Man's eternal struggle between the rational and irrational, which has been extensively covered in disciplines ranging from evolutionary biology, psychology, philosophy, and popular culture. Neoclassical realism brings classical realism back in by assessing the behaviour of the decision-maker as an intervening variable between the international distribution of power and foreign policy. Without a harmony between the contradictory impulses of Man, the state cannot have internal solidarity or efficiently mobilise its resources to pursue calculative and rational interests.

The stability and endurance of civilisation is largely contingent on finding a balance or metaxy between the rational and irrational; universal and particular; society and community. Failure to appreciate the duality and contradictions in human nature, a key weakness in liberalism, triggers a ferocious swing of the Hegelian pendulum from one extreme to another at the peril of civilisation. Understanding the duality of Man is imperative to establish in the following chapters why civilisations rise, decay, and are reborn. The ascendance and current disarray of Western civilisation is better understood by surveying the excessiveness of the rational, and the inevitable response.

2   The cyclical rise, decline, and rebirth of civilisations

Introduction

What explains the rise and fall of civilisations? Civilisations are a puzzle as their ascendency and triumph tend to sow the seeds of their own destruction. Great civilisations and empires rarely perish in an encounter with superior military force on the battleground, rather their downfall is typically caused by socio-economic changes linked to advancement and prosperity. Socially, successful civilisations develop an advanced urbanised cosmopolitan with disdain for conserving the traditional. Economically, successful civilisations develop growing wealth disparity, become excessively materialistic and economic deterministic, while overextending themselves and debasing the currency.

The study of civilisations by historians and political scientists will be framed in this chapter through the theoretical prism of gemeinschaft and gesellschaft. Civilisations are not a static construction; rather they follow a socio-economic cyclical path of rise, decline, and rebirth. Culture is the spiritual scaffolding of civilisations that develops out of the pursuit of meaning, which provides a sanctuary and linkage to the primordial, spiritual, and irrational that reflect human instincts developed over tens of thousands of years in nature. Albeit, much like society outgrows and hollows out the community, the advancement of civilisations eventually exhausts the culture it evolved, leaving behind nihilism and decadence.

This chapter will first survey ancient mythology and religious stories as the oldest recognition of the eternal struggle of civilisation to establish order and engage with chaos. Order is rooted in culture or community, while the borderless complexity of the wider world represents chaos. Thousands of years ago, the various stories of genesis shared the recognition that the chaos of the world incentivised the development of order and traditions for refuge and meaning, while the subsequent erosion of chaos then diminished the requirement for order and thereby reintroduced chaos. The stability and endurance of humanity was therefore portrayed as being contingent upon the ability of the vigorous youth to continuously reproduce the wisdom of the decaying father, by engaging with the chaos of the contemporary world to replenish tradition and order.

Second, the theories on the cyclical development of philosophers, historians, and political scientist will be explored. Italian, German, Russian, English, and

American theorists stood out in the study of great civilisation. Their common findings were that civilisations emerged out of a culture that embraced the heroic, spiritual, traditional, and irrational, while the advancement of civilisation would degenerate the culture it sprouted from. Another commonality was the pessimistic outlook for Western civilisation, which is widely recognised as having entered the era of decadence and pending death.

Third, a theory on the four seasons of civilisations will be developed, framed through gemeinschaft and gesellschaft. Spring symbolises the emergence of culture linked almost exclusively to the community. The fear of chaos, death, and nature compel human beings to establish community-centred entities of governance in touch with the primordial and instinctive for protection and legitimacy. Summer denotes the balance between community and society as symmetrical interdependence is established between the rural regions where culture thrives and the urbanised regions where civilisational advancements are made. Autumn represents the continuous rise of society at the expense of community, with the lack of balance leading to decadence. Civilisation gradually polarises between the urbanised elites committed solely to advancing society, and an internal proletariat attempting to salvage the community. The need to address the ills and divisions within civilisation can be temporarily delayed with expansionism and frontiers as it instils a sense of meaning with the promise of a better future. Winter denotes the death and possible rebirth of a civilisation. Society engulfs the community thereby eradicating the foundation for continued existence. When the materialist and nihilistic civilisation begins to perish, the remnants of the spirituality from the community can be recovered and salvaged by internal elements or reproduced by a peripheral 'barbaric' civilisation that conquers the declining civilisation unwilling or incapable of defending itself.

Civilisational cycle: order reborn out of chaos

The present state of order is not the principal indicator of stability and viability, as civilisations constantly face stagnation and decline. Order is defined as the ability of civilisations to continuously regenerate. Order is born out of chaos, and in the absence of chaos the need to maintain order and borders declines. It is therefore an unremitting necessity to culture the young and vibrant to replace the old and stagnant. The new adopts and builds on the traditions of the old, but with a new vitality and relatability to current realities. Much like the youth who ventures out to engage with the larger chaotic world before rediscovering traditions and returning to the old order, civilisations must also continuously be reborn. Thomas Sowell (2002: 162), an American economist and social scientist, stipulated that the ideals and virtues of American civilisation had to perpetually be rediscovered and reproduced: 'Each new generation born is in effect an invasion of civilisation by little barbarians, who must be civilised before it is too late.'

The mutually dependent and contradictory relationship between gemeinschaft and gesellschaft is a civilisational manifestation of the perpetual rivalry between order and chaos. The rebirth of the ancient and pre-modern offers structure and order by erecting physical, ideational, and spiritual walls between 'us' and the 'other'. The identity, virtues, and order that embody 'us' can only exist in opposition to the unknown and barbarian 'other'. Man is drawn to go beyond the confines and safety of his community to confront an external unknown as he in the process rediscovers and rejuvenates his own virtues that order is founded upon. This eternal and non-linear struggle between order and chaos is at the heart of the creational myths of religions and has made its way through time and is still represented in contemporary culture. For example, even Hollywood tends to reiterate the story of the virtuous protagonist who in the beginning of the tale is in a waning condition due to the lack of purpose, until encountering a barbaric and malevolent adversary. After delving into the chaos and emerging victorious, his spirit and morale are replenished and strengthened.

Religious and mythical stories of genesis function as an intellectual scaffolding for humanity's perpetual struggle between nature and society. Nature represents the chaos of the natural and primordial where meaning and the divine are found, while civilisation represents the endeavour of Man to seek structure and order. The natural habitat of Man is an amalgam between nature and civilisation, yet they create impulses that draw human beings in opposing directions. Paradise and peace in the human consciousness is discovered by accepting these imperishable contradictions and balancing them, while excessive tilt in either direction will eventually cause a destructive dialectic counter-position.

Gods typically represent various primordial and 'irrational' needs, impulses, and personality traits that are permanent in human nature and transcend through time and cultures. Man being created in the image of God suggests that the permanent instincts and features of human beings are manifestations of both the divine and eternal. The ancient Greeks' description of Man as a plaything of the Gods implied that forces beyond the control of human beings dictate their ever-lasting impulses that control personalities and behaviour. God, a paternalistic father figure offering order, embodies the principal idea or ideal of a culture and civilisation. Religions and mythologies across time and cultures largely tells the almost identical story of rescuing and reproducing the legacy of the father as human beings are cultural creatures that live on the past, yet are in constant need of rebirth to rejuvenate history, tradition, and culture that will inevitably decay with time.

The creational mythology of ancient Mesopotamia tells the story of the merger of the two original Gods: Abzu the father representing order, and Tiamat the mother embodying primordial chaos. Harmony and order unravels as their offspring murders the father, and defiantly builds a new home on top of his grave, thereby making it impossible to reproduce him. Following a period of relentless chaos, Marduk eventually restores order and becomes the highest God by slaying Tiamat and her highest monster, Kinu. Marduk then creates human beings out of the blood of Kinu to do the work of the Gods as chaos should not be attempted to be transcended.

Egyptian Gods similarly described the rise, inevitable decay, and rebirth of culture and civilisation. The Egyptian God of Osiris was a great king embodying the paternal spirit ruling with tradition, virtue, and wisdom. His wife Isis was the

Goddess of Darkness and Chaos, which much like the Mesopotamian counterpart ensured a balanced to excessive order as a source of complacency and stagnation. As Osiris got older and began to decay, he became less capable of reinvigorating civilisation. Much like cultures and civilisations, with age king Osiris gradually lost his ability and willingness to recognise and resist the emergence of malevolence threating to undermine order. Osiris' brother, Set, the embodiment of the belligerence of barbarians at the periphery, slayed Osiris when he was weak and vulnerable. Set cut Osiris into 14 pieces and scattered them across Egypt to prevent his resurrection. Nonetheless, Isis became pregnant with one of the pieces of Osiris to give birth to Horus, who went on to revenge his father by killing Set. The eye of Horus, which had been plucked out in the battle with Set, was given to his deceased father. The subsequent common entity of Horus and Osiris enabled culture and civilisation to revitalise due to the convergence of the tradition and virtue of the father, and the youth and strength of the son. The Eye of Horus positioned above a pyramid remains a symbol of this duality of Man that balanced the traditional with the power and vigour of youth.

Greek mythology told a similar story with the phoenix. The long-lived bird would at the end of its life build a nest and set it on fire to shed its weaknesses and decadence, and then be reborn out of the ashes. The phoenix became a symbol in early Christianity due to the analogy of Christ's own death and resurrection to enable the rebirth and renewal of humanity. Christianity as a foundational core of Western civilisation has to a large extent reproduced the dynamics of its religious predecessors. The creational myth of the Garden of Eden, shared by Christianity, Judaism, and Islam, depicts the natural condition of Man as being lodged between nature and society. The Garden of Eden epitomises the purity of wild nature, yet it is organised and protected by a wall and a paternalistic God against uncertainty and barbarity on the outside (Peterson 2007). The balance between nature and society is both threatened and preserved by the presence of a predatory evil. In Asian philosophies and religions, it has also been widely recognised that contradictory impulses can be complementary when they are balanced. For example, Vishnu the preserver ensures stability, yet can only exist with Shiva the destroyer who incites change. Chinese philosophy of yin and yang similarly build on the recognition of the interdependence of contradictive forces in human nature.

The civilisational cycle of gesellschaft undermining gemeinschaft

Civilisations prosper on continuity, by advancing on the foundation of culture. Yet, greatness creates hubris as achievements and affluence cause neglect of the past. Reminiscent of Mesopotamian mythology, a prominent statesman in ancient Rome, Cicero, warned about building the prosperous Rome defiantly on top of the grave of those who came before:

> Before our own time, the customs of our ancestors produced excellent men, and eminent men preserved our ancient customs and the institutions of their

forefathers. But though the republic, when it came to us, was like a beautiful painting, whose colours, however, were already fading with age, our own time not only has neglected to freshen it by renewing the original colours, but has not even taken the trouble to preserve its configuration and, so to speak its general outlines. For what is now left of the 'ancient customs' on which he said 'the commonwealth of Rome' was 'founded firm'? They have been, as we see, so completely buried in oblivion that they are not only no longer practiced, but are already unknown.

(Wood 1991: 163)

The most prominent historians and political scientists exploring former and current civilisations developed their theses on a cyclical pattern of rise, decline, and rebirth. The transition from community to society is the optimal format to understand the socio-economic cyclical development. The common denominator in various studies is the view of civilisation as an entity that continuously gravitates away from the community and towards society, which eventually renders civilisation unsustainable. The Enlightenment was commonly seen as offering great opportunities and challenges to civilisations. Culture and civilisation in the 18th and 19th century were usually referred to as processes, in contrast with the contemporary flawed tendency of depicting them as static. Civilisations were most commonly defined as organic entities that grow out of infancy and reach maturity, and then commence the process of decay and eventually demise. Connolly (2008[1948]: 261) argued that 'the goal of every culture is to decay through over-civilisation':

In spite of the slow conversion of progressive ideas into the fact of history, the Dark Ages have a way of coming back. Civilisation – the world of affection and reason and freedom and justice – is a luxury which must be fought for, as dangerous to possess as an oil-field or an unlucky diamond.

Giambattista Vico (2002[1725]) developed the initial major work on civilisations, which depicted a cyclical process from imagination towards reason. When reason advances and displaces imagination, civilisation begins its decay until rebirth by renewed imagination. Vico identified three stages of the civilisational cycle: the age of the gods, the age of heroes, and the age of humans. In the age of the gods, Man develops culture through poetic wisdom and religion that reflects the innate within human nature, and the subsequent meaning and security produces a gravitational pull towards unifying a culture. As humanity fears the supernatural, rulers initially enjoy a divine legitimacy by acting on a mandate from God. In the age of heroes, larger entities of power emerge, and alliances are formed against external adversaries. The heroes must also repel internal disunity as Man demands greater agency and autonomy. In the last age of the humans, the nascent rationality of Man undermines the authority of the heroes. In the pursuit of equal rights there is an inherent class war, while rationality tears away at the cultural, poetic, and religious spirituality of Man. The internal rivalry and loss of the cultural invites a new barbarism as Man looks back at the innate for order, imagination and meaning.

Brooks Adams (1897) described similar organic cycles in *The Law of Civilization and Decay*. Adams was preoccupied with the incremental and pernicious complexity of advanced capitalist societies. People voluntarily flock towards emerging population centres with the most productive and efficient commercial climate. Albeit, as society becomes increasingly efficient, the community is discarded as inefficient and therefore destroys itself. Greed, distrust, immorality, and nihilism prevails without the community and subsequently tears away at the solidarity and foundation of civilisation.

Konstantin Leontiev's (2014[1885]) *East, Russia and the Slavs* made it common to compare him to Nietzsche by offering a Russian romanticist response to the excesses of the Enlightenment. Leontiev depicted civilisation as an organic entity that passed through three stages: the period of childhood with initial simplicity, the period of adulthood with thriving complexity, and an era of decay with secondary simplicity. The first primitive stage had an unadulterated spirituality that gradually became more sophisticated before culminating in complex high culture. Class distinctions epitomise the maturity of adulthood. Bourgeois culture of the higher echelons of society functions as a socialiser of broader society by establishing an ideal to be revered and emulated. Inequality is the source of aspiration, motivation, and progress. In contrast, the final stage of secondary simplicity is characterised by growing equality and democracy, where civilisation decays due to laziness tolerating the inferior: 'the egalitarian-liberal progress is the antithesis to the process of development' (Leontiev 2014[1885]: 144). The apparent progress towards democracy and equality is pernicious and should be resisted to preserve culture, greatness, creativity, and spirituality. Much like his American counterpart, Brooks Adams, Leontiev believed that the West had entered the stage of decay. Leontiev therefore advocated Russia should reverse its Westernisation initiated by Peter the Great.

Osvald Spengler's (1991[1922]) *The Decline of the West* is allegedly the most dominant work on the cyclical rise, decline, and rebirth of civilisations. Spengler postulated that all cultures are organic entities with a lifespan consisting of birth, adulthood, and eventual death. The birth of a culture is referred to as spring, the burgeoning vitality of high culture represents summer, maturity of civilisation is epitomised by autumn, while senility and decay is symbolised by winter. Spengler defined Europe as a Faustian culture tragically striving for the unattainable that would motivate great exploration and expansion, yet ultimately resulting in nihilism once the creative energies were exhausted. While civilisation develop from cultures, civilisation eventual consume and degrade the culture that gave it nourishment (Spengler 1991[1922]). As efficiency and money eventually decimate culture and spirit, the civilisation begins its decent and exit from history.

Arnold Toynbee's (1946) *A Study of History* identified five stages of the rise and decline of civilisation: genesis, growth, time of troubles, universal state, and disintegration. The first stage of genesis signifies primitive cultures becoming civilisations when a 'creative minority' finds solutions to complex challenges. Civilisation stagnates without sufficient challenges, while failure to overcome challenges causes demise. The creative minority functions as a responsive mechanism to challenges as their success and prosperity incentivises the majority to follow them. The creative minority's ascendance to affluence and power makes them complacent and thus lose their creativity. With diminishing ability to point to current achievements, the creative minority becomes more reliant on pointing to achievements from a glorious past. The celebration of past achievement further undermines the ability to move forward and exacerbates the lack of future-oriented creative solutions. The detached elites, no longer able to legitimise their rule on creativity, eventually become a 'dominant minority' that rely instead on control and coercion. The alienated majority seeks a return to the traditional and spiritual as a refuge, and possibly even establishes a common cause with a rival civilisation at the periphery.

Carroll Quigley's (1961) *The Evolution of Civilisations* postulated that civilisations undergo seven stages from birth to death: mixture, gestation, expansion, age of conflict, universal empire, decay, and invasion. Following a process of mixture between cultures and a period of gestation, the excess energy of civilisation incentivises expansionism. Expansion can take the form of the increased production of goods, increased knowledge and skills, population growth, and geographical expansion (Quigley 1961: 149). Once expansion subsides, the age of conflict unfolds as internal and external skirmishes take centre stage. Focus is diverted towards divisive domestic problems, while large civilisations begin to compete through direct confrontation. Some civilisations perish during the Age of Conflict, and a dominant civilisation may emerge that establishes primacy with a universal empire. Albeit, in the absence of resistance, the lack of meaning and purpose produces anti-social behaviour, division, and decay until eventually conquered by a nascent rival.

Pitirim Sorokin's (1941) *The Crisis of Our Age* similarly depicted a conflict between culture and rational society. Yet, Sorokin distinguished himself from the abovementioned scholars as demise was argued to be avoidable since civilisations could move back and forth between various stages. Sorokin posited that cultures go through three distinct periods, defined by the ideational/spiritual, sensate/ material, and idealistic/integral. The ideational embraces transcendent spirituality, truths, and morality. The sensate stage denotes the belief that only the rational and material world is real, which becomes the organising principle of society. The idealistic aims to find a balance to harmonise the ideational and the sensate as science and spirituality develops best in concert. While civilisations could transition between these categories, it is argued that the West has become increasingly entrenched in the sensate and therefore entering a critical transitory stage of either demise or revival:

> In the twentieth century the magnificent sensate house of Western man began to deteriorate rapidly and then to crumble. There was, among other things, a disintegration of its moral, legal, and other values which, from within, control

and guide the behavior of individuals and groups. When human beings cease to be controlled by deeply interiorized religious, ethical, aesthetic and other values, individuals and groups become the victims of crude power and fraud as the supreme controlling forces of their behavior, relationship, and destiny. In such circumstances, man turns into a human animal driven mainly by his biological urges, passions, and lust. Individual and collective unrestricted egotism flares up; a struggle for existence intensifies; might becomes right; and wars, bloody revolutions, crime, and other forms of interhuman strife and bestiality explode on an unprecedented scale. So it was in all great transitory periods.

(Sorokin 1964: 24)

Sorokin positioned himself as an optimist in terms of the ability of the West to be reborn by moving towards the integral stage:

The disintegration process often generates the emergence of mobilization of forces opposed to it. Weak and insignificant at the beginning, these forces slowly grow and then start not only to fight the disintegration but also to plan and then to build a new sociocultural order which can meet more adequately the gigantic challenge of the critical transition and of the post-transitory future.

(Sorokin 1964: 24)

The four seasons of civilisations

A theory on the cycle of civilisations is developed here with the added value of framing the common abovementioned themes through the prism of gemeinschaft and gesellschaft. Spengler's terminology of the four seasons of civilianisation is utilised, albeit with the content modified.

Spring represents gemeinschaft without gesellschaft. Cultures rise out of the community that primarily centres around the heroic, spiritual, and primordial. Culture, defined as striving towards meaning, is the natural organising mechanism for human beings. The imaginative and poetic builds on the instinctive connectivity with nature, which manifests itself by exploring Man's relationship with nature and God (Vico 1725). Cultures facilitate continuity as the source of order, safety, structure, and meaning. Cultures represent the perpetual endeavour to reach towards the divine and eternal as a source of meaning, rather than attaining utopia. Legitimacy of elites depended on a connection with nature – either priesthood with a mandate from heaven or the poet that elaborates on Man internal complexities (Vico 2002[1725]).

Culture develops out of necessity in response to the nascent human consciousness and the subsequent questioning of the purpose of our existence, which entails fear of nature, the supernatural, and our inevitable demise (Spengler 1991[1922]). Adams (1897) similarly recognised that fear of the chaos in the world created human instincts to seek refuge in the religious, imaginative, artistic, and cultural.

Since memory and traditions of the past are in constant deterioration, there is continuous need for rejuvenation and rebirth by engaging with the anarchic world and thereby rediscovering the past. Fear produces a pursuit for the divine to find our place in the world, expressed in tangible and intangible symbols of a culture. Culture uses imaginative form as 'expressive symbolism' to communicate an inherent truth about humanity or the meaning of human existence (Bell 1975). The architecture of cathedrals reaches towards the heavens, while music and art intend to capture something beautiful within the soul that transcends both time and place. Culture celebrates expansion and exploration of the planet and the universe as the realm of infinite possibilities. Religion encourages morality that mirrors that of heaven, which is rewarded with eternity in paradise. In economics and politics, the aim is to organise society in a manner that perpetually breaks new ground in terms of maximising the human potential. The ability to reproduce one's own culture in terms of kinship, tradition, and language becomes a quest to shed the restrictions in this limited life and aspire for immortality.

Summer signifies advancement to the extent there is a balance between gemeinschaft and gesellschaft. Symmetrical interdependence is established between an urban and rural population (Spengler 1991[1922]). Modern culture captures the need and ability to preserve both the traditions of the Enlightenment and Counter-Enlightenment. Culture is a synthesis of preserving opposites and distinctions, such as reason and religion (Bloom 2008: 197). Rationality enabled the emergence of larger and more competitive units of power with more competitiveness to survive. Simultaneously, honour, traditions, and manners remained central in life as even violence was resolved with duels and mutually agreed formats for warfare in formations. Economic efficiency and an intricate bureaucracy to govern the growing society eliminated previous barriers to competitive society. In Western civilisation, the emergence of the nation-state is indicative of a thriving civilisation. The sovereign state did not eliminate religion and kinship as a rival for loyalty and authority, rather the church and other distinctiveness was embraced as an intrinsic part of statehood and national identity.

Summer continues for as long as a civilisation benefits from greater complexity, either for the prosperity of the people or in opposition to external powers. Albeit, the benefits of complex structures often diminish over time. The population then begins to form new political, social, and economic arrangements at a lower level that fragments and polarises civilisation (Tainter 1990). The era of affluence and intellect is ironically indicative of when civilisations begin to go wrong (Glubb 1976). Economic affluence 'causes the decline of this strong, brave and self-confident people' as virtue, heroism and passion are replaced with excessive self-indulgence (Glubb 1976: 9). The disproportionate focus on the intellect and rationality creates disdain and neglect for the spiritual and irrational.

Autumn denotes gesellschaft exhausting gemeinschaft. Humanity endeavours to reach its potential by progressing towards reasons and perfection, culminating in a relentless push towards an ever-larger and more efficient society. When a civilisation thrives its excessive energy and social velocity, expressed in economic and scientific advancements, undermine the ability to reproduce traditional culture and community (Vico 2002[1725]). Politics is reduced to economic determinism, and decadence looming as reason does not provide meaning. As reason and materialism vanquishes the irrational and founding spiritual ethos, a civilisation commences its deterioration (Adams 1897). The rational and calculative demeanour of civilisation eventually erodes the creativity and organic culture (Spengler 1991[1922]). Nietzsche (1967) likewise argued:

> The high points of culture and civilisation do not coincide: one should not be deceived about the fundamental antagonism of culture and civilisation. The great moments of culture were always, morally speaking, times of corruption; and conversely, the periods when the taming of the human animal ('civilisation') was desired and enforced were times of intolerance against the boldest and most spiritual natures.

Gustav von Schmoller, Friedrich Ratzel, and Adolf Wagner were similarly preoccupied with the durability of culture as civilisation progresses. Georg Simmel even referred to the civilisational advancements of the 19th century as 'the disintegration and perversion of Kultur'. Simmel (1971[1903]: 324) argued:

> The deepest problem of modern life flow from the attempt from the individual to maintain the independence and individuality of his existence against the sovereign powers of society, against the weight of the historical heritage and the external culture and technique of life. The antagonism represents the most modern form of the conflict which primitive man must carry on with nature for his own bodily existence.

Polarisation of civilisation society between the cosmopolitan elites and the 'internal proletariat' is the foremost indication of autumn. Civilisation displays evidence of 'Schism in the Body Social' and 'Schism in the Soul' (Toynbee 1946). The former refers to a division between the elites and the proletariat, while the latter suggests a division between idealising the glory of the past and idealising an unattainable future (Toynbee 1946). 'Two nations' subsequently emerge: the first is an urban and cosmopolitan nation of educated and affluent people who have disproportionately prospered from the increasingly complex economic system. The second nation consists of the 'internal proletariat' who experience relative economic power decline and seek refuge in a deteriorating community. The internal proletariat distrusts the elites, who are believed to betray the foundational values and virtues of the civilisation. The elites scorn the internal proletariat for embracing the irrational and distinctive at the expense of the rational and universal. The working class or 'internal proletariat' carries most of the costs of creative destruction and a diminishing community. As the benefits of complex society lessens, people commence the search for meaning by recreating the community through the rediscovery of religion, ethnic association, cultural kinship, national identity, and the family. The two nations continue to polarise and vilify their counterpart. The interdependence between urban centres and the rural regions becomes asymmetrical as cities can act independently from the rural. The cosmopolitan elites define their own advancement and superiority in contrast with a backward rural region. Yet, cosmopolitanism cannot produce its own culture and art, which results in imitations of previous art and celebration of the frivolous and material. The cosmopolitan elites distract themselves from the growing nihilism by sedating primordial impulses with distractions such as career, wealth accumulation, shallow and vulgar entertainment, obsession with sex, alcohol, and other stimulants. A breaking point becomes evident when there is nothing left of the past to dismantle and no new hope or vision for the future to put in its place.

Nihilism and division incentivises a search for meaning and unity by engaging in chaos. The population grows more susceptible to wars to give life purpose. Decay of civilisation has historically been alleviated with expansionism and the establishment of frontiers as it enables rejuvenation. Civilisations expand for two reasons: to capture new markets and develop more advanced and efficient societies capable of competing against rivals, and as a temporary remedy for the ills of the subsequently declining community. Whether geographical, societal, or technological advancements are made, it instils a sense of meaning as people venture into the unknown with the expectation of improving the future.

Expansionism benefits gesellschaft to the extent it provides a positive return on investment. Kennedy's (1987) thesis on 'imperial overstretch' posited that expanding powers reach the point when the cost of imperial commitments exceeds the income. With resources siphoned from the core to the periphery, the former eventually rots and brings down the entire empire. In contrast, profitable expansionism can delay the need to reform and address internal struggles by extracting wealth from abroad. Machiavelli (2015[1532]: 12) observed great benefits of conquering weaker powers and cultivating them as colonies, in contrast to confronting powerful adversaries:

> A prince does not spend much on colonies, for with little or no expense he can send them out and keep them there, and he offends a minority only of the citizens from whom he takes lands and houses to give them to the new inhabitants; and those whom he offends, remaining poor and scattered, are never able to injure him; whilst the rest being uninjured are easily kept quiet, and at the same time are anxious not to err for fear it should happen to them as it has to those who have been despoiled.

The Machiavellian stratagem to achieve glory while maintaining the appearance of virtue appeals to the duality of Man. Colonisation gave the Europeans an outlet for acting on primitive impulses by exercising brutality and barbaric acts against the 'uncivilised', while remaining civilised among their fellow Europeans. While perpetually seeking new frontiers to expand markets, the encounters with barbarism also rejuvenated community by developing a shared purpose and spirit.

In his influential 'frontier thesis', Fredrick Jackson Turner (2008[1893]) propagated that the progressive, individualistic, and virtuous character of the US was largely the consequence of the American frontier. Westward expansionism sustained a frontier to perpetuate optimism with the promise for a glorious future, and distracted attention away from the imperishable struggle within Man and civilisation. The settler society especially is a powerful remedy for decadence as new lands and markets are acquired by brutally clearing the native population in the name of civilisation. The US, Canada, Australia, and other territories settled in the wake of the Enlightenment, were supported by reproducing ethno-cultural particularities and spreading universal values. English historians and writers ranked societies and civilisations by their development in comparison to Europe. With the Enlightenment and Christian faith as universal values, a civilising mission took place to elevate 'backward peoples' (Moses 2004).

The settler essence of Manifest Destiny embodied the American frontier spirit. The belief that the Americans were building a new Jerusalem in the New World made it a moral mission to conquer North America. Civilisation would perpetually thrust to the West and push the native barbarians backwards. O'Sullivan coined the term Manifest Destiny in 1845 in which he linked expansion and frontiers with morality, liberty, and civilisation: 'the right of our manifest destiny to overspread and to possess the whole of the continent which Providence has given us for the development of the great experiment of liberty and federated self-government'. A similar interpretation of the Monroe Doctrine was provided by the US Secretary of State, Richard Olney (1895): 'civilization must either advance or retrograde accordingly as its supremacy is extended or curtailed'. The idea was upheld that 'it is the function of the Anglo-Saxon race to confer these gifts of civilisation . . . barbarism has no rights which civilization is bound to respect' (Abbott 1902: 10). The genocide of Native Americans has been romanticised since breaking with both the Europeans and indigenous was required to advance the liberal ideals of the American civilisation (Hartz 1955). Thomas Jefferson had similarly advocated that the advancement of civilisation 'justified extermination' of Native Americans (Mann 2005: ix). Later, Theodore Roosevelt also acclaimed that 'extermination was as ultimately beneficial as it was inevitable' (Mann 2005: ix).

Without expansion it was feared that civilisation would decline. When westward expansion finally reached the Pacific coast, and no new frontiers lay ahead, the continuous renewal of America as a settler society with promise of new land and opportunity ended. Turner (2008[1893]) warned that reaching the Pacific Coast would be a pyrrhic victory as the US would have to confront its internal issues and thus accept decline. Turner's argument, not unlike Jefferson, was that democracy relied on the community that maintained strong links to the agrarian society. The loss of 'the meeting point between savagery and civilization' meant the lack of reproduction and rebirth of cultural achievements.

The frontier thesis made a strong case for building an American empire in the Pacific. Henry and Brooks Adams disagreed; Brooks Adams saw expansionism as renewing civilisation, while Henry Adams construed it as sowing the seeds of US decline. Both were largely correct as civilisations that do not grow will stagnate and decline. Yet with excessive growth also follows inevitable decline. In support for the US venturing into the Pacific and imitating European colonialism, Brooks Adams (1900: 25) famously wrote that 'the civilisation which does not advance declines'. Roosevelt believed in the immorality of urbanisation, with society revitalised by greater involvement of the US in international affairs. Empire would reverse the 'grave signs of deterioration in the English-speaking peoples' (Dyer 1992: 149).

Prior to 1898, the US had prided itself on isolationism as a civilisational progress away from the savagery of the Europeans. The American identity inevitably altered as it expanded into the Pacific on an imperial project and became part of the 'West'. The colonisation of the Philippines and other territorial possessions after defeating the Spanish in 1898 converted the US into a colonial power with a civilising mission. Although the Philippines were a Christian nation, the assumed inferiority of Catholicism meant that conversions would take place towards Protestantism. For Mark Twain, the imperial project undermined the essence of the republic and sacrificed the soul of the nation by abandoning the civic uniqueness of the American idea. William James argued that empire had made the US 'puke up its ancient soul' (Atlantic Monthly Press 1921). In short, the US had become a European imperial power. The concept of a shared Western civilisation was gradually embraced as the US emerged as a powerful maritime power with global ambitions, and allies with shared interests were courted. The concept of being part of a Western civilisation was vague and directed mostly towards shaping the world around its own image. Rediscovering the English heritage as 'the English nation, which has been the principal agent in diffusing the influence of Western civilisation throughout the East, has received a great heritage of industrial skill and commercial enterprise from other people' (Cunningham 1900: 2).

Conflict follows the end of expansion as internal cohesion unravels and rivalry with other large actors intensifies. Colonialism was an alternative outlet for competition that mitigated and delayed direct conflict with Europe. Yet, when expansionism eventually subsided, the 'age of conflict' followed (Toynbee 1946). Violence between leading powers escalate as they are compelled to scramble for the same resources to ensure a balance of power or strive for dominance (Quigley 1961: 150). Furthermore, when a leading civilisation stagnates it usually enters relative decline as the periphery continues to grow. Toynbee (1946) denounced the West's expansionist impulses and empire-building as a temporary means to distract from the internal illness of society. Yet, the positive aspect was that Western civilisation would leave behind the spiritual origin, which could form the foundation of a new virtuous civilisation.

While in the past the geographical and societal/psychological frontiers were linked, the lack of uncharted territory and end of colonisation has decoupled the two. Social Darwinism that accepted weaker civilisations perishing to give way to the stronger and more developed lost much appeal after the Nazi atrocities

(Hawkins 1997). An ideological and global frontier was established when the Cold War began. The need to counter the threat of communism made it necessary to expand US power on to all continents. The inherent global expansionism to contain communism become a mission to defend civilisation. Barbarity met again with Civilisation – Christianity against atheism, democracy against authoritarianism, capitalism against communism. Rediscovery of the virtues of democracy, human rights, and free-trade gradually established itself as the core of American identity and creed.

Winter signifies death as a civilisation loses purpose and therefore become unwilling to defend and reproduce itself. The ensuing chaos possibly triggers rebirth by an internal spiritual resurgence or invasion. Conflicts tend to culminate in the emergence of a hegemon or 'universal empire'. As civilisations grow in power and compete for geographic expanse, the number of political units are reduced. Some states are defeated and absorbed, while others voluntarily unite into larger entities of power to benefit from collective strength. The clash between civilisations can result in the victory of a dominant entity. The 'universal state' or 'universal empire' denotes political supremacy or hegemony like Rome. (Toynbee 1946; Quigley 1961: 322). The triumphant unit is capable of subverting efforts by others to collectively balance.

A dominant power did not establish absolute supremacy in modern Europe because of the geographical make-up. The maritime powers in Western Europe could expend their excess energy and compete among each other by taking to the sea and developing colonies, while the presence of Russia as a vast land power in the East denied supremacy to any one power:

> If Europe had been a closed system, some great power would eventually have succeeded in establishing absolute supremacy over the other states in the region. But the system was never entirely closed. Immediately before a would-be continental hegemon could unify the European region by coercion, counterweights on the eastern and/or western wings of the continent emerged to deny a hegemonic victory by introducing new, extraregional resources into the struggle for regional supremacy.
>
> (Thompson 1992: 129)

In modern times, several states aspired to cement their dominance over Europe. The English established a powerful position early in Europe, yet their limited presence on continental Europe remained a key constraint. The evolving maritime strength of the English versus the power of France as a land power established a balanced relationship where a universal empire could not be established. The Hundred Years' War between the English and French eventually diminished English preparedness for engaging in land wars on continental Europe. Britain, and later the US, established an off-shore strategy that aimed to prevent the emergence of a land power that could dominate all Europe and thereby undermine the rule of the maritime state. Napoleon's Continental System brought the continent together with the objective of isolating and devastating the English economy. However, Russia obstructed efforts to conquer the entire continent by repelling the invasions of both Napoleon and Hitler (Quigley 1961: 154). By the early 1900s, empire-building had slowed down. A universal empire under Soviet power seemed possible after the Second World War, but was averted by the incursion of the US into Western Europe. The US had established itself as the unrivalled centre of industrial capitalism and the military protector of Europe, which made a bid for becoming a universal state. The demise of the Soviet Union in 1991 meant that the US became the global hegemon or a unipolar power.

However, the establishment of universal empires has historically been followed by decay. Peace under a universal empire derives from the absence of competing political units, and internal economic harmonisation by eliminating trade barriers and establishing a shared currency. Yet, the absence of rivalry does not produce lasting stability:

> When a universal empire is established in a civilisation, the society enters upon a "golden age". At least this is what it seems to the periods that follow it. Such a golden age is a period of peace and of relative prosperity.
>
> (Quigley 1961: 158–159)

Prosperity is 'deceptive' since the motivations and instruments for expansion have diminished (Quigley 1961: 159). Stagnation and decline follows. When people are born into wealth they tend to be deprived of necessity, often resulting in complacency. Economic problems become more prevalent. The wealth gap causes internal dysfunctions, while an overextended military and imperial obligations transfer funds from the core to the periphery until the latter disintegrates. Poor economics produces irresponsible fiscal behaviour as money is printed until the currency is debased. Economic determinism makes money the core indicator of value, and liberalism unravels citizenship as the populace demands ever-more rights and concurrently rejecting responsibilities such as public service. Nationalism is degraded to a mere tool by the powerful to obtain power, calling for the return to a glorious past or an unattainable future. Furthermore, affluence tends to de-couple power from competence and authority. The 'creative minority', deprived of necessity and creativity, will still command power, albeit without competency and legitimate authority. Animosity and distrust subsequently increase among the public and anti-intellectualism may follow. While barbarians at the gates produce internal unity, barbarians within cause divisions. Culture declines, political structures lose their vigour, and the rulers' legitimacy fades (Weber 1950).

The utopia envisioned in the universal state is paradoxical as human beings find meaning in confronting adversity. If the house is in complete order, Man would destroy it to rediscover his own humanity in the chaos. The concept of utopia is predicated on the false assumption that Man is a rational creature:

> Reason is an excellent thing, there's no disputing that, but reason is nothing but reason and satisfies only the rational side of man's nature . . . Even if man

really were nothing but a piano key, even if this were proved to him by natural science and mathematics, even then he would not become reasonable, but would purposely do something perverse out of simple ingratitude, simply to win his point . . . then, after all, perhaps only by his curse will he attain his object, that is, really convince himself that he is a man and not a piano key! If you say that all this, too, can be calculated and tabulated . . . then man would purposely go mad in order to be rid of reason and win his point.

(Dostoyevsky 2009[1864]: 21, 23)

Without external adversaries, the populace becomes more aware of its internal differences and begins to fragment. Victory breeds hubris, nihilism, and decadence as materialism and consumption become substitutes for meaning and happiness (Toynbee 1946). The increasing wealth gap between the elites and proletariat is temporarily bridged with cheap credit to enable the poor to imitate the lifestyle of the rich. From ancient Rome to the contemporary West, civilisational decline is evident by superficiality and frivolity as a fraudulent culture emerges. A market for distractions grows as the population embraces gladiators or reality TV, while the Romans, Ottomans, and Spanish all made celebrities out of their chefs. An immature obsession with indulgences becomes an indicator of success that masks decline. Civilisation detaches from morality with a 'period of gambling, use of narcotics or intoxicants, obsession with sex (frequently as perversion), increasing crime, growing numbers of neurotics and psychotics, growing obsession with death and the Hereafter' (Quigley 1961: 152). Emotional solitude and loss of social safety nets spur obesity, debts through excessive shopping, and substance abuse (Luttwak 1999: 207–208). Kaczynski (1995) similarly noted that as society becomes sickened by the absence of the inter-personal ties, the modern numbs the symptoms with drugs and mindless television as distraction. The age of decadence is defined by self-absorption, excesses, and unsustainability, which culminates in economic exhaustion and the failure to reproduce culture and the past for posterity (Glubb 1976). People feel insecure and descend into 'a period of growing irrationality, pessimism, superstition, and other wordliness' (Quigley 1961: 150).

Immorality and nihilism generate the impulse to recreate the community:

Period of acute economic depression, declining standards of living, civil wars between the various vested interests, and growing illiteracy. The society grows weaker and weaker. Vain efforts are made to sort the wastage by legislation. But the decline continues. The religious, intellectual, social, and political levels of the society begin to lose the allegiance of the masses of the people on a large scale. New religious movements begin to sweep over the society. There is a growing reluctance to fight for the society or even support it by paying taxes.

(Quigley 1961: 159)

Invasion becomes the final stage of civilisation (Toynbee 1946; Quigley 1961: 328). If the polarisation continues, the internal proletariat will seek cooperation with external actors due to shared resentment towards the elites. The rival civilisation or 'external proletariat' are historically born at the periphery of old. When the old civilisation declines it is usually consumed and replaced by the peripheral civilisation (Quigley 1961:148). The outsiders at the periphery are historically referred to in a derogatory way as barbarians, which eventually overruns the civilisation in decay. Civilisations are built upon the remains of former civilisations as what came before have to fall in order to give way for the next civilisational step. They then often carry on the traditions of the civilisation that gave birth to them.

Conclusion

Humanity's oldest religions convey stories consistent with the academic studies of civilisations that rose to greatness before collapsing. Civilisations rise when the interdependent relationship with the traditional and modern is preserved and nurtured, as the decaying past is reborn in a vigorous and powerful youth. Engaging with chaos is instrumental for replenishing the traditional as it compels people to restore order by seeking ties to the past. Strong culture and spirituality connected with the traditional become the foundation for a strong community, as the prerequisite for a powerful civilisation to emerge.

However, prosperity and greatness are accompanied by hubris as advancement is misconstrued as the modern defeating the pre-modern. Order is conflated with stability and affluence linked solely to gesellschaft, which results in the neglect of gemeinschaft. The ensuing nihilism can be suppressed temporarily with frontiers and self-indulgence, however, eventually the assumed indicators of success reveal themselves as a display of decadence. Civilisations therefore go through four stages before reaching their demise as society exhausts the community from which it sprouted.

The lessons from the literature in this chapter can be applied to the current state of Western civilisation. The failure to harmonise the traditional and modern eventually polarises civilisation between the cosmopolitan elites who benefit disproportionately from complex society, and the internal proletariat who seek to recreate the community. The attempt to revive what has been lost creates desperate support for nationalist rhetoric by anti-establishment politicians who promise what cannot be delivered – a return to a glorious past or promise of an unattainable future. The exasperated internal proletariat seeks common cause with a rival civilisation at the periphery for common cause against the self-serving elites, resulting in the inability or unwillingness of civilisation to defend itself.

Europe has three distinct civilisations at its periphery that can replenish its traditions, ethos, and spirituality – the American, Islamic, and Russian. The American civilisation largely extended the life of European civilisation following the Second World War, albeit itself succumbing to decadence. The Islamic civilisation is making its incursion into Europe by migration with a rapid demographic shift unprecedented in peacetime. The more compatible Russian civilisation inherited and embodies many of the characteristics of Western civilisation and offers the prospect of a return to traditional European traditions, culture, and values. Irrespective of the ability to deliver, Russian conservatism is predisposed to have a strong appeal to an internal proletariat within the decaying Western civilisation, which seeks to revive its community, culture, and ethos.

Part II
Rise and fall of political liberalism

3 Western civilisation as an amalgam of political liberalism and nationhood

Introduction

In one of the most emblematic works on civilisation, *History of Civilisation in Europe*, Guizot (2013[1828]) posited that the unity and advancement of civilisations are founded on conformity to a great idea. Europe was defined by its political pluralism, capable of a variety of great ideas and institutions (Guizot 2013[1828]). More importantly, Western political pluralism facilitated a fragile balance between liberalism and conservativism in response to the contradictory impulses of Man. Balance is imperative as constrained liberalism can advance human freedoms and prosperity, while unrestrained liberalism dismantles internal cohesion and meaning by vilifying ethno-cultural particularities and economic statecraft. Restrained conservativism preserves and reproduces distinctiveness and higher culture, while radical conservativism can descend into blatant xenophobia and harmful protectionism.

Modern Western civilisation has flourished with a delicate balance between conserving ethno-cultural nationhood and advancing liberal civic ideals. The European nation-state became the sturdiest vessel to elevate human freedom and progress as these values were practised within a strong and functioning community. Likewise, the sustainability of nationhood and unity rests on commitment to shared morality, norms, and social justice defined by common liberal principles. Charles de Gaulle famously proclaimed in a radio broadcast in 1942: 'democracy and national sovereignty are the same thing'. The interdependence between nationhood and liberalism coexists with contradictions. Nationhood is contingent on shared identity and kinship to instil a sense of responsibility towards a common political community, while liberalism's quest for equality and liberty perpetually tears away at the social structures that maintain the shared distinctiveness of an identity and citizenship.

The purpose of this chapter is to explore the foundation of the rise of Western civilisation, and the threats from the contemporary dogma of liberal absolutism, universalism, and civic nationalism. Consistent with the flawed assumption that Man is becoming increasingly rational and transcending the instinctive, it is common to portray the development of Western civilisation as a linear progressive development of civic virtues by shedding ethno-cultural nationalism as a blunder from a bygone era. Relegating the significance of the ethno-cultural core of Western civilisation may be political expedient in the short-term to fit with the contemporary narrative of what defines 'us' in the shared Western civilisation. Yet, purging the collective historical memory to advance ideological consistency and universalism fosters a misunderstanding about the rise and fall of civilisations. Civilisations are defined by and evolve out of rational strategic necessity in the competition for power and security, while remaining aware of the irrational emotional human elements that maintains civilisations.

This chapter first argues that the foundation for the rise of Western civilisation has been the balance between ethno-cultural distinctiveness and civic nationalism based on liberal principles. While these impulses were contradictory, they also complemented each other. The false dichotomy between ethno-cultural nationalism and civic nationalism fuels a misconception that progress entails the latter displacing the former. The ideological glorification of a solely civic identity encourages civic absolutism at the West's own peril. A strong and confident ethno-cultural core can be considered a prerequisite for civic nationalism, as it negates the prospect of an ethnic and societal security dilemma. European nation-building largely made the state an entity capable of reinventing and representing a homogenous community. The strength of the state is therefore contingent on balancing the ethno-cultural aspects of the community with the civic virtues required by modern society. The foundation of the US can be conceptualised as a rebirth of a more humane Western civilisation by advancing the liberal ethos to replace malign nationalism with more benign patriotism. Yet, the liberal consensus that underpins statehood and solidarity in the US has undermined political pluralism by recognising its ethno-cultural foundations.

Second, liberal absolutism and universalism unravels the balance between ethno-cultural and civic nationalism. The lure of liberal universalism is to bridge humanity by transcending chaos and the irrational in favour of the rational and orderly. Albeit, by attempting to abandon the distinctive, the homogenising process of nation-building is reversed as people liberate themselves from the arbitrary confines of nationhood. Subsequently, civilisation fragments as social capital and internal cohesion diminish. The state becomes less capable of using common ethnicity, culture, and religion for solidarity, as these expressions of kinship instead becomes divisive as they are harnessed by sub-groups in society. The more diverse society becomes, the more connectivity and morality plummets. Civic nationalism and universalism also produce a failed foreign policy due to the neglect of ethno-cultural and religious authority.

Last, the ability to alter failed policies by constraining liberalism is prevented by the rise of liberal authoritarianism. The liberal consensus converted the generic 'freedoms' into an ever-expanding list of 'rights' and entitlements. An unelected expert class replaces political representatives, and liberal principles are cemented as rights to limit the scope of democratic influence over decision-making.

Western civilisation as a balance between the ethno-cultural and civic

The two longest living institutions of Western civilisation have not been political, but ethnic and religious. A more humane civilisation and nationhood requires more liberal influence, without imperilling the balance between an ethno-cultural and civic identity as a manifestation of the irrational and rational component of Man. An artificial dichotomy and subsequent extreme push towards either an ethno-cultural or civic identity and will continue to be at the peril of the nation-state. Ethno-cultural nationalism entails developing a shared identity and unity based on ethnic, cultural, and religious particularities and kinship. The alternative, civic nationalism, promotes a sense of belonging and patriotism by adherence to specific political values. Civic nationalism is a response to the historical confrontation within ethno-cultural nationalism by instead creating a more inclusive and unifying identity.

The simple binary division between ethno-cultural and civic nationalism is deceptive since there has never been a state with entirely ethno-cultural or civic nationalism. Most states embrace a mixture between the two. A familiar myth is that Western states, especially the Anglo-Saxons, have always embraced a civic identity (Yack 1996; Kuzio 2002). The West only embraced predominantly civic identities from the 1960s, and even then, continued to maintain strong cultural components in their identities and propagate cultural superiority under the guise of common values (Kymlicka 1996). Transcending the ethno-cultural is neither a feasible nor desirable objective. The unity of the US and Europe has through history rested on the ethno-cultural core and shared political values as a gravitational force. With the dilution of particularities to represent a large community, there will inevitably be a rise in nihilism and decline in morality. The embrace of a predominantly civic identity in the West remains a social experiment that neglects ethno-cultural distinctiveness and the irrational.

The narrative of the West prospering solely on liberalism tends to depict the advancement of civic identity as progress, while ethno-cultural nationalism belongs to a bygone era. The great ideas of Western civilisation are therefore commonly argued to have originated in the Greco-Roman civilisations, from the exclusive republican citizenship in Athenian democracy to the inclusive liberal citizenship in the Roman Empire where even conquered peoples could become citizens. The British tend to emphasise the Magna Carta in 1215 as a cornerstone of Western civilisation, which placed the political leadership under the rule of law and led to political and economic freedoms that were eventually exported to continental Europe. The Renaissance and Enlightenment rejected superstition and arbitrary authority in favour of rationality and natural rights, resulting in immense scientific, philosophical, social, and political changes. The Protestant Reformation similarly redistributed power by repudiating the authority of the pope and the ability of the Catholic Church to monopolise representing the Christian faith and practise. The civic and rational evolution of Western civilisation continued into the 1960s with the social revolution and emancipation of marginalised groups.

However, Western civilisation is not solely founded on liberal ideas. Brussels and Berlin railed against Warsaw in 2017 for undermining judicial independence in Poland, which is supposedly a cherished 'European value', yet it is prudent to remember that the separation of power is hardly a longstanding European tradition. European civilisation also developed on a history of religious wars, monarchy, vicious revolutions, Bonapartism, absolutism, radicalism, imperialism, fascism, and Marxism. Portraying this history of Western civilisation as a relic of the past, replaced by the rational, liberal, and civic, contributes to a dangerous liberal delusion. The purpose of recognising the less attractive features of Western civilisation is not to tarnish its accomplishments, but rather to avoid the ideological misconception that the strength of the West has solely relied on enlightened civic nationalism.

As civilisations become more intricate and diverse, they gravitate away from the distinctive to the universal. Distinctiveness of civilisations require virtual or physical borders between 'us' and 'them'. The ancient Greeks did not base their civilisation solely on ethno-cultural distinctiveness, which is evident by Greek city-states or polis not forming a nation-state. The lack of a Greek ethno-cultural identity as an organising principle spawned both benefits and disadvantages due to porous virtual borders. Greek identity and values were universal in nature, and the Greek invaders of Persia therefore faced less opposition as the democratic principles also had an appeal in conquered lands. Yet, the solidarity within Greek city-states also suffered as the ethno-cultural was largely de-coupled from authority. Evident from the writing of Thucydides, it became common for military leaders to switch sides to rival armies several times, and still be welcomed back into the fold. The tolerance and forgiveness of treason is indicative of treachery not being associated with the heinousness of betraying the self in terms of going against one's own people and distinctive culture (Yack 1996: 204).

Human beings act in social groups with distinctive ethno-cultural characteristics and civic values that identify the group and lay the foundation for solidarity. Carl Schmitt (2008[1932]) aptly recognised that identifying 'we' requires identifying the opposite as 'them'. To identify by race, faith, or ideology is powerful, yet it is only cogent if there is a racial, religious, or ideological 'other'. The predicament of group identities is that it appeals to the human need for belonging to a distinct group that can be reproduced and sustains internal cohesion. Ethno-cultural identities are justly criticised for being exclusionary and often hostile by 'othering' non-members, yet attempting to repudiate them ignores the complexities and contradictions within human nature. Preserving the ethno-cultural can be conceptualised as 'societal security', which is the sense of meaning from reproducing immaterial social values such as culture, kinship, language, traditions, religion, norms, customs, and national identity (Wæver 1993).

Focus on particularities is preferable for less powerful civilisations by clearly delineating borders to prevent overlapping authority with stronger foreign powers. Unique and organic civilisations are less mutable and therefore not as easily compromised. The autonomy, internal loyalty, and cohesion of a community is largely contingent on heterogeneity and geography. In contrast, dominant powers are more susceptible to embracing universalism to bring down obstacles for influence.

The paradox of divisive identities is that the more exclusionary they 'naturally' are in terms of ethno-cultural characteristics, the less need there is to demonise the 'other' to defend virtual and conceptual borders. In contrast, civic identities require more upkeep as evident following the collapse of the Soviet Union when the US was under pressure to establish new ideological borders to continue keeping Russia out of Europe. Geographical continental borders are permanent, unequivocal, and do not require a similar Manichean format. Geography has been more ambiguous in defining Europe as the continent is shared with Asia. Ethnicity has since the rise of the nation-state been a strong function in terms of offering an exclusive membership that can reproduce itself across generations and even evoke a sense of immortality (Glazer, Moynihan and Schelling 1975). Ethnic groups defined by shared descent are an exclusionary foundation for identity, albeit dual nationalities of for example Algerian-French or Russian-Ukrainian can dilute the internal cohesion. Religion is more exclusionary in terms of the absence of Muslim-Catholic religious following, yet membership can be shifted through conversation (Huntington 1993a). Cultures are more flexible as they can be closed or remain open to be influenced or influence. Languages can similarly be learned, which was instrumental for example in unifying the Germans into one state. Peter the Great similarly altered the Russian alphabet and imposed dress codes to make Russia more 'European'.

The lure of universalism appeals to both the domestic and international. The purported domestic benefit of universalism is the ability to develop egalitarianism in more ethnically and religiously fragmented states. The assumed international benefit of more porous borders is to establish commonality and reduce belligerence between 'us' and 'them'. Furthermore, as societies become more complex with global interaction, they will inevitably embrace certain universal ideals built on values and norms of human freedom and progress. The delineation of borders diminishes as a global civilisation for the global citizen emerges. Stronger actors have greater incentives to adopt universalism to extend authority over other peoples and create interdependence that maximises both autonomy and influence.

Schmitt (2008[1932]) argued fervently in favour of maintaining the 'political', defined by particularities of political communities to distinguish between 'us' and 'them'. This was an honest recognition of how humanity organises and interacts, rather than an endorsement of the ensuing conflicts. Conflicts between groups and reliance on 'us' and 'them' are polemical and do not need to result in actual war, rather the potential for conflict is enough. Peace is advanced by making the differences between 'us' and 'them' more benign, rather than eliminating the dissimilarities. The initial purpose of the Olympics was not to eliminate the distinctiveness of states as separate entities, but to compete through sports and spirit as a benevolent substitute for lethal means.

The apolitical man is a narcissist and apathetic man that sees nothing higher than himself and becomes a spiritless producer/consumer (Schmitt 2008[1932]). Liberalism encourages shedding an externally imposed identity that defines a community. US Justice Anthony Kennedy, famously said that the edifice of modern liberalism is built on the idea that 'at the heart of liberty is the right to define one's own concept of existence, of meaning, of the universe, and of the mystery of human life'. The reluctance to be defined by any external variables results in an obsession with the self. Already by the late 1970s, Lasch (1979) warned about the emergence of an unhealthy and narcissistic culture:

The new narcissist is haunted not by guilt but by anxiety. He seeks not to inflict his own certainties on others but to find a meaning in life. Liberated from the superstitions of the past, he doubts even the reality of his own existence. Superficially relaxed and tolerant, he finds little use for dogmas of racial and ethnic purity but at the same time forfeits the security of group loyalties and regards everyone as a rival for the favours conferred by a paternalistic state.

Conformity under the European nation-state

The European nation-state is an amalgam between traditional ethno-cultural and liberal civic identity. The subsequent balance between community and society has made the nation-state the most powerful entity, as the distinctive was harnessed by the state as the foundation of unity. European state-building entailed brutal purging of nonconformity to homogenise society, resulting in a common ethnic composition, religious orientation, language, culture, and historical/ancestral myths. The common ethno-cultural and religious core represented or replicated a large 'community' based on shared kinship and spirituality. With a powerful community, a large entity of power could emerge capable of developing advanced society.

Europe was unique as the nation developed before the state, while other parts of the world inherited a state following decolonisation and were then tasked with constructing a nation. Prior to the 1500s, people rarely left their own rural communities, which resulted in regionally scattered identities and loyalties. Therefore the state did not have substantial influence within its own borders that was independent of local feudal lords. In the early modern era, monarchs began to consolidate power with a combination of political alliances, economic statecraft, and violence. Monarchs allied themselves with the rising merchant class and weakened the feudal nobles. As territory and peoples were brought under the authority of the state, a common identity linked to the state was constructed with the flag, anthem, crests, and historical national narratives based on original myths, shared victimhood, and victory vis-à-vis outsiders. Yet, in the absence of state sovereignty, people were subject to overlapping authorities by the Church, kings, barons, trade guilds, and other political actors, which rivalled the state in terms of identity and loyalty. The lack of clearly delineated authority led to the Thirty-Years War between 1618 and 1648, a destructive confrontation between Catholics and Protestants in the wake of the vacuum left behind by the demise of the Holy Roman Empire. Efforts were made to convert subjects to Catholicism to extend authority over the populace, which mobilised a countering alliance by Protestants. The English civil war ended, and solidarity was restored when Protestantism was established as the dominant religion.

The Peace of Westphalia in 1648 established the full sovereignty of the European nation-state, which resolved the problem of overlapping authorities and conflicts between internal ethno-cultural groups. The state became the highest sovereign by stripping rival groups of autonomy and integrating them under the authority of the state. The faith of the prince became the religion of his realm and foreign states could not intervene to aid minorities (Mann 2005: 49). The state became a stable and powerful actor once it claimed supreme sovereignty within specific borders, and purged rivals to establish a cogent ethno-cultural, religious, and linguistic core. National education, military service, national economy/industry, and railways further augmented assimilation and loyalty to the state. The state incentivised conformity through conversion and penalised non-conforming citizens as second-class (Mann 2005: 49). Constructing a homogenous society in France was challenging as rural peasants outside of Paris had overwhelmingly local and regional identities. Protestant were thinned out by compelling them to either convert to Catholicism or face expulsion, while local cultures, traditions, and languages were eradicated under the mission of nationalising the identity of the people.

The nation-state mirrored the community by harnessing and representing the distinctiveness of the people. Yet, the nation-state brandished a powerful society capable of advancements and competing in the international system. The nation-state did not eliminate ethnicity, culture, and religion as sources of identity, but decoupled precept from authority. The state then became the dominant authority by absorbing and shaping these ethno-cultural identities. When the state is unable to provide security or a distinct identity for the population, religion can be harnessed as an ally. Otto Von Bismarck recognised the imperative of Christianity to develop compatible values and enhance legitimacy when unifying German states (Kissinger 1968: 898). When Poland was under the intrusive influence of the Soviet Union, peaceful resistance by the Solidarity labour movement included developing a distinct and opposing identity by establishing links to the Catholic Church. Similarly, the Russian Orthodox Church provided peaceful support for Yeltsin as he faced the threat of removal by the communist authorities (McDougall 1998). Religion ended its rival influence once the sovereignty of the state was restored. In Russia, the Christian Orthodox Church was imperative to restoring national identity and stability after the collapse of the Soviet Union. Religion as an ally or adversarial authority to the state is therefore contingent on the strong foundation of statehood and the state's willingness to accommodate religious faith.

The nation-state subsequently became the most powerful political force as a large tribe representing the traditional of communities. Kennan (1993: 76–77) recognised nationalism to be 'the greatest emotional-political force of the age'. The strength of nationalism as a political community is explained as representing the 'essence of our being which defines us against the background of the world' (Lippman 2008: 66–67). Nationalism appeals to the irrational for meaning, which we neither can nor should aspire to eradicate. Nationalism encapsulates both love and hate as 'a cluster of primitive feelings, absorbed into a Man and rooted within him long before conscious education begins' (Lippmann 2008: 60). The instinctive impulses of Man for the past thousands of years have organised humanity based on kinship. The sense of shared destiny and aspiration for immortality by reproducing the community encourages altruistic behaviour towards the ethno-cultural collective. Stability and durability is contingent on the presence of a homogenous ethno-cultural core to allow the state to represent the identity that the primordial and instinctive gravitate towards.

Nationalism can take various forms, with romantic nationalism more closely linked to the community and patriotism to the society (Kennan 1993: 77–81). Romantic nationalism builds political legitimacy on the organic and natural by ascribing qualities to ethnicity, religion, culture, or language. Reproducing the traditional and spiritual for historic continuity appeals profoundly to the human condition as a source of meaning and solidarity. It is also appealing for the state to establish clearly defined borders between 'us' and 'them' to ensure autonomy. Yet, romantic nationalism tends to embrace excessive collective self-admiration at the peril of empathy and relations with the 'other'. Furthermore, reforms for rational advancement are constrained as the organic defines the greatness of the people and their relations with the state. Patriotism in contrast is less preoccupied with the organic as affection and loyalty to the state is built upon civic ideas rooted in values and norms. Patriotism is more conducive for rational reforms and advancements as the state must abide by certain ideals and the imperfect state can air its mistakes and improve. Peaceful relations with the 'other' are likely to be more benign as the borders between 'us' and 'them' are more permeable. Yet, the porous borders can weaken internal cohesion and invite interference into domestic affairs. Cohen (1991: 47) argues:

> Malign nationalism seeks national goals relentlessly, even at the expense of others; benign nationalism, by contrast, is prepared to compromise national policy priorities where necessary to accommodate the interests of others. The difference between these two types of nationalism lies in the willingness of a country to identify its own national interest with an interest in the stability of the overall international system. Benign nationalism acknowledges a connection between self-interest and systemic interest; malign nationalism ignores or denies it.

The liberal rebirth of Western civilisation

The American and French Revolution started the liberal rebirth of Western civilisation. American civilisation initially attempting to shed the decadence and corruption of its European past. Reborn, the US intended only to preserve the strengths inherited from European civilisation. The conception of the American identity was predisposed to dismiss ethnic characteristics as the American Revolution was fought almost exclusively by men with British origin, and some even with British identity (Gleason 1980). The objective of the revolutionaries was to narrate a different Anglo-Saxon identity. Rather than contesting the English identity, the revolt built on the notion that the colonists were acting consistently with liberty in accordance with English ideas and principles (Hannan 2013). The narrative of splitting from the British was to seek a purer liberty where the full potential of freedom could be reached by decoupling from the monarchy. Liberty was a pragmatic identity to distinguish from the British royalist by exposing the civic inconsistencies of the British.

While the American Revolution and French Revolution were fought about the same time and for the same liberal principles, the US was distinctive – defined by strong institutions and values, not strong leaders. The principal distinction was between the constrained and the unconstrained. The French Revolution gave unconstrained powers to the representatives that would advance the liberty of the people, which rested on the belief that the right people should be empowered. The American Revolution, in contrast, expected liberty to prevail when the leaders themselves were constrained by checks and balances (Sowell 2002). Burke (2012[1790]), a cogent supporter of the American Revolution and fierce opponent of the French Revolution, therefore distinguished between the barbarity of the French mob rule that could destroy French society and the US experience with continuity by conserving traditions and property.

As a child of the Enlightenment project, the US embraced a more liberal ethos. The destructive rivalry of ethno-cultural nationalism was sought to be replaced with civic patriotism. Liberalism is the source of solidarity by establishing a political centre that implicitly delineates acceptable political discourse and its philosophical, cultural, social, and political foundations. Liberalism was to be balanced by preserving morals, which would be based on culture and faith. In George Washington's farewell address in 1796, he proclaimed: 'Of all the dispositions and habits which lead to political prosperity, religion and morality are indispensable supports'. Manners can be said to mirror morals, and the importance of manners was best expressed by Edmund Burke (2012[1796]): 'Manners are of more importance than laws. Manners are what vex or soothe, corrupt or purify, exalt or debase, barbarize or refine us, by a constant, steady, uniform, insensible operation, like that of the air we breathe in.'

A civic identity was instrumental in distinguishing American civilisation from European. The US situated itself as a unique civilisation until the end of the 19th century, with American virtues and liberty in the New World being juxtaposed on to European vices and the despotism of the Old World. Paternalism, collectivism, and decadence contrasted with self-help, individualism, and purity. The American civilisation was seen to be built as an improvement of the remnants of European civilisation, much like modern Europe was built on the flawed but valued relics of the Roman Empire. Scholars popularised the notion of US exceptionalism by arguing that liberty was a founding principle (Lipset 1996). The American identity was aimed to be civic to avoid the divisive ethnic identities that had fragmented Europe. American Man was defined as a European or descendant of Europeans who had left 'behind him all his ancient prejudices and manners' and a new identity born out of commitment to values of liberty (Gleason 1980: 33).

Yet, the US inherited a strong homogenous ethno-cultural configuration of European civilisation, which was to be harmonised with its liberal constitution. The civic identity of the US was evidently restricted to the European origin, as a strategic and rational choice. The US after 1776 was never a purely civic state as a distinct White Anglo-Saxon Protestant (WASP) ethno-cultural core was constructed as the foundation for internal cohesion. It was determined that no territory would obtain statehood in the union unless WASP outnumbered the minorities to be capable of a forceful gravitational pull over the rest of the population (Glazer 1983). Whiteness distinguished the American from the Native Americans and Latin Americans, while Protestantism developed clear religious differences from the Catholic French. Max Weber's (1958) idea of Protestant ethics was therefore adopted and became popular among American intellectuals. Yet, the ethno-cultural identity produced cleavages within the US as WASP male supremacy resulted in most of its adult population not enjoying full citizenship in terms of political rights and responsibilities (Smith 1997). Inheriting English identity did not entail a completely civic nationalism as non-whites could become British, but never English (Kuzio 2002: 27–28). The US similarly established its own civic restrictions as 'we the people' was, much like in ancient Greece, largely a reference to white men with property. The blacks were not considered a race suitable for assimilation, and the main challenge was perceived to derive from Southern and Eastern Europeans as they differed from the ethno-cultural core of the initial settlers.

The liberal reversal of conformity in the nation-state

Liberalism's perpetual push towards advancing the rights of the individual at the expense of responsibilities towards the community, has traditionally been balanced by a formidable conservative movement. The Enlightenment project assumes that progress entails a linear progression towards the rational thereby gradually displacing the past. Progress is thus defined not by a balance between the progressive and conservative, but rather by the former defeating the latter. The nation-building process of homogenising the population is subsequently undergoing a reversal. Hobsbawm (2007: 93) posited that the process that turned peasants into Frenchmen and immigrants into American citizens is reversing, and it crumbles larger nation-state identities into self-regarding group identities.

The victory of liberalism over classical conservativism eventually leads to the demise of both as the common cause of the liberal nation-state erodes. The delicate balance in the US between ethno-cultural and civic identity has gradually unravelled. From 1815, the large-scale immigration from Catholic Germany and Ireland diluted the WASP majority. By the 1830s, anti-Catholicism sentiment rose as the US protestant identity suffered and became more insecure in its ethno-cultural core. Yet, in 1900 the 'old American', consisting of Protestants, still made up 55 percent of the entire population (Kaufmann 2004). The Protestant identity has declined, yet the US remains the foremost Christian nation among developed states.

The process of diluting the WASP majority was countered in 1882, when immigration restrictions were placed upon specific races (Smith 1997: 118). While American borders had remained largely open, this changed drastically in the 1920s. With a declining WASP majority, the political debate changed by increasingly making a distinction between desirable and undesirable immigrants

(King 2009). Yet, by the 1940s, US borders were increasingly opening to Asians. Not only did the ethnic composition fragment, but the political followed as elites tended to favour more immigration as advanced society was prioritised above the preservation of the community. Besides the interest-driven variable of adopting a civic identity with a larger immigration pool, the ideology of a liberty-based identity also limited the ability to uphold the ethno-cultural core at the heart of the American identity.

The decline of the WASP majority resulted in a fragmented ethno-cultural identity in the US (Schrag 1971). By the 1950s, 'identity' had become a central term to discuss ethnicity in the US (Gleason 1980: 31). In the 1960s, a provocative thesis submitted that Americans had fragmented into ethnic identity groups. In *Beyond the Melting Pot*, Glazer and Moynihan (1963) identified the pernicious development that immigrants to New York largely maintained their ethnic identities. Substantial social differences were recognised between various ethnic groups as for example the African Americans and Puerto Ricans were over-represented on social welfare, while the Asian (particularly Indian) side demonstrated higher human capital (Glazer and Moynihan 1963). Primordial attachment became a social construction for many ethnic groups seeking to rediscover their ethnic identity distinctive from other Americans. While inter-racial marriages had traditionally facilitated biological and social assimilation, identities remained more resilient. For example, Americans identifying as 'Native Americans' increased almost four-fold between 1960 and 1990, which contrasts with the reduction in biological ethnic distinctiveness as 70 percent of Native Americans marry outside their race (Patterson 1993: 28–29).

The American 'melting pot' for assimilation has been replaced by a 'salad bowl' model. The term 'Americanization' after the First World War was a policy aimed to assimilate immigrants, by gravitating towards the core to be considered 'more American'. The exclusionary component of the ethno-cultural core of American society therefore functioned as an incentive to assimilate and homogenise the population. White America was imitated by speaking the same language, attending the same churches, and adopting the local culture to ensure acceptance (Hsu 2009). Yet, assimilation was gradually denounced as a form of totalitarianism since minorities were expected to conform to the majority. New liberal ideals instead advocated that minorities should have the right to preserve their native culture and not conform to the nation (Glazer 1993: 123). Glazer (1993) noted that in discussion about ethnicity with students at Harvard, the term 'assimilation' had become overwhelmingly a negative term equating it to cultural genocide. While through its history ethno-cultural nationalism in the US has dominanted over the civic, this changed in the 1960s (Kaufmann 2000).

The ideology of multiculturalism rejected the melting pot integration model as a totalitarian structure that excludes and denies the ability of people to maintain their native culture. Multiculturalism has the virtuous objective of promoting tolerance and inclusion, yet inevitably fragments the state by failing to use the ethno-cultural as a common identity. The liberal concept of citizenship advances the right to exercise and preserve any culture, which is prioritised above the responsibility of adapting to the dominant community. Society is intended to work as a distinct patchwork of cultures and find strength in diversity. 'Soft multiculturalism' recognises a nation-centric culture that accepts a variety of other cultures as dominant, with the expectation that they will gradually gravitate towards the national culture. In contrast, 'hard multiculturalism' dismisses a hierarchical ordering of cultures and expects all domestic cultures to coexist as equals. Confusion between the two has allowed the former to persevere (Albrechtsen 2009).

By the 1990s, the ethno-cultural identity being balanced with a civic identity was increasingly abandoned in favour of civic absolutism. The decline of an ethnic majority was praised by President Bill Clinton (1998) as advancement:

> Today, largely because of immigration, there is no majority race in Hawaii or Houston or New York City. Within 5 years, there will be no majority race in our largest State, California. In a little more than 50 years, there will be no majority race in the United States. No other nation in history has gone through demographic change of this magnitude in so short a time . . .

Basing the argument principally on economic development, Bill Clinton (1998) suggested that meaning and identity would strengthen by diluting the ethno-cultural core and establishing a reversed frontier:

> [Immigrants] are revitalizing our cities. They are building our new economy. They are strengthening our ties to the global economy, just as earlier waves of immigrants settled the new frontier and powered the Industrial Revolution. They are energizing our culture and broadening our vision of the world. They are renewing our most basic values and reminding us all of what it truly means to be an American.

As the US became more powerful, there were greater incentives to experiment with and embrace the virtues of civic absolutism as a source of legitimacy, loyalty, solidarity, and influence. Powerful states have incentives to focus on the universal rather than the distinctive to promote to sovereign inequality because the more powerful state benefits from overlapping authority. Furthermore, state-building based purely on civic nationalism developed as an excessive response to disastrous unfettered ethno-cultural nationalism. The virtuous objective of embracing universal and civic ideas is largely aimed to overcome the harmful 'us' versus 'them' divisions that has been the source of most conflicts in human history. Germany, with its particularly brutal ethno-nationalist past, is also more inclined towards developing civic identity based on 'constitutional patriotism' and asserts its leadership in Europe under the banner of 'shared values'.

The ethno-cultural as a rival authority

The failure of the state to harness and represent ethno-cultural distinctiveness results in it becoming a rival authority. A civic identity is therefore more stable when it is founded on a strong ethno-cultural majority, rather than attempting to transcend the distinctive. While preserving a gravitational pull towards an ethno-cultural core is controversial in contemporary society, it is nonetheless widely recognised as a necessity. Social security is:

> the ability of a society to persist in its essential character under changing conditions and possible or actual threats. More specifically, it is about the sustainability, within acceptable conditions for evolution, of traditional patterns of language, culture, association, and religious and national identity and custom.
>
> (Wæver 1993: 23)

The exposure to and mixture of ethnicities, cultures, and religions can make a state more benign by reducing the unknown, anxiety, and fear as key sources of conflict. Albeit, threats are not only misperceptions but also realities. Without a dominant core that remains unchallenged, ethno-cultural particularities can become a domestic organisational principle for competition for resources. A 'societal security dilemma' can develop when the state's effort to homogenise in order to strengthen internal cohesion conflicts with the ability of sub-groups to reproduce themselves in terms of traditions, culture, religion, and language (Posen 1993; Roe 2004). The equal status of all cultures within a society may enhance their exposure, but also elevates them to a threat. As minority cultures obtain the status equal to the titular majority culture, the competition for resources and political capital intensifies. The weakening of an overarching identity based on a strong ethno-cultural core with a gravitational pull does not create a shared civic identity, rather refuge is sought in identity politics. The Soviet Union and Yugoslavia both sought to transcend the ethno-cultural and create a supra-national identity, yet they maintained ethno-federalism due to the recognition that its civic aspiration would be a lengthy process. The collapse of the Soviet Union and Yugoslavia unfolded when the diverse ethnic identities rivalled the communist state for legitimacy.

Secularism in the West, defined as the détente between the state and church, has provided stability. The church as the representative of Christianity has in the past exercised significant power that was utilised to compete for influence. Secularism ensures the primacy of the state, yet the government can use the influence of religion to promote meaning, a sense of community, and commonality among the populace. Evoking a mandate of Heaven can inspire greater loyalty and sacrifice by the people, which can also 'make warriors of zealots and martyrs of peacemakers' (McDougall 1998). Yet, secularism is under threat as the state begins to eschew the church. The state's relationship with religion is fraught as religion can enhance the legitimacy and power of the state or become a rival influence.

As religion functions as a moral compass for many citizens, it is prudent for all US presidents to express their devotion to the Christian faith and to link American values with Christian virtues. Jimmy Carter appealed to the common precepts of Judaism, Islam, and Christianity when he encouraged support by religious leaders to embrace the Camp David Accords (McDougall 1998). Truman, Eisenhower, and Reagan used religion to strengthen the moral undercurrents of the Cold War by depicting the West as on the side of God, against the ungodly and atheists of the East. In contrast, the Soviet's derision for religion as 'opium for the masses' made the Christian identity incompatible with the national identity and therefore a rival loyalty. Christianity could also not be used by the Soviets to mobilise international support, and atheism alienated Catholic Latin American countries where communism appealed as resistance to the US.

The decline of Christianity as a shared religion in the West diminishes its function as an instrument for connectivity and 'we-ness', and makes it a divisive sub-identity. Much like Bill Clinton celebrated the decline of the ethno-cultural core as progress, Obama proclaimed that 'we are no longer just a Christian nation'. The Right defends Christianity as one of the last vestiges of the traditional and the preservation of civilisation itself. Tocqueville (1945[1839]: 319–320) famously expressed his belief that religion contributes to the glue in American democracy. Europeans had viewed the deterioration of religion as the consequence of the progress of the enlightenment, liberty, and freedom. Yet in the US, ahead in both liberty and freedom, religion was dominant (Tocqueville 1945[1839]: 319–320). Religion is important as a form of networked community that enhances social capital, which encourages altruism. Religious Americans are therefore better neighbours, more trusting, and active citizens in terms of enhancing social capital (Putnam and Campbell 2010). Religion also instils Americans with a sense of meaning and satisfaction/happiness with their lives in comparison to atheists (Putnam and Campbell 2010: 492). The Right recognises that reproducing religion as an imperative component of gemeinschaft is imperative to sustain civilisation. Buchanan (2010) posits that when faith declines, the culture and population also begins to die. President Reagan (1984), an icon for the American Right, warned that all great civilisations that eventually collapsed had one thing in common:

> One of the significant forerunners of their fall was their turning away from their God or gods. Without God, there is no virtue, because there's no prompting of the conscience. Without God, we're mired in the material, that flat world that tells us only what the senses perceive. Without God, there is a coarsening of the society. And without God, democracy will not and cannot long endure. If we ever forget that we're one nation under God, then we will be a nation gone under.

The argument that diverse populations and multiculturalism produce civic strength, expressed with the popular mantra of 'strength in diversity', is not supported by evidence. A more mobile and diverse workforce in certain high-skill professions can offer competitive advantage as the dissimilarities heightens the consideration for other experiences and perspectives and encourages individuals to question their own innate beliefs. (Page 2008). However, as the homogeneity of the community declines, human beings experience a growing need for traditional values and kinship by rediscovering or inventing new exclusionary identities linked to religion, ethnicity, culture, and language that will fragment diverse societies. Reducing ethno-cultural homogeneity does not eradicate the distinctive as a source for an identity, rather the ethno-culture becomes a rival authority to sub-groups. Putnam's (1995) research demonstrated how complex society has undermined 'social capital', defined as the social networks found in communities as an indicator of civic vigour. Social capital is the well-being resulting from personal connectivity with family, friends, neighbours, and the wider community. Strong social capital in homogenous societies correlates with happiness, empathy, care for fellow citizens, trust in neighbours, civic engagement, and voting (Putnam 1995).

Putnam discovered that 'the only two things that go up as the diversity of your census track goes up are protest marches and television watching' (NPR 2007). From 1973 to 1994, attendance at public meetings in the US reduced by half. While more than half of Americans stated in the early 1960s that most people can be trusted, this number plummeted to less than a third in the 2000s (Sander and Putnam 2010; Cillizza 2014). Furthermore, large diverse societies correlate with wider wealth gaps and increased crime. Putnam (2007: 150) posits that:

> Inhabitants of diverse communities tend to withdraw from collective life, to distrust their neighbors, regardless of the color of their skin, to withdraw even from close friends, to expect the worst from their community and its leaders, to volunteer less, give less to charity and work on community projects less often, to register to vote less, to agitate for social reform more but have less faith that they can actually make a difference, and to huddle unhappily in front of the television.

Diversity also diminishes morality. There is less generosity and willingness to look after the poor when they are not considered part of the same community (Alesina and Glaeser 2004; Putnam 2007). The immense differences in social welfare spending between the US and Europe can therefore largely be attributed to the greater ethno-cultural diversity in the US (Alesina and Glaeser 2004). Traditionally heterogeneous Scandinavia is thus expected to downsize the vast welfare state as the population rapidly becomes more diverse and disconnected. Diversity can also reduce internal cohesion during conflicts with external actors. For example, within the US Union Army, there were markedly higher desertion rates among soldiers serving in companies with greater varieties in age, occupation, and birthplace (Costa and Kahn 2003).

The failure to represent kinship and spirituality results in a vacuum to be filled by competitive ethno-cultural enclaves. The decline in religion makes it a societal sub-group that subsequently makes it politicised and divisive. The 'God gap' refers to religion having become a divided partisan issue in the US (Putnam and Campbell 2010: 369). While the religious community is more generous and has higher social capital, religious people are less supportive of civil liberties than their secular counterparts as they seek to conserve and reproduce their own traditions (Putnam and Campbell 2010). Religious and atheist fundamentalists see each other as rivals as human progress and peace is believed to be contingent upon everyone adopting their belief system. Interestingly, religious and atheist fundamentalists seem to find common ground in their adversity by commonly resorting to the argument that religion is not only a spiritual community as the religious text and practises should be interpreted literally without recognising changes in time.

Similarly, ethnic diversity across the West is indicative of the state losing its ability to represent the irrational, rather than the ethno-cultural being transcended. The destruction of the family as the cornerstone of gemeinschaft has resulted in the demographic death of Europe. European states account for 18 out of the 20 nations with the lowest birth rates, which is balanced with mass migration (Buchanan 2010). The EU long prided itself on the virtues of tolerance and civility as defining characteristics, yet they have since become the key vulnerabilities (Krastev 2017: 38–39). Liberal excesses achieve the opposite as ethnic identity becomes more domineering when it is perceived to be under threat. In 2011, a few years before the Brexit referendum, a Yougov poll demonstrated that 62 percent of British people agreed with the following statement: 'Britain has changed in recent times beyond recognition, it sometimes feels like a foreign country, and this makes me feel uncomfortable'. However, these results were commonly interpreted and dismissed as a rise in xenophobia, rather than unease about the ability of British society to reproduce itself.

Multiculturalism is, however, increasingly recognised to have failed. By October 2010, German Chancellor Angela Merkel, announced that multiculturalism had 'utterly failed' and created parallel societies within Germany. British Prime Minister, David Cameron (2011), in his 2011 Munich Security Conference speech warned that multiculturalism had divided rather than united:

> Under the doctrine of state multiculturalism, we have encouraged different cultures to live separate lives, apart from each other and apart from the mainstream. We've failed to provide a vision of society to which they feel they want to belong. We've even tolerated these segregated communities behaving in ways that run completely counter to our values. So, when a white person holds objectionable views, racist views for instance, we rightly condemn them. But when equally unacceptable views or practices come from someone who isn't white, we've been too cautious frankly – frankly, even fearful – to stand up to them . . . we must build stronger societies and stronger identities at home.

Cameron's successor, Theresa May (2016), similarly called for a narrower definition of citizenship: 'if you believe you're a citizen of the world, you're a citizen of nowhere. You don't understand what the very word "citizenship" means'.

While the West, where the nation came before the state, is incrementally abandoning the ethno-cultural and religious aspect of its identity, other rising powers are developing as nation-states. Even India has begun to embrace a strong Hindu nationalism. There could be 130 million Christians in China, already surpassing the practising Christians in Europe (Ferguson 2011: 278). While churches are torn down across Europe due to lack of attendance, and often converted into mosques, China builds churches at a rate like nowhere else in the world. The Christian community in China contributes to Weber's work ethic and becomes a source of community among sub-groups that also encourages fewer contractual business practises among its membership in terms of creditworthiness or trust as a mechanism for cooperation (Ferguson 2011: 285). In Russia as well, Christianity is taking a centre state in the national identity.

Engaging with the world with recognition for the ethno-cultural

The West's delusion that the ethno-cultural can be transcended has contributed to a disastrous relationship with the Islamic world. The failure in the West to recognise the continued role of religion has produced dangerous and failed military adventures in the Middle East, and made Europe unprepared for the identity crisis caused by mass migration from Islamic countries. Religion is dominant in the culture and identity of Islamic countries, partly due to weak statehood. This makes Islam an important mechanism to defend sovereignty, and it also makes ethno-cultural assimilation of Muslims in the West less feasible. The rise of political Islam in Iran, Saudi Arabia, and Afghanistan are pertinent examples of weak statehood that succumbs to religious authority. In all instances, weak governments relied on the authority of religion to establish or restore statehood, yet Islam became the principal source of authority.

Iran's political Islam arose from foreign suppression of national sovereignty, resulting in independence movements forming an alliance with the religious leadership as an alternative source of legitimacy. Iran can still be said to have a relatively benign form of political Islam due to the ability to restore the supremacy of the state over religion. Iran had relatively stable statehood based on centuries-long traditions of the relatively unified Persians, until the democratically elected president of Iran, Mossadeq, was toppled by the US and UK in 1953. The installed US-allied Shah used the ominous and brutal SAVAK security forces to limit any political opposition. Islam, a strong source of identity, could not be adequately harnessed and controlled by the Shah and it could not be suppressed. Subsequently, political discussions and political organisations drifted into the Mosques as the sole social meeting-place out of the government's reach. The religious leadership thus asserted its political leadership of the revolution and established the Islamic Republic of Iran. Since the revolution, Tehran has acted as a rational state and the revolutionary sentiments have largely been instrumental in expanding state power by attempting to 'liberate' allied Shia majority populations living under Sunni minority dictatorships.

Saudi Arabia's political Islam is much more belligerent due to the inability to elevate the state above religion. However, the patronage by the US has also contributed to the elevation of this destructive state. The Saudi family pursuit of the initially calculated/rational objective of increased political power required a partnership with the Wahhabists, a fundamentalist and militant branch of Islam that preaches extreme puritanism. While fomenting a clearly delineated religious Wahhabist identity, its exclusionary nature fuels sectarianism and conflicts with the other branches of Islam. The establishment of one leader for all Muslims, the Caliph, required a brutal purge of heresy to establish strict conformity and homogenise the Muslim world. The reliance on Wahhabism as an indispensable ally for Saudi statehood has also perpetuated weakness. Saudi Arabia has been reliant on directing Wahhabism abroad to fight Iran-aligned Shia influence with Sunni extremism, often with Western support. Yet, the contradictions between rational interests of the state and Wahhabism is not easily reconcilable, and the stability and viability of statehood is challenged by religious extremism. Channelling extremist forces abroad is therefore also a necessity to direct focus away from the Saudi-Wahhabist pact that is unfolding domestically.

Afghanistan similarly experienced religion being used to organise opposition and undermine the legitimacy of the Soviet-leaning authorities in Kabul. The violent US-backed insurgency by the Muhadjeen in Afghanistan before and during the Soviet invasion strengthened a post-national religious identity, albeit, the religious authority remained after the Soviet Union withdrew. The broken relationship between the state and religion in Afghanistan may also consume Iraq. Saddam Hussein, a secularist, depicted himself as religious to augment his authority in the religious community and as a source of unity. Yet, his efforts to establish a stronger sense of unity within Iraq by employing Islam also represented a challenge, as Islam could be utilised as an alternative authority. Furthermore, if religious groups break into Sunni and Shia sects it undermines commonality. Western invasions or other reasons for state collapse in Iraq, Somalia, Libya, and Syria, have enabled religious groups such as ISIS to fill the vacuum by organising post-national political entities.

Liberal authoritarianism

Correcting and constraining the liberal impulses of the West is problematic due to liberal authoritarianism. While the strength of the US derives from a consensus on liberal principles, the subsequent ideological constraints limit the scope of debate. Liberalism has made the US truly exceptional, yet it is also suffocating the US (Hartz 1955). The underlying Lockean liberal consensus functioned as a source of unity to avoid upheavals, yet it also posed the 'danger of unanimity' by limiting possibilities and pragmatism for thought and policies due to the 'deep and unwritten tyrannical compulsion' of conformity to Lockean doctrine (Hartz 1955: 12). The paradox is that American ideology celebrates the individual, yet the reliance on ideological conformity and its civic identity represented a very anti-individualistic ethos.

The famous historian, Hofstadter, remarked that the US has the misfortune of being an ideology rather than having one (Kennedy 2013: 623). Ideologies are useful by mobilising political support and resources in support of rational interests of society, to preserve the irrationality of community, and to harmonise the two. However, when ideology becomes too prevailing by constraining or dictating policy, it can become a source of irrational behaviour. The US is less capable of altering its civic idealism when it no longer serves a pragmatic purpose since this would entail abandoning the idea of America. Deviations from the liberal consensus cause excessive fear and radical responses. The Red Scare and subsequent McCarthyism demonstrated that the US responded disproportionately with illiberal means to defend its liberal ethos. Another contradiction of the US is that it is liberal and conservative, by seeking to conserve its liberal traditions (Hartz 1955: 50). The conservative aims to maintain the existing way of life against alienating changes. Balancing the contradictions were indeed recognised to be at the heart of American culture: 'it looked forward to the future but that it worshiped the past as well' (Hartz 1955: 51). Yet, the strength of liberalism in the American political consciousness also makes it more difficult to constrain.

The ideological conflicts of the 20th century made liberalism instrumental in the competition between great powers. Liberalism was in a ruthless competition with fascism, and then communism and the Cold War ironically introduced one of the more illiberal chapters of American history as allies were demoted to vassals. Yet, the liberal identity was preserved and heightened in comparison to the US foremost rivals. The hubris of the ideological victory after the Cold War and the ideological foundations for the unipolar moment incentivised liberal absolutism or neoliberalism consensus as the uniform answer to all the world's problems. Liberalism is embraced to its fullest extent as it is no longer treated as an imperfect ideology, but as the natural condition of Man. The former political pluralism between conservativism and liberalism has given way to a liberal authoritarianism that strikes down on dissent contesting the virtues of liberalism and the institutions that purportedly upholds these values.

Liberal authoritarianism has cemented itself as the principles of liberalism are embraced to such an extent they cannot be challenged. Liberal authoritarianism is implemented by the increasing reliance on government to provide 'rights'. The philosophy of liberalism constrains the power of the government by placing individual freedoms at the centre. Yet, unfettered liberalism also liberates the individual from the all arbitrary authority and constraining collective identities related to nation, culture, family, religion, gender, and spiritual community. Free from the dependence on traditional inter-personal ties of the community, the state increasingly becomes a law-based substitute.

Subsequently, liberalism incrementally evolved from a philosophy of individual freedoms to an ever-expanding list of rights. An expert class emerges that replaces the elected officials to ensure these rights are shielded from democratic pressures (Babones 2018). The experts wield genuine authority due to their specialised knowledge and experience as civic rights activists, human rights lawyers, medical professionals, environmental scientists etc. The relative power of experts increases in complex societies as political representatives cannot possibly harness all the required knowledge. The new expert class rule with the authority of representing liberal principles that cannot be challenged by democratic means. Liberal authoritarianism is subsequently established as the liberal elites develop new 'rights' that increasingly limit the power of political representatives that can be elected and removed by the ballot box (Babones 2018). The impotence of political representatives that are incapable of altering failed policies causes a growing distrust by the populace. The population recognise that 'establishment politicians' are constrained by the liberal authoritarianism and neoliberal consensus. Hence, there is a growing attractiveness of non-political and radical populists that are prepared to tear the political system up at its roots to implement the required changes.

Conclusion

The disarray and identity crisis of the West is largely the result of the ambiguity surrounding its own historical teleology. The narrative that the West was born out of reason and the spirit of the Enlightenment suggests a neglect of the ethno-cultural birthplace of the West in the natural. The rise of Western civilisation can be attributed to the balance between the natural/primitive and reason/modernity. The decline of Western civilisation is caused by the belief that advancement entails shedding the traditional and irrational completely. Efforts to construct a common Euro-Atlantic political community is a social experiment in the process of failing, since it neglects that ethnicity and religion are the two most durable institutions of Western civilisation. Diverse and traditional ethno-cultural and religious identities are displaced with an ideologically liberal democratic civic identity.

The new civic absolutism posits that preservation of the ethno-cultural is exclusionary and contradicts Western values. The decay of intellectual pluralism has dumbed down as informed philosophical debates on contradictions in human nature have disappeared from the discourse in politics, academia, and the media. Re-conceptualising a shared Western civilisational as commitment to liberal democracy and laissez-faire capitalism is problematic as these are relatively recent principles. A crisis in democracy and nationhood is evident as solidarity diminishes. Political pluralism no longer allows the best ideas to float to the top and facilitate peaceful transition of power, instead each side seeks to vanquish the other. On the Left, there is a demand for permanent revolution, however with increasingly less of the past to discard and little ability to point to a better future. On the Right the conservatives have become permanent reactionaries as classical conservativism was abandoned with the neo-liberal consensus from the 1980s and 1990s. Liberal foundations for a shared 'Western Civilisation' incentivises a shift to liberal authoritarianism that suppress opposition. Yet marginalising the platform for legitimate concerns by ethno-cultural nationalists will empower radical alternatives prepared to reject the entire liberal platform of the West.

4   The postmodernist graveyard of Western civilisation

Postmodernism is the epitome of excessive 'liberty' as cautioned by ancient Greek philosophers, as people seek to free themselves from institutions and responsibilities that instil civilisation with order, purpose, and meaning. Postmodern art mirrors the flaws and dangers of postmodern political theory as a painting depicting Man's contradictory relationship with nature or God is replaced with a meaningless canvas splattered with ketchup or a bicycle glued to a wall. By abolishing arbitrary objective features or structures of art that could obstruct creative expression, the technical skills acquired by artists over a long period of time and the meaning art conveyed is abandoned with the argument that everything can be interpreted as art. Postmodernism aptly recognises that there are infinite ways to interpret observations as the world comes to us filtered through our senses and not objectively, which is why it is imperative to deconstruct and challenge the rationale of established truths. However, in art and in life, meaning and progress derive from striving towards establishing certain transcendent truths that reveal something about ourselves and the world. Yet, for the postmodernist, one definition and a higher truth cannot be established as elevating one interpretation above another is a form of arbitrary authority and dominance.

Premodernism worshipped the ancient and spiritual as a refuge for the irrational and instinctive impulses of Man, which has ever since been incorporated into culture. Christianity became a prevailing authority and source for organising a shared identity and purpose. The repudiation of the rational and calculative obstructed socio-economic advancements at the peril of both affluence and competitiveness vis-à-vis rival powers. Modernism developed as a response to deficiencies of premodernism as the Enlightenment project in Europe substituted arbitrary authority with governance based on the rational. The philosophy of modernism considered the traditions and hierarchies of the past, based on non-rational ideas, to limit the advancement of the freedom of Man. The French Revolution and the American Revolution were the most radical expressions of the Enlightenment project, with liberalism setting the political and economic rights of the individual as a core idea. In the 20th century, three modern political theories rivalled: liberalism, fascism, and communism. All three political theories shared an assumption about a linear development of humanity that resulted in utopian and absolutist initiatives to transcend the evils of the past.

While the modernist era sought to free humanity from arbitrary authority by establishing a society based on rational governance, postmodernism challenges all social institutions and traditions to eliminate intrinsic exploitative relationships. In a neo-Marxist fashion, postmodernism views the world as a competition between the privileged and exploited, a relationship that can be exposed and eradicated through deconstruction. Postmodernism is inherently nihilistic as it rejects any fundamental truths and rejects by dismissing all social paradigms as social constructions. Efforts to deconstruct human relationships and even language to eliminate a flawed past and establish a new Man results in also abolishing meaning.

This chapter will first explore postmodernist efforts to deconstruct and delegitimise meta-narratives in favour of mini-narratives. The benevolent intention of creating tolerance for alternative interpretations and culture codes results in a relativism that challenges the common truths of a society. Promoting comprehensive equality requires redistributing wealth, equalising the voice of fools with the wise, and challenging the narrative of the dominant. All cultures and morals are not equal. Promoting the equality of unequals therefore entails surrendering the defence and advocacy of bourgeois culture as a superior way of organising society. Nihilism ensues, and people are less willing to defend the meta-narrative that sustains civilisation.

Second, the rise of identity politics is surveyed as a manifestation of postmodernism. Well-intentioned efforts to create a more egalitarian society divides society and fuels animosity. Dominant groups are shamed for being exploitative, and weaker groups are victimised by being portrayed as being oppressed. This logic compartmentalises people arbitrarily into identity groups that undergo a homogenisation as internal differences are brushed over and group loyalty is demanded, while new conceptual walls are established to 'other' externals. Systemic pressures arise for competition between identity groups, with victimhood being the main currency to compete for the redistribution of political, social, and economic resources. The focus of victimhood incentivises hyper-sensitivity, polarises society, and eventually legitimises violence against opposition.

Last, American university campuses are assessed as the experimental laboratory for liberalism and postmodernism. It is found that the growing influence of the new Left on campuses has led to growing hostility towards the ethno-cultural core of the US and conservativism. Rather than engaging with competing ideas to peacefully harmonise a balance between liberalism and conservativism, debates are won by vilifying and delegitimising opposing views as evil. It will be concluded that by rejecting higher truths and demoting all ideas and values as relative, postmodernism deconstructs the great unifying ideas of Western civilisation.

Postmodernist philosophy: deconstructing meta-narratives and meaning

Postmodernism responds to modernism's pernicious utopianism, absolutism, scientism, and revolutionary violence that contributed to inciting totalitarianism

(Shorten 2012). The philosophy of postmodernism sprung into academic thought from the 1970s and 1980s under key scholars such as Jean-François Lyotard, Jacques Derrida, Michel Foucault, Louis Althusser, and Jacques Lacan. Postmodernism questions the existence of any objective reality and truth in the effort to liberate people from arbitrary authority. The postmodernists accurately identify that interpretations of reality can be subjective, albeit the reluctance to recognise immutable truths is its radical and destructive feature. Postmodernism represents a radical step in the effort to rid the world of the totalitarianism and social hierarchies, resulting in the deconstruction of institutions and traditions required to sustain civilisation.

Postmodernism is tasked to deconstruct the 'meta-narratives' of modernism, a repudiation of positivist and cohesive elucidation for major phenomena (Lyotard 1984). With no reality independent from interpretation, human categorisation is construed to principally be about power. The different versions of truth are merely a display of power as we compete for interpretation to assert dominance over other groups. Postmodernism and Marxism shares the view of the world as a struggle between the oppressors and the exploited. All truths are 'social constructions' to acquire power, with totalitarianism and oppression being built into meta-narratives of religions, ideologies, or societal institutions. The postmodernists therefore fight for social justice by 'deconstructing' narratives used by an oppressor group to exploit the marginalised.

The 'oppressive' meta-narratives are replaced with 'tolerance' for more personal mini-narratives that recognises cultural and moral relativism to avoid one group from asserting their narrative to construct a power hierarchy. Through the prism of totalitarianism, all structures are divided into the oppressors and oppressed. Deconstructing the meta-narratives and cancelling traditional forms of identities is believed by the postmodernist to be imperative in overcoming the totalitarianism of the modern era. For example, the narratives of the superb achievements of Western civilisation are dismissed as justifying authority and exploitation of other peoples, while gender roles that developed from a historical division of labour due to biological differences are denounced as narratives to legitimise the dominance of men over women. Postmodernism is therefore typically hostile to Western civilisation, traditions and shared identity, and fuels radical feminism and identity politics.

By positing that ideas and identities are socially constructed to constrain and limit our freedoms, advancement of freedoms entails deconstructing and denouncing civilisation as an oppressive construct. Equality for all requires the deconstruction of civilisations, states, cultures, ethnicities, religion, the family unit, gender roles, and other widely shared values and institutions that provide meaning and unity and are deemed to be an artificial social construction imposed by a dominant group. Postmodernism is inherently nihilistic by dismissing values and traditions that give life meaning, direction, and societal cohesion. Grand unifying narratives and value-structures that define a civilisation are demoted to artificial social construct to assign privilege to some groups at the expense of others. While there are various branches and degrees of absolutism within postmodernist theory, the harm can be observed as the ideas leap into society in the form of moral and cultural relativism.

The pseudo-science, bleakness, and cognitive nihilism associated with postmodernism earned it fierce and well-deserved contempt from academics on both the Left and the Right. Chomsky purportedly scorned postmodernism as 'extremely pretentious, but on examination, a lot of it is simply illiterate . . . and a good deal of plain gibberish' (Wolters 2013). Dawkins (2004: 45) defined the postmodernist as 'an intellectual impostor with nothing to say'. Habermas (2015) argues that postmodernism contradicts itself by presupposing concepts they seek to challenge, such as freedom, creativity, and subjectivity. Efforts to expand postmodernism from social science towards the natural science has aroused criticism and ridicule. Sokal and Bricmont (1998) denounced the efforts by postmodernists to deconstruct the natural sciences to reveal totalitarianism as a descent into absurdity. Their case studies included a feminist postmodernist claiming that Newton's principal was a 'rape manual' and Einstein's $E=mc^2$ was sexist as 'it privileges the speed of light over other speeds that are vitally necessary to us' (Sokal and Bricmont 1998: 81–83).

Tolerance as cultural/moral relativism

Tolerance, defined by support for mini-narratives, has become the new absolutism in the West. Tolerating diversity has risen to the height of what defines Western societies, and ironically a civic value that allegedly upholds unity. Efforts to justify dissenting positions questioning the virtue of tolerance is paradoxically not tolerated as it is deemed to be a sign of intolerance. The virtue of tolerance becomes indicative of civilisational decline as it represents the lack of willingness to defend one's own culture. Plato warned about tolerance as a precarious feature of democracy, as everything and everyone is acclaimed to be tolerated equally irrespective of merit: 'Such is democracy; – a pleasing, lawless, various sort of government, distributing equality to equals and unequals alike.' Aristotle similarly stated ominously more than 2,300 years ago: 'tolerance is the last virtue of a dying society'. Tolerance threatens to undermine all principles of Man. In more recent times, Chesterton once wrote that 'tolerance is the virtue of a man without convictions', culminating in moral relativism undermining principles and traditions to advance humankind. Toynbee (1946: 629) similarly posited that Europe's time of troubles began during the 1700s due to tolerance as the equality of unequals:

> It was because the toleration achieved by 'the Enlightenment' was a toleration based not on the Christian virtues of faith, hope, and charity but on the Mephistophelian maladies of disillusionment, apprehension, and cynicism. It was not an arduous achievement of religious fervour but a facile by-product of its abatement.

Liberal tolerance is paradoxical as it advocates for more openness and acceptance for diversity to the extent it promotes cultural and moral relativism, while concurrently having a narrow definition of morality. Recognising competing moralities is imperative as people do not act on rational decision-making. When scanning the brain, it is found that people reach conclusions based on moral instincts, and then selectively apply reason to justify their predetermined inference (Haidt 2012). Societal cohesion is not possible without the recognition for a broader conservative understanding of morality, as people act on moral intuition rather than reason as an independent variable. In other words, liberals do not recognise the immorality of tolerance when it assaults the traditional and the community.

Morality tends to be defined narrowly by liberals as care for others by detesting harm, seeking fairness and reciprocity. Conservatives share these categories of morality, but interpret morality more broadly by also including in-group loyalty, authority/respect, and sanctity/purity in terms of exercising restraints and control over what is done with the body (Haidt 2012). The liberal and conservative definition of morality can conflict as for example welfare programmes and feminism are moral expressions of care and fairness, albeit they can dilute the dominant role of the family as the principle institution for in-group loyalty, authority/respect, and sanctity. Similarly, multiculturalism is reasoned with inclusion as a form of care and fairness, yet it undermines the morality of an assimilation and social capital deriving from in-group loyalty. Conservatives are more attuned to preserve gemeinschaft as they instinctively interpret morality as maintaining physical and conceptual borders to strengthen the familiarity, safe, and dependable that instils a sense of meaning and order. In contrast, liberals tend to push towards gesellschaft by being more open to reduced borders, allow more diversity, and embrace greater exposure to new knowledge and experience (Haidt 2012).

In short, the morality of the Right entails building walls to ensure order, while the Left links morality to fairness by bringing walls down. When states grow in prosperity, it is found that values change as well (Haidt 2016). When people move up Maslow's hierarchy they are less reliant on values linked to mere survival, such as in-group loyalty by reproducing the traditional, community, and family. The increasingly affluent and urban population instead adopts cosmopolitan values and morality such as tolerance and openness (Haidt 2016). The former morality linked to in-group loyalty and preserving order through walls is subsequently replaced with a moral ethos that deems walls to be immoral. Globalisation has intensified the rift between the Left and the Right as prosperity grew rapidly by tearing down walls protecting the community, which also left many people behind.

In the contemporary integrated world, the competition between the new Right and the new Left subsequently manifested itself as a rivalry between nationalism and globalism. For the new Right/nationalists, it is imperative to preserve the moral order with patriotism. For the new Left/globalists, the idea of patriotism is conflated with unacceptable racism. The paradox of globalisation is that it makes the world more interconnected, yet it segregates the population into liberal and conservative enclaves. In a more specialised economy, the segregation is geographical along urban/rural lines and industry, while social media further intensifies the echo chambers. The lack of exposure to their counterparts results in a diminished ability to reach a common understanding with rational discourse. There is consequently a shift towards the psychology of a team sport, resulting in seeking to defeat rather than engage the moral and intellectual counterpart. Efforts by the new Left to eviscerate the arbitrary authority and immorality of nation-state create an authoritarian counter-reaction by the new Right to preserve order. A balance is required as an excessive virtue in either direction becomes a vice.

Postmodernism is pernicious due to the hostility towards the morality within traditional institutions that radically polarises society. While liberalism's failure to understand conservatives derives from prioritising care and fairness as the principle tenets of morality, postmodernism conceptualises in-group loyalty, authority, and sanctity as a nefarious establishment of a power hierarchy. Narrow moral arguments cripple intellectual diversity and political discourse as the arguments of the opposition are not engaged, rather the discussions are won by identifying and revealing their evil intentions (Sowell 1995). The opposition is not to be engaged with civility as it is perceived to normalise their platform of hate, while compromise is tantamount to treacherous appeasement. Intolerant of competing views, political groups withdraw into echo chambers that offer protection from morally unacceptable positions and thus fuels their cognitive dissonance.

American society has polarised into two nations, an affluent and cosmopolitan liberal elite and a struggling underclass. The underclass is crippled by tolerance for the normalisation of declining virtues in terms of illegitimacy, crime, and unemployment (Murray 2012). In contrast, the upper class embraces the virtues of hard work, intellectual achievements, and to marry and raise children together. However, the liberal tolerance, political correctness, and kindness of the elites prevents them from judging alternative lifestyles and preaching the virtues of their bourgeoisie culture (Murray 2012). There is a tense relationship between equality and freedom as disproportionate inequality can impede on the freedoms of the weaker, yet is also to some extent incompatible. Nikolai Berdayev argued that 'freedom is the right of inequality' as equal wealth means taking from the rich, and equal voice entails equalising the fool with the clever. Leontiev's (2014[1885]) advocacy of class distinction and healthy inequality within society was reasoned by the importance of a bourgeois class establishing benchmark for societal values to influence the lower classes. Bourgeois culture provided a social stability by maintaining the primacy of the community and preparing the population for participation in complex society. Bourgeois culture advocated and shamed deviance from the ideas that one should:

> Get married before you have children and strive to stay married for their sake. Get the education you need for gainful employment, work hard, and avoid idleness. Go the extra mile for your employer or client. Be a patriot, ready to serve the country. Be neighbourly, civic-minded, and charitable. Avoid coarse language in public. Be respectful of authority. Eschew substance abuse and crime.
>
> (Wax and Alexander 2017)

Revamping bourgeois culture and civic responsibilities requires the recognition that all cultures are not equal. Restoring bourgeois culture requires people to 'relinquish multicultural grievance polemics and the preening pretence of defending the downtrodden' (Wax and Alexander 2017). For example, illegitimacy is a dominant indicator of societal wellbeing. Across all races and social groups, there is a strong correlation between growing up in a single parent household and anti-social behaviour such as drugs, violence, alcoholism, and rape (Fagan 1995; Kendall and Tamura 2010). Crime and anti-social behaviour is also found to be lower in religious neighbourhoods (Fagan 1995). Asked about the greatest change occurring during his academic and political career spanning over four decades, Moynihan argued in 2000 that the 'family structure has come apart all over the North Atlantic world' (Ravven 2013: 15). Even the education of children is stripped by authority due to the belief that children must be free to develop their own minds rather than reproducing the ideas of the parents as authoritarian figure: 'teaching must renounce the authority of the teacher' (Stenhouse 1971). Cultural relativism was largely a benign response to racism, recognising that hierarchical ordering of cultures led to discrimination. However, the result is that the dominant culture is not emulated, rather the superior culture is deemed to be exploitative.

The sound aspiration of social mobility is replaced by denouncing the concept of social classes. Society advocates tolerance for cultures that advocate single-parent homes, abortion, gender identity, gay marriage, and other practises that degrade the community. Cultural adaptation become taboo as it could be depicted as claims of cultural superiority and racism. Traditionally, adaptive cultures have been able to prosper by learning traits from other cultures. However, in the era of cultural relativism, liberals cannot identity or address cultural weaknesses within 'other' cultures. This does a disservice especially to African Americans where for example illegitimacy is not addressed despite plummeting numbers of children born within marriage. The illegitimacy rate of African Americans was 25 percent in 1965, this had surged to almost 75 percent by 2015 (Williams 2015). Addressing the issue could easily be labelled as an affront to African Americans and women/single mothers. Similarly, anti-social behaviour and 'anti-American' attitudes within the Muslim community is not addressed because it is vulnerable to accusations of Islamophobia.

In the US the upper-middle class must serve its traditional and required role of being more vocal in the defence of superior cultural practises and resist the inferior culture such as 'the single-parent, antisocial habits, prevalent among some working-class whites; the anti-"acting white" rap culture of inner-city blacks; the anti-assimilation ideas gaining ground among some Hispanic immigrants' (Wax and Alexander 2017). The Republicans in the US are more capable of conserving traditional values, and therefore more likely to be in stable and happy marriages, have children within wedlock, and are less likely to get divorced (Wilcox and Menon 2017).

The seemingly benign and virtuous act of standing up for the vulnerable and oppressed becomes a vice in its excesses as it entails shedding responsibilities and deconstructing superior bourgeois culture. The global dominance of Western culture results in 'justice' usually having an inherent anti-Western bias as restoring equity entails elevating the weaker culture and constraining Western culture as the source of oppression. The idea that the dominance hierarchy is a Western social construction that can be dismantled can be disproven by the natural sciences as human beings have competed and organised themselves in dominance hierarchies for thousands of years, culminating in evolutionary history imprinting hierarchies in the nerve system by rewarding upward and punishing downward movements in status. Immigration is imperative for the multicultural philosophy as the demographic shifts and dilution of the dominant culture prevents the suppression of minority cultures. The lost irony of the multiculturalist is that the unity found among minority groups is caused by the systemic pressure to collectively balance the ethno-cultural core, and with the demise of the majority there are fewer reasons for unity among identity groups. Instead of creating a harmonious society, multiculturalism encourages a 'clash of civilisations' within states (Huntington 1993b: 190).

The West does not assert a civilisational model that should be emulated, rather equality is proclaimed with anti-social behaviour and inferior culture. Cultural and moral relativism destroys the West's universal claims by being just another culture on a par with and equal to others (Bloom 2008: 39). Cultural and moral relativism is destructive to Western civilisation as the great philosophers and ideas of the West are devalued. Superior rationalism cannot succeed in a culture that is unable to defend itself against lesser ideas (Bloom 2008: 196). 'Unfortunately the West is defined by its need for justification of its ways or values' (Bloom 2008: 39). Tolerance and openness used to imply seeking improvement by using reason, while under relativism tolerance suggests accepting everything. The abandonment of belief in one's own civilisation is inaccurately portrayed as moral progress. In other words, nihilism is depicted as moralism (Bloom 2008: 239).

Identity politics and victimhood

Identity politics was a response to the xenophobia deriving from exclusive ethno-cultural identities, which had marginalised disenfranchised minorities. Marginalised constituencies are empowered by strengthening their collective bargaining power. These sub-groups construct a community where the individual feels they can belong (Hobsbawm 2007: 428). Communities are constructed by adopting and imitating symbols and narratives that bring together the group and establishes clear boundaries between 'us' and them'. Identity politics initially appealed primarily to ethnic groups, yet identity groups also emerged for women, religious groups, and sexual minorities. In US politics, identity politics translate into concrete political advantage as it has even been built into the language that politicians for example seek the 'black vote', 'woman vote', 'Hispanic vote', 'evangelical vote', or 'gay vote'. The lack of solidarity and common cause with broader society epitomises what Aristotle referred to as a 'deviant democracy', where it is the rule of the many, yet the self-serving masses only seek to advance their own interests.

The repudiation of meta-narratives as the foundation for traditions, institutions, norms, authority, and shared national identity does not eradicate human's need for belonging, rather civilisation regresses towards smaller and rival sub-identity groups within the state. Realist theory recognises that human beings act in social groups that compete for redistribution of wealth to enhance their power and security. Social groups represent a primordial instinct in human nature for material security in a hostile world, community, recognition, and possible a longing for immortality. People are biologically predisposed to seek belonging in an identity group to avoid standing alone (Patterson 1993: 28–29). While the state is the highest sovereign in the contemporary international system and therefore attempts to harness this community identity, rival sub-groups with distinct identities undermine its capacity to act as a sovereign and unitary actor.

States held together by civic identities are vulnerable when the ideology loses its appeal and people seek refuge in a competing ethno-cultural identity. The weakening of a shared identity and subsequent state authority creates a gravitational pull towards rival identities: 'The breakup of the traditional authority structures and the previous affective social units- historically nation and class . . . make the ethnic attachment more salient' (Bell 1975: 171). A dilemma thus emerges between racial self-segregation and community cohesion (Lasch 1979). The loss of state control over the economy further amplifies the fragmentation of identities as 'independent market power made it easier for youth to discover material or cultural symbols of identity' (Hobsbawm 2007: 328). Subsequently, the state risks fragmenting into ethnic enclaves unless a liberal civic nationalist agenda can emerge that transcends ethnicities (Lind 1995).

The emancipation movements in the 1960s originated with the liberal notion of individual responsibilities and rights, as people should not be categorised and judged as a group. Liberty through 'individual rights' was considered to enable social mobility as a necessity for greater equality. As declared in Martin Luther King Jr's famous speech: 'I have a dream that my four little children will one day live in a nation where they will not be judged by the colour of their skin, but by the content of their character.' The attempt to shift focus from the ethnic group to the individual has been reversed as collective autonomy and influence is sought as a tool against discrimination. Minorities recognised that collective bargaining power in various ethnic, national, religious, and gender groups augmented their strength and representation to obtain social justice (Crenshaw 1991: 1242).

Identity politics does not liberate the individual, rather identity groups undergo their own internal homogenisation and 'othering' of externals to become a political force. Identity politics within a state shares similarities with ethno-cultural nationalism due to:

> the insistence that one's group identity consisted in some existential, supposedly primordial, unchangeable and therefore permanent personal characteristics shared with other members of the group, and with no one else. Exclusiveness was all the more essential to it, since the actual differences which marked human communities off from each other were attenuated.
>
> (Hobsbawm 2007: 428–429)

It is imperative to recognise that people want to belong in social/identity groups as the inability of the state to harness a strong unifying identity results in dissolution into smaller divisive groups. Agency is assigned away from the individual as arbitrary representatives of identity groups emerge who proclaim the right to speak on their behalf, while internal dissents are shamed as a betrayal of loyalty to their group.

Rivalry emerges within the state, which mirrors the competition for resources between states caused by international anarchy. Each identity group benefits from distinctiveness from the rest of society since their power is largely contingent on using 'political leverage of group loyalty' (Hobsbawm 2007: 428). The durability of any identity group is sustained by 'othering' rival identities and groups. Replicating the realist logic of cooperation, in the absence of a supreme sovereign capable of resolving problems and ensuring security, group A and B collaborate to balance group C as a more powerful adversarial. Different states of social groups are principally united by a common enemy, implying that the shared interest and partnership is suspended when the adversary is gone. Translated into identity politics: Blacks and Hispanics for collective autonomy and influence vis-à-vis Whites. In an increasingly complex identity politics, the Left becomes a coalition of the disenfranchised based on ethnic, gender, religion, or cultural identity.

Postmodernist obsession with less transparent forms of oppression intensifies animosity and rivalry between identity groups as equality is replaced with equity. The former suggests equal opportunity and the latter entails equal outcome. Equity is at the heart of the postmodernist inclination towards liberal authoritarianism. With the assumption that everyone is the same, the different performance by identity groups is indicative of one group exploiting another. Freedom defined as equal opportunity is therefore not sufficient for the postmodernists as the oppressors have 'institutionalised' their historical privilege and dominance over the oppressed. It is therefore warranted to even out the playing field by offering 'positive discrimination' favouring marginalised groups. The government's task of ensuring equal opportunity ensures a more intrusive role as high-performing groups are punished and low-performing groups rewarding as victims. Overcoming 'institutionalised discrimination' suggests special rights instead of equal rights, by demanding affirmative action and quotations based on membership in a minority group. The irony is that the civil rights movement has shifted from aspiring to a colour-blind to a colour-conscious society where people are judged based on the privilege or victimhood of their identity group (Huntington 1993b: 190).

Identity politics creates new power structures by redistributing political and economic power in accordance with victimhood. The practice of equity inevitably encourages a victimhood mentality as 'positive discrimination' implies that a group is discriminated against. The characteristics of each group are defined broadly, and the different groups in society are ranged into a hierarchy and divided into oppressors or victims. Victimhood is translated into political currency and competition for victimhood emerges as groups are incentivised to look for ways they are offended and declare oppression. In contrast, the oppressor groups are

No men's fear of woman, the stronger gender & "womb envy" of Women, the creator vs Man the killer warrior

shamed and demanded to recognise their privilege, typically 'white privilege' or 'male privilege'. While identity politics is intended to reconcile by correcting historical abuses, it unavoidably divides as people are divided into competing groups.

Victimhood and violence

Western civilisation is undergoing its second transition in moral culture, towards a victimhood culture (Campbell and Manning 2014). The first transition occurred in the 18th and 19th centuries as Western civilisation began transitioning from honour culture to dignity culture. Honour culture denotes revenging insults, while dignity culture signifies that people are not required to earn respect and therefore leave the punitive actions to legal institutions. The contemporary second cultural shift is towards victimhood culture where the oppressed 'underdog' has the moral authority and status, and social justice is advanced with retaliation against any insult. The victimhood culture does not entail a return to honour culture, as it is more conducive to draw attention to one's own weakness rather than strength. While the honour culture deems self-help and individual responsibility to be a virtue, the victimhood culture seeks support from a stronger third party by attempting to campaign for public attention for any grievances (Campbell and Manning 2014).

Postmodernism is an attractive political philosophy as it embodies what Nietzsche referred to as 'slave morality'. The weak rationalise their position of weakness as a virtue by suggesting there is something intrinsically good about the underdog, while the powerful and assertive epitomise evil. The seemingly benign intention to stand up for the little guy can inadvertently encourage victimhood narratives. There is a tendency to bestow authority to marginalised people, suggesting that whoever is most oppressed has a greater understanding for the faults in society and is therefore correct and virtuous. There are strong incentives to become offended rather than resolving disputes as victimhood becomes a political, social, and moral currency. The subsequent outcome is high sensitivity to any offence, and the weakening of the individual as there is a growing moral dependency on third parties.

Converting victimhood into political currency does not necessarily empower the weaker groups in society by rewarding individual responsibility and hard work, rather it tends to infantilise people by blaming oppression and looking to the state for social justice. Most virtues can become a vice in their excesses. Compassion for the marginalised can similarly divide the world into victims and predators. When the schoolteacher or employer delivers a negative assessment of the performance of their students or employees, the response can either be constructive by aiming to improve oneself or destructive with the sense of being a victim of unprovoked belligerence. The former creates self-improvement, while the latter conflict.

Plato's definition of democracy as the rule of the poor suggested that the people would eventually despise the rich. Conflating economic, intellectual, or political authority with exploitations produces an anti-elitist and anti-intellectual wave.

draw!

The rich would use the language of the poor to take power. The currency of victimhood fuels condition such as the mental disorder known as 'Munchausen syndrome', when a patient mimic an illness to drawn attention to themselves and gain sympathy. The victimhood paradigm reverses the American Dream as social mobility does not entail emulating the culture and practises of the successful, rather success leading to a rise in the dominance hierarchy is denounced as oppression and an attack on the principle of equality. The fight against social equality in India has also reversed the incentives for upward social mobility because being classified as a lower caste is beneficial in terms of being at the favourable end of redistribution of opportunities and wealth (Hobsbawm 1996).

The hierarchy of victimhood produces a 'victimhood Olympics', which is encapsulated in the postmodernists' reference to 'intersectionality'. The theory on intersectionality suggests all systems of victimhood are interconnected and addresses the hierarchy among disenfranchised groups ranging by gender, race, religion, sexuality, etc. The argument behind intersectionality is that those who are more oppressed have access to deeper and more authentic knowledge about life and society (Andersen and Collins 1995). For example, black feminists have certain victimhood authority over white feminists as they are not subjected to the same oppression. Intellectual or elite authority can be dismissed as indicators of oppressors, and authority is transferred to the victim. The oppressor must listen to the victims as victimisation is conflated with wisdom, moral authority, and prestige (Andersen and Collins 1995). Victim groups obtain certain immunity from critique and questioning the immunity is seen as an indication of continued oppression. The subsequent political correctness supports 'separating people according to culture and eschewing any criticism of minorities' (Albrechtsen 2009). White Christians are criticised for oppression of gays, while Muslims are to some extent exempted due to their status on the victimhood hierarchy. Obama's reluctance to use the term Islamic terrorism for fear of insulting Muslims effectively made it impossible to even identify the adversary the US was aiming to defeat. Likewise, the attempt by the Swedish Foreign Minister to criticise the lack of women rights in Saudi Arabia was scorned as Islamophobia.

The obsession with controlling the language is the source of a new liberal authoritarianism. Liberalism initially embraced the famous statement of Voltaire about free speech: 'I disapprove of what you have to say, but I'll defend to death your right to say it.' However, in the postmodernist victimhood culture, language is depicted as an instrument of oppression. Political correctness imposes self-censorship to control and limit what is considered to be acceptable political discourse. Competing views are framed as xenophobic, offensive, and therefore illegitimate in a liberal democracy (Chait 2015). The paradox of political correctness is intolerance disguised as tolerance: 'Political correctness, aimed to curtail totalitarianism, is approaching on the totalitarian' (Chait 2015). The 'creative minority' that finds solutions to the challenges of civilisation needs intellectual freedom and pluralism, which is suffocated by the inability to call a spade a spade.

Virtue signalising represents the other side of political correctness, the expression of support for causes linked to tolerance for cultural and moral relativism. Virtue signalling is the recognition and atonement for class guilt by recognising membership in a privileged group and subsequently for being an oppressor. Virtue signalling is the superficial expression of moral values and subsequent political position in solidarity with another group. Virtue signalling is the cosmopolitan expression of understanding and tolerance for everything to communicate their advancements, moral superiority, and disdain for the traditionalist rural communities. Virtue signalling represents a perversion of morality as ethics is demoted to expressions of support for popular causes. Often the demand for signalling virtue undermines the ability to resolve the problems as intellectual pluralism and freedom of speech is sacrificed at the altar of political correctness. Political discourse can be limited by for example labelling political parties as racist or misogynous, which compels people to distance themselves from these parties to signal their virtue. Even debating the merits of the accusation becomes treacherous and a betrayal of the liberal consensus. Virtue signalling is a lazy and self-righteous form of politics as the purpose is to show how good you are, and it demands no effort in terms of contributing with sacrifice and solutions (Bartholomew 2015). Morality is expressed by posting a picture on social media about homelessness, rather than volunteering at a soup kitchen. It should not be conflated with compassion as its function is to satisfy one's own narcissism, rather than proving societal benefit or improved condition for the vulnerable.

In the dignity-based culture, the response to the use of force is outsourced to legal authorities, while tolerance is advocated for verbal assault by encouraging people to develop thick skin. In the victimhood culture, intended and unintended insults are depicted as a form of violence. Another paradox of the liberal authoritarianism is evident as liberal principles traditionally advocate tolerance and non-violence. Yet, if liberalism represents tolerance, its opposition is considered hostile to tolerance. Subsequently, the logic suggests that there should not be tolerance for intolerance. The intellectual groundwork for this brand of liberal authoritarianism was laid in the 1960s, with scholars such as Herbert Marcuse (1965) from the Frankfurt School arguing that there should not be free speech for fascism. In *A Critique of Pure Tolerance*, Marcuse posited that 'liberating tolerance' means 'intolerance against movements from the Right, and toleration of movements from the Left'. The argument was that if Hitler had been fought rather than given a platform, the Third Reich would not have taken power. The argument becomes especially pernicious as the definition of fascism can be expanded. As Marcuse suggested, American capitalism exhibits resemblances with Nazi Germany and should therefore be resisted rather than debated. Barrett (2017) argues free speech should be restricted as words can cause stress, and stress produce physical harm to the body. Her logic is therefore that offensive speech should be equated to violence. The Under-Secretary-General of the UN and Executive Director of UN Women similarly equated words with violence:

> Cyber touch is recognized as equally as harmful as physical touch . . . Whether you are dead because your partner shot you or beat you up, or you killed yourself because you couldn't bear cyber-bullying, or you were

exposed to many of the sites that lead people to suicide pacts—bottom line, we lose a life.

(Alter 2015)

The incentive to become offended in order to censor intellectual opposition is dangerous beyond the threat to free speech and political pluralism, as people who perceive themselves as victims are often predisposed to accepting violence in return. Violence often derives from hypersensitivity by interpreting everything as derogatory and offensive, unjustified self-esteem, and idealism that justifies violence:

> Hypersensitivity to insults also makes it possible to understand what might otherwise appear to be senseless violence . . . Many violent people believe that their actions were justified by the offensive acts of the person who became their victim.
>
> (Baumeister 1999)

Hypersensitivity about words, specific words that are seen to socially construct relationships between the privileged and serfdom, fuels a sense of inferiority. The victim of insults perceives the right to self-defence as responding with violence. Or in the lingo of the new Left, 'microaggressions' may justify 'macroaggression' as a response. Victims of oppression tend to embrace their identity as good because they are in opposition to evil. The virtuous is therefore entitled to use violence to repel evil (Baumeister 1999).

American campuses as the laboratory of liberalism and postmodernism

American university campuses can be observed as a social experiment of postmodernism, and the ensuing contractions. Tolerance and openness have become established as guiding principles, while conservative ideas and morality are marginalised and vilified. Ethno-cultural and gender diversity is celebrated as strength, yet intellectual and moral diversity is diminished as the social sciences departments have increasingly been filled with liberal academic staff. Universities have traditionally been experimental labs for critical thinking to advance liberal and progressive ideas by challenging orthodoxies and conventional wisdoms, however, universities have incrementally narrowed the scope of acceptable conclusions and sought to protect students from competing ideas as they offend. While American university campuses were the staging ground for the emancipation movements in the 1960s, they have also become a laboratory for postmodernism as the push for liberation also deconstructs and eradicates traditional structures of authority.

Much like the fascists and communists, the postmodernists are using education for indoctrination. The radical increase of new courses and practises in the humanities and social sciences at universities indicates that the purpose of universities is undergoing a shift away from the pursuit of truth and towards political conformity. For example, passing a course on women studies or ethnic studies would be unlikely unless the conclusion by students conformed to the narrow scope of acceptable victimhood narratives. While there can be established certain truths within these studies, postmodernism rejects that there are any truths as narratives are merely used to assert power. For the postmodernists, the purpose of these studies and university is therefore not to discover inherent truths, but to shift the narratives and thus power structures in favour of the oppressed and against the oppressor.

In other words, universities are instrumental in indoctrinating students with narratives that deprive the privileged of their power, with white, heterosexual males in the West at the top of the exploitative hierarchy. The contradictory effort to fight racism was displayed at Evergreen State, a small liberal arts college in Washington. The college tradition of a 'Day of Absence' that allowed black students to consensually leave campus to demonstrate the emptiness of the community in their absence, was sought to be altered by instead demanding that white students leave campus. When a professor proclaimed the initiative to be oppressive, students rioted in protest against the professor, attacked his supporters, and cursed other white professors. At Yale University, students sought to protect the culture of minorities from being contaminated by protesting against the use of certain Halloween costumes as a form of 'cultural appropriation'. Even the authority of the academic staff was challenged as students 'discovered that the pompous teachers who catechized them about academic freedom could, with a little shove, be made into dancing bears' (Bloom 2008: 315). › chastised ?.

Postmodernist efforts to deconstruct and control language eventually regulates thought. At American universities, political correctness has already been formalised into the concept of 'microaggressions' – speech that may be offensive and therefore interpreted as aggressive. At the University of North Carolina, microaggressions was categorised by the 'social identity group' who may feel targeted and offended. For example, the use of the term 'Christmas holiday' must be avoided as it marginalises non-Christians. Inviting colleagues to a round of golf was also recognised to be offensive as it made assumptions about their financial resources and can be perceived as someone asserting dominance (Richardson 2016). Similarly, microaggressions includes asking where someone comes from or complimenting their accent as it excludes based on origin. Referring to 'you guys' or 'mankind' can likewise offend women. Mansplaining, a new postmodernist word to enter the dictionary, depicts a man assertively explaining something to women as a way of asserting his dominance and perpetuating patriarchy. Women, ethnic, and religious minorities cannot be guilty of the same actions, as they are on the other end of the oppressor-victim dichotomy. Declaring that America is 'the land of opportunities' can be considered a verbal attack on people who feel they have been denied opportunities. White people claiming to be 'colour blind' in terms of race can paradoxically be deemed racist and offensive since it neglects their own 'white privilege'. Microaggresssions are not only verbal, but also 'environmental'. For example, if all the pictures on the wall in a chemistry building are of famous white male chemists, it is exclusionary and offensive to those who do not identify as white male (Saul 2016). The assertion of two genders, as empirically recognised in the natural science of biology, is denounced as a binary social construction that is offensive to perpetuate dominance. At the City University of New York, employees have been forbidden from addressing students with using Mr and Ms as it could be offensive. These speech codes have since been pushed out into broader society, as for example the New York subway no longer use the phrase 'ladies and gentlemen' in their announcements as it may alienate people who identify as neither male nor female. In Canada, this liberal authoritarianism has been taken a step further with Bill C–16, which added 'gender identity' to the Canadian Human Rights Act and the Criminal code. The law makes human rights a zero-sum game by compelling people to use an ever-growing range of gender-neutral pronouns as opposed to 'he' or 'she'.

Self-segregation and victimhood are also perpetuated by developing 'safe spaces' and 'trigger warnings'. Safe spaces are physical facilities on campuses for women, people of colour and other groups, where students can feel safe from perceived dangers. This includes the threat from speech or ideas that may feel offensive. Trigger warnings are demands usually put on professors to warn students of topics or even words that may trigger unpleasant feelings. The intellectual space crumbles as students self-infantilise. Students who find comments troubling or have their beliefs challenged can complain before withdrawing to safe spaces equipped with cookies, colouring books, blankets, toys, and videos of puppies (Shulevitz 2015; Lindsay 2016). To shield sensitive students from potentially offensive ideas, prominent guest speakers have been cancelled, such as former Secretary of State, Condoleezza Rice, and Managing Direction of the International Monetary Fund (IMF), Christine Lagarde. The promotion of hyper-sensitivity correlates with the inclination to censor free speech and use violence. A survey found that one-fifth of American college students believed it is acceptable to use violence to prevent a speaker with offensive arguments from speaking (Villasenor 2017).

Postmodernism and the deconstruction of the international system

Postmodernism is also deconstructing and destroying the interactions between states in international affairs. After the demise of the Soviet Union, the severely skewed balance of power of the unipolar era incentivised postmodernist deconstruction of legal and moral constraints on Western power. Unconstrained, the US and the collective West had strong inducements to embrace ideas and ideologies advocating flexibility and sovereign inequality. The promotion of democracy, humanitarian interventionism, the responsibility to protect, and the global war on terror shared the idea of a post-Westphalian and hierarchical ordering of the world, where the West could interfere in the domestic affairs of other states but not the other way around. Without a shared morality to guide foreign policy, 'common values' are applied inconsistently and pragmatically to achieve narrow interests. International order subsequently declines as consistency and reliability are key currencies to advance trust. Domestic order also diminishes since the deconstruction of a shared morality eventually undermines internal cohesion.

Adopting postmodernist thinking in foreign policy enabled greater flexibility, at the expense of predictability. Postmodernism challenges the Westphalian system by deconstructing universal language and rejecting absolute truths that underpin stability in the international system. Words are important as they allow people to communicate with a similar language, which is required to clearly define challenges and to find the best solutions. Credibility and reliability are indispensable to avoid misunderstandings and establish predictable behaviour between states. The erosion of a common vocabulary camps reduces engagement as each side polarises into unsympathetic camps that talk past each other.

The legal and moral relativism of post-Cold War foreign policy of the West is largely the result of postmodernism. Legal relativism is evident as ambiguous notions of 'common values' replace unambiguous concepts like sovereignty. Sovereignty of the state and the individual are treated as competing principles, and legality and legitimacy have similarly been decoupled. The universal principles of Just War are substituted with postmodernist views on war, which deems war to be just if enough people believe it is just. The power deriving from creating and disseminating narratives has increased since legitimacy is defined by public opinion (Kortunov 2017b).

The West's invasion and dismemberment of Serbia was a violation of international law, justified by conceptually decoupling 'legality' and legitimacy'. In the name of liberalism and freedom, 'legitimacy' takes precedence over 'legality'. Support for the unilateral declaration of Kosovo's independence was also illegal from a legal standpoint, but supposedly legitimate. Furthermore, the narrative spun is that Kosovo was a 'unique' case and did therefore not set a precedent, which is problematic as the requirement for comparison and consistency is deeply rooted in law. Legitimacy displacing international law is divisive since at most it is conceded that the West may do the wrong thing for the right reasons, compared to Russia that at best would do the right thing for the wrong reason. The 'legitimacy' of being a liberal democracy allows NATO to ignore Russian and Chinese vetoes in the UN Security Council, while the number of states participating in a 'coalition of the willing' make it just to ignore the UN altogether (Kortunov 2017b).

During the Arab Spring, support and respect for sovereignty or use of military force to topple the leadership was contingent on geostrategic interests. Humanitarian abuses when Gaddafi was in power were unacceptable, while the substantially worse human rights abuses after NATO toppled him by force were considered tolerable. The criticism of Western support for armed groups in Syria was limited to whether these groups were 'moderate'. In the era of terrorism, the notion that one man's terrorist is another man's freedom fighter has also enabled moral relativism by dividing terrorists into 'good' or 'bad'. The concept of a freedom fighter and terrorist are not mutually exclusive as the former is a reference to the objective, while the latter denotes the means. Albeit, focus on the means or ends is determined by narrow national interests.

The erosion of a common language has perilous effects and was a key variable causing the crisis in Ukraine and obstructing it from being resolved. 'Sovereignty' is used almost solely as a reference to the right of Ukraine and its neighbours to join Western economic, political, and military blocs. Sovereignty seemingly does not refer to non-interference into Ukraine's domestic affairs to install a government that aspires to join the EU and NATO. A conceptual vacuum becomes evident as Russian influence beyond its borders can only be conceptualised as a 'sphere of influence', in contrast with the West's 'European integration'. European integration entails Ukraine de-coupling from Europe's largest state as Brussels has reinvented and monopolised the concept of 'Europe'. The support for a democratic 'revolution' in Ukraine entailed support for toppling a democratically elected government by backing the riot and then rescinding on the commitment as guarantors to the ensuing negotiated unity government. 'Revolution' is usually defined by fundamental alteration to power structures, in contrast to a 'coup' defined as the use of force to transfer power to the established political opposition who lost the election. Yet, even the word 'coup' to describe the removal of Yanukovich from power is dismissed as Russian 'propaganda', a term equally ill-defined to denounce opposing views. While the coup was illegal according to the Ukrainian constitution, the pro-Western rebellion was deemed legitimate due to their virtues, values, and European aspirations, in contrast with the Russian-leaning population. Under a new government, the West placed its support behind Kiev's 'anti-terrorist operation' against the people revolting against the legality of the coup.

The deconstruction of language and rejection of absolute truths result in contemporary 'truthiness' and alternative facts devoid of principles. It is conspicuous that during the Cold War against the Soviet Union as a formidable power with diametrically opposite ideology, the US was more cautious with its language. The idea of describing the more moderate Soviet leaders as a 'new Stalin' would be peculiar. Yet, following the Cold War, the constant comparisons and labelling of Putin as another Stalin or Hitler has become commonplace. While possible nuclear war with a Soviet Union that sent its dissidents to the Gulags did not prevent cordial interaction, Russian restrictions on gay parades and moderate human rights abuses culminates in animosity that borders on the absurd. Moral relativism is evident in the selective outrage of illiberal policies. The West's tirade of critique and partial boycott of Russia's 2014 Olympics over discrimination of homosexuals similarly displayed the absence of common standards. While homosexuality is not a crime in Russia, it is criminalised on more than 80 countries, including in India and among other Western allies.

Conclusion

Postmodernism attempts to liberate Man by deconstructing meta-narratives that perpetuate what is interpreted as exploitative power relations, which include the social institutions and traditions of Western civilisation. The society becomes ungovernable when radical and aggressive individualism produces narcissism and discourages self-restraint. Rules are considered to constrain freedoms and should be resisted or ridiculed. Lack of purpose and absence of commitment to the transcendent fuel discontent and radicalism. The subsequent criminal and anti-social behaviour transition from being scorned to becoming acceptable or even glorified as a struggle against oppression.

The fight for society in the West has primarily been between the modernist and postmodernists. The former seeks to employ classical Western traditions of science and rationality to advance humanity, while the latter considers Western civilisation itself to be an oppressive construct that must be overcome to enter the next stage of human progress. The morality of in-group loyalty, authority, and sanctity is castigated as an oppressive social construct, rather than simply deemed to be inferior to care and fairness. In the absence of any objective truths, postmodernism aims to deconstruct shared knowledge and unifying narratives as they are perceived to be imposed by the oppressors over the oppressed. The extremely negative emotions and self-righteousness of postmodernism fuels hostility that polarises society and eschews the rational debate and political pluralism that has sustained Western civilisation. Modernity is not adequately equipped to counter the invasive and destructive influence of postmodernism as the demise of classical conservativism results in the failure to genuinely advance a broader concept of morality that balances the rational and irrational.

Part III
Rise and fall of economic liberalism

5 The rise of Western geoeconomics as the tool for neo-gesellschaft

Introduction

This chapter explores the limited utility of economic liberalism as an instrument to advance and maintain civilisation. Western powers have achieved greatness by skilfully employing various strands of economic statecraft, while economic liberalism has been used once the state has been elevated to a dominant position in the international system.

Laissez-faire economics amounts to economic anarchy and deprives states of an important source of power. A rational approach to economics demands state intervention in the market to create asymmetrical interdependence, thereby maximising both autonomy and influence. A development strategy aimed to advance political autonomy and influence in the international system requires the state to control strategic industries, transportation corridors, and mechanisms for international economic cooperation. Once control has been obtained over these levers of geoeconomic power, economic liberalism functions as a veiled economic statecraft by integrating the world into a global economy administered by the hegemon. Committing to the ideology of economic liberalism is dangerous for weaker powers as it limits the ability to develop, while the liberal delusion makes the hegemon complacent and unprepared to defend its power once challenged by rising powers.

Economic statecraft has evolved from classical mercantilism to a more sophisticated process in response to changes in the international system. Colonialism enabled European powers to compete and augment their relative economic power without engaging in direct conflicts with other European states. However, German efforts after the First World War to rationalise the economy radically altered the conditions of economic rivalry, to which other states had to adapt. By developing a powerful economic role for the state, the competition for controlling markets and establishing favourable global value chains was altered and intensified.

Rationalising the economy to become more efficient is imperative to create a competitive society capable of surviving in the international system, yet the economy must concurrently serve the instincts and inspirations of Man. Complex economic systems decouple people from their traditional communities, reduce the

autonomy of the worker, concentrate wealth, increase inequality, and can deprive
Man of a sense of function and meaning. Both the US and Russia initially sought
to remain an agrarian society to preserve the traditions and spirituality of the
community, and thus avoid sharing the fate with the morally decadent manufacturing
societies in Western Europe. Albeit, from the early to mid-19th century, both the
US and Russia recognised the dilemma of either emulating the Western European
economic model to become competitive or have their political autonomy and
possibly sovereignty eviscerated.

This chapter first explores the basic assumptions of geoeconomic theory, the use
of economic statecraft to create favourable symmetry in economic interdependence.
Four indicators of geoeconomic power are presented that advance a complex society
and assuage the impact on the community. First, great powers must control strategic
industries. Second, competitive transportation corridors are developed under the
dominance of the state. Third, the state establishes a privileged position in financial
and economic mechanisms for cooperation. Last, the state must ensure that morality
is aligned with its economic interests by the preserving the community.

Second, this chapter surveys the geoeconomic rise of the West. Britain initially
rose to prominence with skilful economic statecraft by protecting and developing
competitive industries, establishing dominance over maritime trade corridors, and
establishing dominant banks and a powerful trading currency. The US and
Germany employed the economic nationalist policies of Friedrich List to
modernise their economies without integrating into a British-dominated system.
The US was largely successful with the American System, benefitting from state
intervention to develop a manufacturing base, physical economic connectivity
with transportation, and a national bank. After establishing its independence from
Europe, the US aspired to global power by asserting its influence in the Pacific
Ocean from the early 20th century. By contrast, Germany was limited by
geography. The economic statecraft that had been used domestically to unite
Germany in the 19th century could not be employed for region building to become
a global power. Inadequate transportation corridors and mechanisms for
cooperation resulted in aspirations for autarchy and territorial expansionism,
culminating in war. However, after the Second World War, Germany was set to
ascend as it was integrated into a collective Western geoeconomic model in
opposition to the Soviet Union.

Geoeconomics and the delusion of economic liberalism

Geoeconomics can be defined as the economics of geopolitics, advocating state
intervention in the market to enhance the geostrategic position. While geopolitics
entails control over strategic territory and military power, geoeconomics denotes
controlling strategic industries, economic transportation corridors, and international financial/economic mechanisms for cooperation. Geoeconomics as a
form of power grew to prominence as the world economy became increasingly
interdependent. Furthermore, new and more destructive technologies made wars
more perilous: when 'military conflict between major states is unlikely economic

power will be increasingly important in determining the primacy or subordination of states' (Huntington 1993c: 72). Luttwak (1990) superbly outlined the transition to geoeconomics in the post-Cold War era: 'Everyone, it appears, now agrees that the methods of commerce are displacing military methods – with disposable capital in lieu of firepower, civilian innovation in lieu of military-technical advancement, and market penetration in lieu of garrisons and bases.'

The principal foundation of geoeconomics builds on the realisation that economic interdependence is about relative gain (Heckscher 1955; Hirschman 1945). Economic interdependence is not a liberal source of peace, but a realist tool for power as autonomy and influence derive from constructing uneven or asymmetrical economic interdependence. When one side is more dependent on the other, asymmetrical economic reliance can be converted into political influence (List 1885). The realist underpinnings economic interdependence was further advanced by Hirschman (1945: 16), who posited:

> The power to interrupt commercial or financial regulations with any country, considered as an attribute of national sovereignty, is the root cause of the influence or power position which a county acquires in other countries, just as it is the root cause of the 'dependence on trade'.

Geoeconomics therefore captures the essential and rational policies aimed to manipulate and skew the symmetry in interdependent economic relationships to maximise both influence and autonomy. Influence is augmented by making other states more reliant, while reducing one's own dependence. Political freedom implies 'shaking off commercial dependence on foreigners which was continually becoming more oppressive' and developing 'economic autarchy' (Schmoller 1897: 76).

Geoeconomics derives from different strands of economic statecraft developed in response to contemporary realities. Mercantilism refers to the French economic model of the 17th century, which applied a market-based logic with government intervention. Mercantilism's obsession with gold and ships reflected the realities of the time, as gold was the principal currency to preserve wealth and a navy was required to assert control over trade corridors and establish a privileged position in markets to extract resources and export manufactured goods. The state would intervene, often with military force to acquire natural resources and gold and use this economic power to further strengthen the administrative state and the ability to win wars. Mercantilism was an early and extreme form of geoeconomics by using state power to establish staple ports and expand overseas colonies, to which rival powers were forbidden access. The colonial powers accrued gold and silver, while banning the export of these precious metals. The era of mercantilism largely ended as war lost some of its ability to conquer new markets. Neo-mercantilism built on maximising exports and minimising imports with less military intervention. Neo-mercantilism still entails climbing the value-chains by subsidising manufacturing and exports, and repressing wages to enhance competitiveness. Neo-mercantilism therefore has many commonalities with economic nationalism, which emerged as a development strategy to escape to obtain economic and political autonomy in an economic system dominated by the British. As the godfather of economic nationalism, Friedrich List (1885) developed economic nationalism as policy, arguing that survival of the state in the international system hinges on the aptitude of the state to intervene in the market to create competitive economic structures.

A new economic world order began to emerge after the First World War, spurred by the 'Rationalisation Movement' in the German economy. The German state was transitioning from having a political to an economic role by ensuring strategic industries were state-owned or state-guided. The 'Rationalisation Movement' in the economy with the destruction of the middle class, caused a 'revolution in the minds of men' and forcibly altered the relationship between people, corporations, and the state (Du Bois 1941: 383). Mass inflation followed by deflation destroyed incomes, property values, and savings, while large industry could repay their debts, transition away from old equipment and rebuild. Industry was organised into large and specialised units, which transformed Germany into a leader in technology and manufacturing.

The economic revolution pre-dated Hitler, yet the ascendance of the Nazis put resulted in a mixture with crude xenophobia, militarism, and juvenile theory of race. Power would be structured by an international division of labour under German leadership, which was expected to be influenced by race. Eastern Europeans would be used for hard manual labour, while Germanic peoples in the Netherlands, Belgium, and Scandinavia would be structured higher in global value-chains. While the Nazis could be defeated, the new economic order could not be eliminated as states had the option of either adopting the new political economy championed by the fascists or being marginalised. Du Bois (1941: 383) recognised that 'unless England and the Unites States follow the footsteppes of Germany, they can never expect to rival her in technical production and distribution'. The fascist political economy was simply more competitive, and states could either abide by it or become marginalised. Once the war was over, competition between states to control industry was destined to shape the international order. In the new order, states were confronted with a dilemma: large industries were required to compete in international markets, yet huge corporations would become too powerful domestically by usurping political influence and possibly pursuing business interests conflicting with the state. The only solution would be to develop a powerful and assertive state with intrusive economic leadership, capable of owning or controlling key industries.

Du Bois (1941: 386) recognised severe implications for his native US. Political freedoms and democracy had been contingent on 'economic anarchy' by limiting the economic role of the state. It was nonetheless imperative for American industry to be 'rationalised' and controlled by the state, which would conflict with unconstrained democratic rights of the individual. At best, the US should aspire to being a benign industrial democracy to rival the nascent oligarchic technocracy of Europe. Recognising Germany's flaw of alienating potential partners with its racial hierarchies, the US should attempt to make the rest of the world beneficiaries of a US-led international system (Du Bois 1941: 386). Following the Second World War, large competitive American corporations entered Western Europe and established US-dominated value-chains that would benefit the US for decades. The Cold War contributed to public and state support for US influence across Europe, which meant that the US relied less on authoritarian means to advance and maintain its geoeconomic empire. Academics would later refer to the US-led international system as 'empire by invitation' by providing economic benefits and security guarantees (Lundestad 2003).

Geoeconomics builds upon the fundamental assumptions of its precursors, albeit it emerged in the globalised world economy after the Cold War and makes economics a key tool for geostrategic rivalry due to the increased destructiveness of weapons. The proliferation of the logic behind the German 'Rationalisation Movement' in the economy nonetheless persists, as states must either embrace radical efficiency or experience a relative decline in power. States are required to develop increasingly sophisticated economic structures to remain competitive in great power politics, and concurrently assuage an ailing community in an era of declining frontiers.

The free trade argument rests on the liberal assumption that states cooperate for absolute rather than relative gain. Economic statecraft entails competition for relative economic power to enhance security, which is consistent with the main assumptions of realist theory. Geoeconomics mirrors the realist understanding of trade as economic activities must be harmonised with rather than rival state interests. Geoeconomics 'recognises the anarchic nature of international affairs, the primacy of the state and its interests in international affairs, and the importance of power in interstate relations' (Gilpin 2011: 14). The intellectual godfather of economic nationalism, Friedrich List (1827: 30), recognised the robust arguments in favour of free trade, albeit he rejected that the market logic of the domestic market could be extended internationally due to the international anarchy resulting from the lack of a centralised world government:

> As long as the division of the human race into independent nations exists, political economy will as often be at variance with cosmopolitan principles . . . a nation would act unwisely to endeavour to promote the welfare of the whole human race at the expense of its particular strength, welfare and independence.

The ideological component of the Cold War contributed to drawing an artificial binary dichotomy between free-market capitalism and socialism, neglecting the historical role of economic nationalism and geoeconomics as a middle ground. Advocating the virtues of free trade as an absolute truth and disparaging socialism as a failure produces historical amnesia as conservatives have traditionally protected domestic industries from international competition. A pure form of economic liberalism was not even advocated by the intellectual godfathers of lasses-faire capitalism and has never been embraced by a major rising power. Adam Smith recognised the state as an important facilitator of social obligation by investing in education, healthcare, infrastructure, and other common goods (Agnew and Corbridge 2002: 110). State support for education and infrastructure constitutes a form of subsidy for industry and development of transportation corridors. Adam Smith and John Stuart Mill were advocates of the Navigation Acts to ensure trade was restricted by the state to uphold national security (Baldwin 1985: 85). State intervention in the economy was therefore advocated to the extent it enhanced security.

Economic liberalism has historically veiled economic nationalism by the dominant power. Countries have throughout history ascended to greatness with state intervention in the market avoiding unfavourable asymmetrical interdependence. Once a dominant position has been established there are greater incentives to preach the virtues of economic liberalism. Henry Clay, a prominent US statesman, warned in 1832 that 'free trade' equated to succumbing to British colonial power:

> What was meant by free trade, was nothing more nor less than, by means of the great advantages we enjoyed, to get the monopoly of all their markets for our manufacturers, and to prevent them, one and all, from ever becoming manufacturing nations.
>
> (Williams 2011: 221)

List (1885: 295–296) similarly referred to British advocacy of free trade and vilification of economic nationalism as a strategy to 'kick away the ladder':

> It is a very common clever device that when anyone has attained the summit of greatness, he kicks away the ladder by which he has climbed up, in order to deprive others of the means of climbing up after him. In this lies the secret of the cosmopolitical doctrine of Adam Smith, and of the cosmopolitical tendencies of his great contemporary William Pitt, and of all his successors in the British Government administrations.

The 'stickiness' of ideology can, however, result in irrational behaviour as decision-makers continue to act on their convictions even when the utility of economic liberalism declines. Chamberlain's efforts to implement a tariff from 1903 to 1906, and subsequent election loss to free-market liberals was indicative of a state that had lost sight of free-trade being the policy of the hegemon.

Indicators of geoeconomic power

Modern geoeconomic power is enhanced by skewing the 'balance of dependence' (Diesen 2017: 52). One's own reliance on other states is reduced by diversifying partnerships, while the dependence of other states is increased by attaining monopolistic position in strategic industries and services that are indispensable, and problematic to diversify away from. Regionalism has become a key geoeconomic tool to enhance collective bargaining power vis-à-vis adversaries by negotiating favourable conditions for trade and finance or controlling transportation corridors. In *The National System of Political Economy*, List (1885) advocated several policies to use economic statecraft for nation-building and region-building.

With some modifications, four key objectives for creating favourable symmetry in economic interdependence are outlined here. The balance of dependence is skewed by asserting control over 1) strategic industries; 2) transportation corridors; 3) mechanisms for cooperation; and 4) preserving gemeinschaft. The state has an important role to play in supporting domestic industries against rival powers, helping them grow in global-value chains by recognising that know-how and skills set the conditions for future growth and can provide people with meaning.

First, obtaining control over strategic industries. Strategic industries, defined by monopolistic characteristics, are opportune to shift the symmetry as it augments autonomy and other states cannot as easily diversify away from their dependence. Traditionally the state has principally had the incentive to grow a cogent manufacturing base and be self-sufficient in agriculture and make neighbours dependent. Albeit, stimulus for innovation and technological leaps are of growing importance in the contemporary economic climate. Natural resources, manufacturing, and high-tech industries are prevalent examples of strategic industries where economic power can more easily be converted to political capital. Higher education is also indicative of a moral society. Besides providing geoeconomic power, high-tech industries also have synergy effects on a strong infrastructure and military might.

The state can intervene by temporarily using tariffs and subsidies to protect infant industries until they become competitive in international markets (List 1827). It must be reasonable to expect a foreseeable moment to remove state support to prevent a perpetual drain on other industries through taxation and tit-for-tat trade restrictions by adversaries. Due to 'creative destruction' caused by the introduction of new technologies and global markets, the state is also tasked with redirecting capital and labour into high-skilled and high-wage industries. The fallacy of economic liberalism is the belief that structural changes should be welcomed when imports are cheaper and replace domestically produced goods, as the saved labour and capital can be diverted to more productive and competitive industries. This misunderstanding is based on the liberal and cosmopolitan preoccupation with absolute gain. Looking towards the industrial revolution as an example also breeds misperceptions as the innovations then enabled the transfer of capital and labour from agriculture to urban manufacturing centres. In contrast, over the past few decades, the demise of American manufacturing saw the transfer of excess labour and capital towards low-skilled and low-paid retail and service industries (Luttwak 1993b). Governments therefore have a great responsibility to either protect strategic industries or ensure that uncompetitive professions are redirected to high-skilled and high-wage professions.

Second, control over transportation corridors. Control over transportation corridors has historically been linked to state-building and region-building by advancing both trade and societal connectivity. Great powers require control over physical infrastructure to obtain reliable access to vital resources and safe transportation corridors by land or sea, and to extract political influence by extending or denying the same access to other powers. Naval powers have historically been more favourably disposed towards laissez-faire capitalism as they benefit from controlling trade corridors, have less to risk by becoming dependent on trade, and can open distant frontiers. Societies become more resilient and capable of radical change by creating open systems, most notably by embracing trade to the fullest (Bertalanffy 1975). Inversely, land powers had to be more careful to embrace free trade as survival depended on their adversaries upholding freedom of navigation (Hirschman 1945: 8).

The ancient Silk Road consisted of a myriad of land-routes throughout the Eurasian continent, which endowed the Eurasian civilisations with profound advantage for the economy and military. The Mongol Empire, the last empire to administer the ancient Silk Road, owed its effectiveness and durability to the nomad infrastructure. The disintegration of the Mongol Empire and the demise of land-corridors made control over sea-lanes imperative to obtain global power. Western civilisation prospered from the continuum of controlling transportation corridors. The Ancient Greeks and the Roman Empire fought for control over regional ocean passages as flexible and rapid troop movement ensured security and power, while trade allowed prosperity and connectivity. Western European nation-states then rose to global prominence by establishing maritime trade corridors from the early 1500s. The Americans similarly became a global force from the early 1900s when the Pacific fell under US domain.

Third, influence over mechanisms for financial and economic cooperation. Immense geoeconomic power can be extracted from influence over international institutions and investment banks that develop or dictate trade rules, regulations and technical standards, trade/reserve currencies, and financing. Writing the rules and restrictions for trade is imperative for competitive advantage as there has never been completely free trade. Strong banks and currencies are also imperative for skewing the autonomy/influence balance in international interdependent economic partnerships. Investment banks can issue the debt, demonstrate bias in competing projects, and wield political influence by setting conditions for funding.

Fourth, preserving gemeinschaft and social cohesion. Morality and the community are under increasing pressure as society expands and increasingly complex economic structures cause Schumpeter's creative destruction. The state has an important role to negate social strains as market forces detach people from their traditional communities and family. For example, state support for local industries enhances social capital by reducing the need for worker mobility, while paid maternity leave and tax benefits to encourage one parent to stay home strengthens the family. Encouraging population growth is imperative to ensure the ability to reproduce the traditions and spirituality of the community. In contrast, advanced economies with a declining demographic become dependent on immigration that dilutes domestic culture and social cohesion in the community. Both the US and Russia sought to preserve the traditional agrarian society as it was morally sound and in opposition to the morally decadent manufacturing societies of Western Europe.

Conversely, List (1885: 374) was critical of a purely agrarian and rural society as 'the whole range of intellectual and moral powers is virtually nonexistent'. Advanced industries provide workers with high-skilled and high-paid professions as a source of self-realisation for the individual and human capital for the state. An educated population is often linked to a moral people embracing bourgeois principles. Similarly, a strong currency, such as the Deutschmark, or a national bank can be a symbol of independence and a source of pride and solidarity within a society. The 'export of bicycles or steel rails is no longer the cold-blooded thing it looks like in statistical reports of commerce. It is integrated with our passion' (Lippman 2008[1915]: 76).

The airline industry epitomises the non-material value of an industry that is protected by strong regulation. Besides providing ample high-skilled jobs, the airline industry has for a long time been a symbol of national pride, another symbol of the state much like the flag and the anthem. The development of strong reputable airlines in the Gulf States is widely recognised as being important to develop national pride as a component of state-building, in addition to being profitable as the region is a geographically convenient transit point. The ability of the state to strongly regulate competition is also present as only carriers operating in the state of origin or destination are permitted to fly a route. Furthermore, the safety aspect enables the state to set high conditionality for operating.

The state ensures societal cohesion by supporting education, infrastructure, health, and development. The authorities need to ensure the rise of a middle class as the condition for political stability, entrepreneurial capabilities, and intellectual power. There are inevitably conflicts of interests within the state and the authorities therefore have a profound responsibility in terms of intervening to ensure unity within the state and harmonise interests. Economic nationalism has traditionally been recognised as moral and benign when it is employed to uphold the social responsibilities of the state, such as a welfare state. An unequal distribution of wealth within the states leads to fragility and fragmentation, fuelling resentment among various groups within society (Baru 2012). The excessively wealthy can challenge the authority of the state and pursue competing interests at the expense of the population, and even align themselves with the strategic interests of competing states.

Geographical expansion is a reference to the imperative of frontiers in the absence of a strong community, which gives settler states a competitive advantage. Expansionism and the establishment of frontiers function as a temporary remedy for a decadent community. Linking morality to conquest is imperative to instil a sense of meaning for commercial exploits. Empires need to justify the unprovoked conquering of foreign lands in the name of advancing civilisation. The Roman Empire used the language of law and order, the Spanish used salvation, the British would proliferate civilisation as the white man's burden, while America's transition from republic to empire was done under the name of spreading freedom, democracy, and being the moral guardian of the world (Garrett 1961).

The rise of Britain

Britain and France led the European mercantilist era when Western Europe rose to global primacy. The mercantilist policies entailed formidable support for domestic manufacturers with subsidies, high tariffs, and wage suppression, while gold and silver were primarily accepted for payment to develop skills in return for accruing wealth. The promotion of asymmetrical interdependence to climb up the value-chain was supported by opening up exclusive markets with staple ports and colonies. Britain and France competed for primacy, with the former eventually taking the lead.

Britain rose to dominance with government intervention in industries and the mercantilist policies advocated by James Steuart (1770). Cunningham (2008[1905]: 133) argued:

> For a period of two hundred years [1600–1800], the English nation knew very clearly what it wanted. Under all changes of dynasty and circumstances the object of building up national power was kept in view; and economics, though not yet admitted to the circle of the sciences, proved an excellent servant, and gave admirable suggestions as to the manner in which this aim might be accomplished.

A strong manufacturing base was built with the support of the state, as high tariffs protected domestic producers. England enjoyed geographical advantage as an island state in terms of getting a head start on the industrial revolution. Unlike European continental powers with more adversaries within proximity, England did not require a large standing army during peace time. The government therefore had less coercive power that could be used to subdue its population, which made the authorities more vulnerable and therefore more disposed to accept greater diffusion of power (Quigley 1961). Parliament's strength vis-à-vis the monarch led to greater land rights and enclosures, which contributed to intensifying the efficiency of the agriculture industry. Excess labour and capital could therefore be directed towards urban manufacturing, providing Britain with a lead in the race to industrialise. The repeal of the Corn Laws in 1846 became one of the final acts to open the British market to agricultural competition as its economy was making its transition into manufacturing. Exclusive access to markets through colonisation developed strong British banks with global reach and a trusted international currency, producing both favourable conditions for its manufacturers and social stability at home. British banks remained dominant long after the US economy had surpassed it.

Control over transportation corridors was achieved in a rivalry between the English and the French by building powerful navies to ensure privileged access to natural resources and exclusive markets for its manufactured goods. The emergence of the powerful nation-state in Europe and maritime power in the early 1500s began the gradual progress of re-establishing Eurasian and then global economic connectivity through maritime corridors. As a maritime power, an offshore balancing strategy was more efficient that deploying large land-based armies. The lack of a requirement for a large standing army meant that the funds could instead be diverted to construct a powerful navy with both military and economic advantages. During conflict, the British could block transportation corridors to stun mobility of troops or starve an adversary's population. Rather than deploying a large force capable of holding land, the purpose of British troops on the continent was merely to ensure that a balance of power was maintained to prevent the emergence of a continental superpower capable of conquering Britain (Mearsheimer and Walt 2016).

Control over transportation corridors concentrated power in the West and have became the foundation for Western dominance ever since. The emergence of the trade-post empires gave European powers privileged or exclusive control over markets and corridors. For weaker powers such as Portugal, taxing the use of their ports in Asia became a source of revenue. Christopher Columbus' efforts to establish a trade corridor between Spain and East Asia through the Atlantic led to the discovery of America, which expanded Western powers' control over maritime corridors. British control over the seas eventually brought down China as the dominant economy. While China remained the leading economy in the world until the mid-1800s, the loss of control over the regional sea-lanes spurred its downfall. The British were in a position to defy China's demand for precious metals as a currency and replace it with opium. Following the two Opium Wars, the spoils of war included the transfer of Hong Kong and special status in Chinese ports and sea-lanes.

Control over transportation corridors proved to be imperative in the competition between colonial powers. Britain seized French merchant ships when there were disputes over territory in Northern America. Similarly, Britain threatened to impose a naval blockade to cripple the German economy when Germany interfered in Britain's Boers War in Africa. During the First World War, Britain starved to death a million German civilians to undermine their war efforts, and to weaken Germany in the future. Churchill proudly announced in Parliament four months after Germany surrendered: 'We are enforcing the blockade with rigor, and Germany is very near starvation' (Buchanan 2017). The opening of the Suez Canal in 1869 epitomised the imperative of Britain's control over transportation corridors. The construction of the Suez Canal had been met with fierce opposition by the British, as it was feared it would diminish their control over transportation corridors. London was concerned the canal would be open for all states and subsequently enable interference in Britain's privileged trade with its colonies, most importantly India. The construction of the Suez Canal was sabotaged by protesting against the use of slave labour and inciting a revolt. The eventual opening of the canal occurred under French control, a key colonial rival. Britain, conspiring with the French and Israeli, responded in 1956 to Egypt's nationalisation of the canal by invading to reassert control over the canal. US demand for withdrawal meant the British finally had to abandon the canal, followed by the US stationing forward deployments in the region to assert its influence over important maritime choke points. The UK's struggle to find a new post-colonial role in the world resulted rationally in embracing a 'special partnership' with the US.

British colonisation had a distinct civilisation component by augmenting both competitive advantage and assuaging the community. Exclusive markets were opened where Britain enjoyed competitive advantage. While the community diminished in industrialising society, the frontier reinvigorated the sense of meaning and enabled the barbaric to be harmonised with the advancement of civilisation. Colonialism represented brave Europeans expanding civilisation by conquering nature and 'uncivilised' peoples. Colonialism had its virtues in both the distinctive and the universal as an inherent expression of racial superiority and under the name of exporting universal values and civilising barbarians abroad.

The ascendance of the US

The development of the US was largely influenced by the dilemma between gemeinschaft and gesellschaft. President Thomas Jefferson's aim to preserve the morality and virtues of the community translated into advocacy for the US remaining an agrarian democracy, rather than maximising economic output by advancing an industrialised society (Griswold 1946: 667). The morality of agrarian society was consistent with Jefferson's tendency to romanticise Anglo-Saxon mythology. Jefferson rejected that there should be a discrepancy between private and public ethics and morality, and cautioned against developing like Europe (Tucker and Hendrickson, 1992: 60).

Yet, a powerful society was required to advance political independence. Alexander Hamilton, the first US Secretary of the Treasury, persuaded President Jefferson that it was necessary to embrace the rational/calculative industrial society to increase relative power against other states (Szlajfer 2012: 51). Hamilton posited that the US could not preserve political independence if it remained economically reliant on Britain. Political independence is contingent on economic autonomy and influence, which was unattainable as 'free trade' equated to 'unfair trade' under a British-led international system (Mott 1997: 22). Washington was concerned about asymmetrical interdependence as Europe had little dependence on the US, while the US was extremely reliant on European manufactured goods and banks. Economic nationalism was a rational policy as the British aimed to maintain American subservience by ensuring it remained an exporter of raw materials. British statesman and prime minister, William Pitt, stated in parliament: 'If the Americans should manufacture a lock of wool or a horse shoe, I would fill their ports with ships and their towns with troops' (Van Tyne 1927: 33).

Hamilton's ideas eventually culminated in the 'American System', which rested on three pillars to establish a competitive economy: manufacturing, transportation, and financial infrastructure. The state-interventionism of the American System devised by Alexander Hamilton and Henry Clay was reconfigured and followed in the administrations of James Madison, James Monroe, John Quincy Adams, Abraham Lincoln, William McKinley, Theodore Roosevelt, and Franklin Roosevelt.

The first pillar of developing a manufacturing base was supported with tariffs and subsidies. Free trade was frequently scorned as immoral as it exposed American workers to intolerable foreign competition, while subordinating the country to Britain. Theodore Roosevelt wrote in 1895: 'Thank God I am not a free-trader. In this country pernicious indulgence in the doctrine of free trade seems inevitably to produce fatty degeneration of the moral fibre' (Eckes 1999: 30). High tariffs from 1865 to 1932 under the Republicans increased domestic industrial power, which elevated the US from mediocrity to leadership. With growing relative American commercial strength, there were strong incentives to promote free trade and anti-colonialism to challenge the privileged position of European colonial powers. Free trade as an American ideology cemented after the Second World War as its war-time industries were converted into commercial industry, large competitive corporations replaced minor retailers, and new technologies emerged. Even those recognising the societal ills of free trade had to accept that the fight against communism had to be prioritised. President Eisenhower posited in 1953 that harmful free trade should be tolerated as 'all problems of local industry pale into insignificance in relation to the world crisis' (Eckes 1995: 165).

The second pillar of the American System, transportation corridors, was constructed for domestic development and international influence. The development of railroads across the US throughout the 1800s, most importantly the transcontinental railroad from the Atlantic to the Pacific, was imperative for settlement, to bind together the vast regions of the country, and to industrialise by creating larger markets and a more mobile workforce. In the late 1800s, Captain Alfred Thayer Mahan wrote his influential work with the conclusion that control over the world required establishing dominance over the seas. Controlling transportation corridors was argued to provide the US with economic competitiveness and enhance its security by becoming an offshore balancer. The spoils of war from the victory in the Spanish-American war in 1898 endowed the US ownership over the Spanish colonies of the Philippines, Guam, Puerto Rico, and temporary control over Cuba. This was followed by annexing and purchasing a variety of islands in the Pacific. Furthermore, by coercing the secession of Panama from Colombia in 1903, the US could build a canal under US sovereignty to connect the Pacific with the Atlantic. The US initially set its eyes on controlling Latin America and East Asia as the Europeans had already divided Africa and the Middle East (Wiebe 1967: 239). Increasingly aware that the US had fallen behind in the colonial race, Brooks Adams argued that 'the pinch will come when all else has been absorbed and we must take China with its mines, or be undersold' (Wiebe 1967: 234). The economic argument for expansionism was rooted in economies of scale. US Senator, Albert Beveridge, advocated geographical expansionism to increase efficiency:

American factories are making more than the American people can use; American soil is producing more than they can consume. Fate has written our policy for us; the trade of the world must and shall be ours ... We will establish trading-posts throughout the world as distributing points for American products. We will cover the ocean with our merchant marine. Great colonies governing themselves, flying our flag and trading with us, will grow about our posts of trade. Our institutions will follow our flag on the wings of commerce. And American law, American order, American civilization, and the American Flag will plant themselves on shores hitherto bloody and benighted but by those agencies of God henceforth to be made beautiful and bright.

(Bowers 1932: 67)

double! ?

Following the Second World War, the US expanded its maritime expanse globally, providing immense commercial and military benefits at a relatively low cost. Key transit corridors and critical choke points fell under US control: the Suez Canal, Bab el-Mandab, the Strait of Hormuz, Strait of Malacca, Cape of Good Hope, and the two 'island chains' in Asia-Pacific to contain China and the Soviet Union. A moderate influence was also established in the Danish Strait, Mediterranean, and Bosporus to constrain Soviet access to the Atlantic. After the Cold War, NATO expansionism further strengthened the US in the Baltic Sea and the Black Sea.

The third pillar of the American System was influence over financial infrastructure and other mechanisms for economic cooperation. The initial task was to establish a national bank to reduce financial dependence on the British. Recognising the imperative of governments' capacity to harness economic statecraft, Adams (1947[1900]: 80) predicted that states in the future would become 'a gigantic corporation whose business is to materially benefit its members'. A small government with legitimacy from the foundational principle of not stepping on individual freedoms was largely incapable of developing a powerful administrative state capable of harmonising state interests with the market (Adams 1947[1900]). Systemic incentives thus emerged for the US to develop a larger and more intrusive government to become more 'European'. Roosevelt's attempt in 1904 to establish US financial industry in China to rival the Europeans was futile, as J.P. Morgan was motivated by profits rather than augmenting state power (Wiebe 1967: 251). The Bretton Woods system ensured that state power was closely aligned with market power; the gold-backed US dollar would reign supreme, and the US would be dominant in the International Monetary Fund (IMF) and the World Bank as the principal international financial institutions.

The US aimed to cement its unipolar position after the Cold War by integrating the global economy under US stewardship. Efforts to recuperate the Bretton Woods institutions have centred on establishing American control over global standards and trade rules. The Trans-Pacific Partnership was an important initiative to resuscitate American primacy in the Asia-Pacific. The treaty consisted of maritime states along the pacific, with the notable exception of China and Russia. Obama (2016) outlined the central objective of the TPP:

> America should write the rules. America should call the shots. Other countries should play by the rules that America and our partners set, and not the other way around. That's what the TPP gives us the power to do . . . The United States, not countries like China, write them.

The geoeconomics of Germany and Western Europe

Germany embraced the economic nationalist policies of Friedrich List for state-building and region-building. Germany protected its infant industry from its more mature British counterpart and avoided integration into a British-dominated international system. Bismarck's protectionism from the 1870s was then emulated by France, Italy, Austria-Hungary, Sweden, and Spain (Matthias et.al. 1989: 62).

Both physical transportation connectivity and financial infrastructure were imperative to bring together the German regions and create a common state. List famously referred to the economic instruments of railways and economic union as the 'Siamese twins' of German state-building (Earle 1943: 442).

The history of German militarism, expansionism, and attempted autarchy mirrors the systemic pressures for a burgeoning land-power confined at the centre of Europe. Constrained by its geography, Germany was without reliable transportation corridors, access to markets, or colonial expansion to compete with rival European powers and establish a civilisational frontier against barbarism. State-building therefore became reliant on successful region-building in terms of constructing a common Europe to extend its power further. Comparing Germany with the US, Adam Brooks stated: 'the Germans cannot increase their velocity because they cannot extend their base, and augment their mass – we can and do' (Wiebe 1967: 234).

After prospering under Napoleon's Continental system, Germany sought to recreate a shared market through a customs union that was also open to non-German states. Reliance on trade routes controlled by adversaries was recognised as an intolerable vulnerability, which became evident as the German population starved under the maritime blockade during the First World War. Transportation corridors were sought by sea and land, which threatened to upset the regional balance of power. Efforts to establish itself as a maritime power led to a naval arms race with the British, while the Berlin-Baghdad Railway threatened Britain, France, and Russia. The alternative was to become self-sufficient. Mirroring the US decision to venture into the Pacific, Haushofer's advocated that Germany had to attain autarchy and become a global power through territorial expansion to obtain more living space (lebensraum). Two failed world wars later appear to indicate that Germany had failed.

However, the foundations for harmonising German with 'Europe' was achieved following its defeat in the Second World War, as the Cold War provided a common 'Western' security architecture. German industry could be exported across the West, the US ensured safe transportation corridors and access to resources, a powerful Deutschmark was developed, and the European Coal and Steel Community set the condition for a shared trade regime in the European Community. Helmut Schmidt, the former German Chancellor, argued in 1978 that it was imperative to 'clothe ourselves in this European mantle . . . we need it also to cover these ever-increasing relative strengths, economic, political, military, of the German Federal Republic within the West' (Bundesbank 1978). Bismarck famously articulated in the previous century: 'I have always found the word "Europe" in the mouths of those politicians who wanted from other powers something they did not dare to demand in their own name.' Positioned on the frontline in the ideological Cold War, Western Germany benefitted from the US subsidising its security, while Washington also tolerated European state support for infant industries to conquer market share from the Americans.

After the Cold War, the EU emerged as a dominant geoeconomic institution by using collective bargaining power to protect the strategic industries of its member states, while concurrently pressuring its trading partners to open their markets and abide by EU regulations and laws (Raza 2007). The EU became a geoeconomic 'regulatory power' as economic power was converted to political influence by establishing the standards and conditionality for favourable trade agreements (Eberlein and Grande 2005; Bradford 2012: 65). The more the EU expanded, the more European non-member states at the periphery were faced with the dilemma of integrating into an EU-led system, or alternatively becoming an isolated and weak hermit kingdom. European states such as Norway and Switzerland that are part of the Single Market by declining membership are compelled to abide by a 'pay-without-say' model as instructed by EU directives, yet do not partake in decision-making. Using more coercive language, the EU Commissioner for Energy, Günther Oettinger, threatened to isolate and marginalise neighbouring states that did not fall in line: 'whoever leaves the Energy Community indirectly leaves the partnership with the EU. It becomes the next Belarus' (Keating 2012). The EU's EU2020 initiative intends to further amplify support for the strategic industries of member states by endowing Brussels with 'powerful tools to hand in the shape of new economic governance' (European Commission 2010).

The common currency, the Euro has been a key source for further integration and federalisation of the union. The common currency was deceptively launched as an economic initiative, with deliberate structural flaws embedded. Without a fiscal union and political union there would inevitably be structural problems that could only be resolved with fiscal and political integration (Bergsten 2012; Spolaore 2013; Stockhammer 2014). An architect behind the common currency explained the intended political purpose of the common currency: 'The road toward the single currency looks like a chain reaction in which each step resolved a preexisting contradiction and generated a new one that in turn required a further step forward' (Padoa-Schioppa (2004: 14).

Conclusion

In contravention of the ideological devotion to economic liberalism and globalism, Western powers rose to prominence with economic statecraft and strategic integration. It is imperative to recognise the source of geoeconomic power and not be consumed by liberal delusion in other to sustain the advancement of society and preserve the community. Furthermore, assessing the geoeconomic rise of the West offers a better understanding for the ongoing relative decline. Resurgence of the West depends on asserting influence over strategic industries to augment autonomy and dependence by others. This entails energy resources, agriculture, and innovative high-tech industries such as robotics, automation, and cyber technology. The West also needs to maintain its influence over strategic transportation corridors as more efficient and cheaper transport endows less natural advantage to local production. Physical economic connectivity between large Eurasian powers such as China, Russia, India, and Iran were underdeveloped during communism, however, they are now developing rapidly to escape reliance on transit routes under US control. Mechanisms for international economic cooperation that were developed at Bretton Woods will increasingly be challenged in terms of new trade/reserve currencies, investment banks, and trade regimes. Last, the solidarity and collective hegemony of the West based will deteriorate as the share of trade with non-Western countries increases, and political interests and loyalties eventually follow.   *awkward*

6 Unconstrained economic liberalism: death of community and society

Introduction

Unfettered market forces are decimating both gemeinschaft and gesellschaft. The withdrawal of the state from the economy is paradoxically occurring at a time when state intervention is needed more to defend the transcendent within the community and the competitiveness of society from the unforgiving pressures of global markets forces and new technologies. States are faced with the formidable task of striking a balance between opportunity and equality, industry/social stability and technological innovation, prosperity and environmental preservation, dynamic economic structures and stability, efficiencies or full employment, economic efficiency, or the reproduction of culture/social norms. The absolutism embedded in the ideology of free-market capitalism ignores this delicate balance, while the push towards standardised global practises and rules that limits the ability to experiment with these balances to find the best outcome.

While the nation-state has been the foundation for preserving a balance between community and society, the demand for increasing economic efficiency is eschewing the nation-states as a hindrance to seemingly greater economic potential. The radicalism of economic liberalism is the belief that markets are self-regulating. The view of the nation-state as an out-dated political organisation has become commonplace among Western elites. This worldview neglects the instinctive and irrational aspect of human nature, and fuels a growing disconnect between the elites and the regular citizens they govern. The liberal delusion is grounded in the undisputable fact that the ever-growing economic efficiency within an increasingly globalised world has increased prosperity and lifted millions of people out of poverty. It is also aptly recognised that in an increasingly interconnected world, it is imperative to establish new global formats for collective action. The new challenges presented to humanity such as global warming and international terrorism are accurately recognised to require global solutions. However, the radical view that the world must abandon the state-centric system fails to recognise that the nation-state is indispensable to facilitate both the community and society. While it is recognised that many have been disadvantaged by the forces of globalisation, the elites remain convinced that this problem can be solved within the framework of globalisation by merely reimbursing those that have been disadvantaged.

The West's descent into free-market ideology as a source of creative destruction will first be explored. The transition from controlled capitalism from 1945 to unfettered capitalism in the 1980s was caused by both ideology and pragmatism. Perpetual economic growth became a leading source of political legitimacy after the Cold War, and the elites then responded to the stagnation of the 1970s by lessening state control in the 1980s. Following the demise of communism in the 1990s, the West had further incentives to embrace the ideology of free-market capitalism to integrate the world under a Western-led international system.

Second, the subsequent decline of the community will be surveyed. Carl Jung (1969) considered God to represent the highest ideal and was therefore reluctant to resists gravitation towards religion that has across time and cultures placed moral virtues at the centre. In an economically deterministic society where economic efficiency is the highest ideal, morality and the community inevitably decline. Even the family as the most sacred institution for human interaction and intimate community, disintegrates when it no longer enjoys economic utility. Global markets have created an international division of labour due to comparative advantage that erodes the middle class. New technologies similarly spur creative destruction and eschew loyalty to the community and the nation-state.

Third, the reduced competitiveness of Western society is assessed. Geoeconomic rivalry between Western powers is intensifying, while the non-Western world is re-discovering economic statecraft and becoming increasingly competitive with the West. It will be concluded that there are growing incentives for the world to protect both the community and society from global markets and new technology by dividing into regions.

From controlled capitalism to unfettered free-market capitalism

The strand of capitalism that reigned in the West from 1945 until the 1980s can be defined by contemporary jargon as 'controlled capitalism'. Western states intervened in the market to augment the competitiveness of society by protecting strategic industries, and to uphold social responsibilities by shielding the community. The experimentation of various modes of capitalism in the West was evident. The US favoured intervention for stability in the economy with strict regulation to control competition between corporations and protect strategic industries such as agriculture, energy, transportation, telecommunications, and financial services from disruptive competition. In Western Europe, there was more protection for the workers and groups vulnerable to volatile market forces and creative destruction. Besides ensuring protection for strategic industries, the Western Europeans were concerned about the welfare of employees by advancing employee rights, health care, and other efforts to ensure economic development did not upset the stability for workers. The logic in favour of state-controlled capitalism across the leading capitalist states was consistent: capitalism makes society increasingly efficient by shedding inefficient structures, yet some limitations have to be put in place to account for the people and state reliant on the ineffective structures.

[handwritten margin note: rather incessant "innovation" is crushing creativity]

After the Second World War, continuous economic growth became a decisive indicator for political legitimacy during the rebuilding and opening of markets to capitalist allies. The bourgeoning economic affluence, social opportunities, and support by the welfare state initially outweighed the social costs of dislodging the population from the community. Yet, the arrogance of governments and economic stagnation during the 1970s made a strong case for diffusing power by allowing a greater role for the market. The Thatcherism of the 1980s largely responded to these challenges as a more 'flexible labour market' was advanced by repudiating national ownership of industry, regulations, and the welfare state. The concurrent Reaganism similarly assisted in reinventing conservative philosophy. The efforts by Ronald Reagan to rejuvenate the American economy by maximising efficiency removed much of the regulatory power of the state to uphold societal responsibilities. Traditional capitalism in the US came under assault from rapid deregulation, the willingness to accept higher unemployment, scaling back the unions, and dismissal of the state's societal responsibilities (Davidson and Davidson 1988: 138). Economic liberalism as a response to the challenges of the 1970s had become a delusional and absolute truth that could be applied to all scenarios.

Traditional conservatism, an imperative balance to liberalism promoting continuity, thus began its rapid decline in the 1980s. While unrecognisable today, conservatives of the past had a strong communitarian aspect. Unconstrained market forces have since decimated the institutions and traditions that traditional conservatives sought to preserve. Genuine traditional conservatism today must paradoxically be revolutionary by restoring the traditional rather than merely conserving it. Western civilisation has become defined almost exclusively by liberal virtues, and any meaningful opposition advocating continuity of the traditional is vilified as an attack on Western values and civilisation itself. Furthermore, as the West developed a strong middle class the attractiveness of political extremes rescinded. The distinction between political parties became less profound as a consensus developed in terms of where countries should go and how to get there. With growing national solidarity and a limiting scope of acceptable policies, the communists on the extreme Left or fascists on the extreme Right had lost their significance and value to political debate. Political representatives are regularly changed, yet with only a narrowly accepted scope for legitimate discourse, the political philosophy and policies remain constant.

By the 1990s, the incentive for embracing the ideology of unfettered capitalism was further supported with the process of globalisation. Free-market capitalism meant integrating the entire post-communist world into a Western-led world order. As Sergei Lavrov (2012) posited, the demise of communism and the Soviet Union had convinced Washington that 'the developed Western countries and large corporations would freely spread their influence around the world and that the liberal-democratic system would be the only beacon for all peoples "lagging behind".' In other words, the geoeconomic power of the West reached new heights as globalisation largely translated into 'Americanisation' or 'Westernisation'. The incentive for the West to embrace the new globalist doctrine was immense as Western states were dominant in all geoeconomic spheres: the strategic industries, transportation corridors, and mechanisms for economic and financial cooperation.

Under the Clinton administration, the Left began abandoning the traditional platform of economic justice. Committed to unconstrained capitalism, the Democratic Party distances itself from the Unions and the discourse of the redistribution of wealth (Rorty 1998). Clinton's repeal of the Glass-Steagall Act suspended the separation between commercial banking and investment banking, setting the stage for exacerbating the looming financial crisis of 2008 that devastated the middle class.

Decaying gemeinschaft: global markets and new technology

Capitalism is unrivalled and revered for its ability to maximise efficiency. Social institutions, family, friends, neighbourhoods, cities, and even nation-states that are not economically efficient will see their value dwindling in an economic deterministic society. Economic liberalism has developed into an unchallenged orthodoxy as the ability to become rich is a virtue, while failure to do so is a personal failure. Economic strength does not translate into stronger communities and sturdier families, rather demographic decline is indicative of their diminished economic utility. Spouses and children are a burden to the career, while the elders in society without economic function are stored in retirement homes until they expire. Personal relationships are demoted to instruments for social mobility, consumer choice is maximised at the expense of commitment to local and domestic industries, and abortion is normalised to increase inconvenience rather than morality. Economic determinism even reduces the immigration debate to a question about whether it grows or stunts the economy, while arguments for reproducing the culture and preserving the community is secondary or even dismissed as xenophobia. The West is subsequently transitioning from being a collection of states with economies to becoming economies with states.

Until the 1980s Western governments were tasked with protecting the community by responding to Schumpeter's creative destruction, a reference to the social problems caused by entire professions and industries disappearing due to technological innovations and market forces. Complex economic structures disconnect people from their traditional communities, to the extent that society develops independence from the community. The solution is not for the state to obstruct technological progress or subsidise out-dated industries as the result would merely be relative geoeconomic decline in the international system, which reduces security and the prospect of survival. Yet, creative destruction presents the state with an important responsibility in terms of mitigating the social strain as skills become redundant and jobs vanish.

Economic liberalism after the Cold War is best described by the retreat of the state as global markets opened and revolutionary new technologies were unleashed. The systemic retreat of the state occured at a time when more state intervention was required to manage the rapid societal changes caused by complex economic structures. Unaddressed, such developments are likely to concentrate wealth, impede social mobility, increase creative destruction, and cause estrangement and divisions. While public ownership previously signified the reassurance of collective benefit, the state has since become vilified as a symbol of inefficient bureaucracy and technological stagnation. Both depictions are to some extent accurate. Regulations, public ownership, and centralised planning are accurately recognised to stifle the efficiency of capitalism, yet they manage to have a negative impact on people. Furthermore, new technologies also appear to reduce the need for government as communication technology enhances transparency. Burgeoning society has always burdened the community, yet the changes in the post-Cold War era are unprecedented: *or ??? Censorship*

> Structural change, with all its personal upheavals and social disruptions, is now quite rapid even when there is zero growth, becoming that much faster when economies do grow. The engine turns, grinding lives and grinding down established human relationships, even when the car is stopped; and reaches Ferrari-like rpms at the most modest steam-roller speeds.
>
> (Luttwak 1993a)

The neo-liberal consensus that followed the Cold War could not be balanced, as classical conservativism had committed suicide:

> The desolation of settled communities and the ruin of established expectations will not be mourned and may well be welcomed by fundamentalist market liberals. For them, nothing much of any value is threatened by the unfettered operation of market institutions. Communities and ways of life which cannot renew themselves through the exercise of consumer choice deserve to perish. The protection from market forces of valuable cultural forms is a form of unacceptable paternalism. And so the familiar and tedious litany goes on.
>
> (Gray 1995: 100)

Instability ensues when the middle class struggles. Aristotle recognised that the rule of the middle class offers an alternative to the extreme of the rule of the rich and the rule of the poor. In the American experience, the middle class rested on manufacturing jobs, which have incrementally been replaced by the service industry with retail jobs, bartenders, and waitresses. Furthermore, large and complex global value-chains tend to concentrate wealth, while the populace loses autonomy and community due to the decline of local private ownership. This trend puts more pressure on the state to address the ensuing gap between rich and poor, diminishing social mobility and societal instability by harmonising community with society. Yet, through the prism of the free market versus socialist dichotomy, the mitigating capacity through state ownership and intervention is discredited. While in the past the state was endowed with the status as a guarantor of public interest, the state has in present times become a symbol of corruption, inefficient bureaucracy, and technological inertia (Luttwak 1993a). **?**

Unfettered market forces of global markets, spurred by free-trade agreements and cheaper transportation costs, compel a further division of labour as states must take advantage of competitiveness and maximise economies of scale. Globalisation is often crudely presented as a binary between nationalism or globalism, while neglecting that economic connectivity has historically been based on controlled capitalism and strategic integration. The radical embrace of Ricardo's concept of competitive advantage has resulted in growing domestic inequalities and social breakdown. The transition from manufacturing to a service economy in the US has been a failure, evident by the enormous trade deficits. Capital and labour saved from outsourced manufacturing has mostly been directed towards low-skilled and low-paid jobs, while growing economic inequality is eroding the middle class and undermining economic innovativeness, adaptability, and resilience (Luttwak 1993b). US commercial strength is evidently in skilled high-tech industries and the priority has therefore been to open these foreign markets to superior American corporations. In trade negotiations, the US has been willing to reciprocate by opening its less competitive lower-tech and manufacturing industries to more competitive foreign rivals. Subsequently, a powerful high-tech industry grew while low-tech manufacturing died. The US population has become increasingly divided as the country was split into a super-rich educated class, and a dying middle class due to stagnating or declining skills and wages. Krugman (2007), a Nobel Prize-winning economist, argued 'it's hard to avoid the conclusion that growing US trade with Third-World countries reduces the real wages of many and perhaps most workers in this country. And that reality makes the politics of trade very difficult.'

Global markets liberate people from the confines of their own borders, yet there is also more demand on workers to be increasingly flexible in terms of time and location of their employment. Informal associations have historically created closed markets and limited efficiency, yet without the necessity to adopt to new standards and format, there has been less need for flexibility of the work force. The more complex an economic system becomes, the weaker the community becomes:

> Repeated interaction and community norms work best when markets are mostly local and small scale, when people do not move around much, and when the goods and services traded are simple, standardised, and don't have to travel over long distances. But as economies grow and geographical mobility increases, the need for clear and extensive rules and more reliable enforcement becomes paramount.
>
> (Rodrik 2012: 15)

A globally mobile workforce makes it imperative for states to raise the standard of living to prevent a brain drain. The problem for states with highly developed economies is usually negative demographic development, which entails reliance on a flow of migrants that incrementally replaces the native population. While migration has drastically increased, migrants have also become less committed to their new host country. Ease of travel reduces the necessity for cutting ties with the original homeland as prosperous migrants travel between homes.

After the Second World War, there was a growing consensus that 'each nation's citizens take primary responsibility for enhancing the capacities of their countrymen for full and productive lives' (Reich 1991). Without unity based on the recognition of a shared fate, the state would not be able to compete against other states. Yet, with more affordable travel and global mobility, immigrants have become less likely to sever ties with their countries of origin and commit/ integrate into the new community. Globalisation undermines the morality as in-group loyalty within the state declines:

> No longer does their well-being depend exclusively or primarily on his productivity, purchasing power, or wage restraint exercised by the other four-fifths of the population. The American executive software engineer, linked to his world-wide web by computer, modem and facsimile machine, is apt to be more dependent on design engineers in Kuala Lumpur, fabricators in Taiwan, bankers in Tokyo and Bonn, and sales and marketing specialists in Paris than on routine production workers in a factory on the other side of the town.
>
> (Reich 1991: 250)

New technologies also tend to weaken the community by rendering entire professions and industries obsolete and reducing inter-personal social interactions. Communities are especially disrupted without a slow generational shift to transition from one technology to another, as people's skills are made redundant and re-education is required. This was true with the internet revolution and may become more profound with automation and robotics. Mimicking the IT industry, human capital will in the following years change in terms of a continuous need for updated education as the work environment and technology changes rapidly. The era of being prepared for a life-long career after finishing education in the early 20s is ending.

The new pending industrial revolution within automation, robotics, and energy production is set to dramatically amplify creative destruction (Karaganov 2016: 461). The pending launch of autonomous cars could eliminate 5 million jobs in the US alone (Greenhouse 2016). After revolutionising operations of warehouses with robotics, Amazon's possible venturing into grocery with its rapidly evolving robotics and automation technology could eliminate about 75 percent of the ordinary staff in grocery stores (Herman 2016). An estimated 47 percent of workers in the US have jobs considered at a 'high risk' of being automated. As middle class jobs are increasingly vulnerable to being automated, there is a pending 'job polarisation' as the population will be pushed towards either low-skilled/low-paid jobs or high-skilled/high-paid jobs. However, eventually robots will also be used for high-skilled jobs (Ford 2015).

The predictable result is a large workforce without influence due to out-dated skillsets, and greater concentration of wealth in enormous corporations that inevitably attain strong political influence. The state will need to extract taxes from powerful corporations to iron out the growing domestic inequalities and fund the re-education of workers with out-dated skills and direct them towards high-skilled and high-paying jobs. Concurrently, the state needs to ensure a competitive low-tax business environment to attract large automated corporations that are more mobile and have a thinner workforce due to robotics. Hence, states will be incentivised to anchor companies within the country by imposing protective measures such as tariffs, to reassert influence over corporations without losing them to competitors.

Automation and robotics will undermine the development strategy of poor industrialising states that enter international market with a cheap workforce as a competitive advantage. The 'duck formation' development model employed by the Asian Tigers and China, in which they commenced with low-quality products and incrementally developed more technologically advanced products to grow in global value-chains, will be weakened. Up to 137 million workers in Indonesia, the Philippines, Thailand, Vietnam, and Cambodia, approximately 56 percent of their entire workforce, could be replaced by robotics due to the reliance on low-skilled professions such as the garment industry (Chang, Rynhart, and Huynh 2016). In other words, countries could also be redivided into super-rich and super-poor, thus eliminating the process of evening out since de-colonisation.

New communication technology adversely affects the social interaction that keeps communities together. During the revolutionary changes in the information space in the 1990s, Sagan (1996: 25) made a pessimistic prediction about how technology would also contribute to make the world worse:

> Science is more than a body of knowledge; it is a way of thinking. I have a foreboding of an America in my children's or grandchildren's time – when the United States is a service and information economy; when nearly all the key manufacturing industries have slipped away to other countries; when awesome technological powers are in the hands of a very few, and no one representing the public interest can even grasp the issues; when the people have lost the ability to set their own agendas or knowledgeably question those in authority; when, clutching our crystals and nervously consulting our horoscopes, our critical faculties in decline, unable to distinguish between what feels good and what's true, we slide, almost without noticing, back into superstition and darkness.

Modern technologies further enable personalities and interactions to be used rationally/instrumentally in the pursuit of material interests. Modern technology 'elevates narcissists to prominence' in politics and cultural life and 'elicits and reinforces narcissistic traits in everyone' (Lasch 1979: 235). The election of Trump to the presidency, a narcissistic host of a reality TV show, is a political consequence of the self-absorbed floating to the top of modern communication. While technology deprives people of their primordial and instinctive needs, it also provides sedatives to distract. Kennan (2014: 119) posited that 'people [were] drugged and debilitated by automobiles and advertisements and radios and moving pictures'. Case in point, social media responds to the human need for connectivity, yet exacerbates the condition as people become more isolated. The ability to achieve instant gratification and release of serotonin has diminished patience for investing in the time to develop inter-personal relations. The preference for a socialising device that cannot form deep and trusting relationships, has produced a proven correlation between spending time on social media and suffering depression. Digitally created personas replace authentic and reliable social interactions, causing society to become more alienated. Anti-social behaviour proliferates as for example bullying becomes more pervasive on social media due to the impersonal digital nature of the interaction.

The combination of global markets and new technologies are causing 'the completely unprecedented personal economic insecurity of working people' (Luttwak 1993a). The disconnect between the urban elites and those valuing the traditional is expected to only exacerbate: 'This world economy will soon be owned by a cosmopolitan upper class which has no more sense of community with any workers anywhere than the great American capitalists of the year 1900' (Rorty 1998). In the 1990s, Harvard economist Rodrik (1997) predicted that the intensification of globalisation would make the world more efficient but impose intolerable social costs. As tariffs and trade barriers were de-constructed, wages would be forced downwards, employee protection laws would be scaled back, regulations suspended, and more demand would be placed on an increasingly flexible labour market. Social costs had been rising since the 1970s and continued accelerating with globalisation. Since the 1970s, lower-skilled American and European workers have experienced a radical fall in the real value of their salaries. Furthermore, there was less job security, higher unemployment, longer and more volatile working hours. Unrestrained economic integration was expected to cause 'social disintegration' that would have severe political consequences. Instead of scaling back economic liberalism, Paul Krugman purportedly warned Rodrik that his books would embolden and provide 'ammunition to the barbarians' seeking to challenge the status quo (Rodrik 2012: 294).

Uncompetitive gesellschaft: competition with allies and adversaries

Geoeconomics were exercised more moderately during the Cold War than feared by Du Bois (1941) during the German Rationalisation Movement of the economy. The bipolar global rivalry negated tensions between allied capitalist states, while the West's foremost adversaries were communist states largely decoupled from economic statecraft. With the end of the Cold War, there were systemic incentives for increased competition within the West, and the eventual rise of adversarial non-Western powers utilising economic statecraft.

While the Cold War deferred the geoeconomic era that started after the First World War, the revolution was unleashed again when the Soviet Union and communism collapsed. Seemingly building on the work of Du Bois, Luttwak (1993a) made a renowned and controversial prediction in his article *Why Fascism is the Wave of the Future*. The unfettered free-market capitalism that took shape in the 1980s and become further unhinged in the post-Cold War era, revealed the flaws of economic liberalism when implemented to its fullest extent. Some aspects of the economic policies of fascism make a forceful return in lieu of the failures of economic liberalism. Dictatorial powers and extreme racism represented the most destructive and reprehensible aspects of fascism, which should and could be de-coupled from the fundamental ideas behind the economic policies as an alternative to economic liberalism and socialism.

The utopianism and absolutism of 20th-century modernist ideologies resulted in the failure to recognise the strengths and weaknesses of liberalism, fascism, and socialism. The German Rationalisation Movement, which was hijacked by the fascists, built upon economic nationalism and the socio-political philosophy of Heidegger and his contemporaries. However, the xenophobia, concentration of power, and brutality of European fascists largely discredited the fundamental ideas, irrespective of the same economic policies being implemented by the worlds' leading geoeconomic powers after the war. The strength of fascist economics was to build on the ideas of List (1827) that rejected cosmopolitanism due to the competition in international anarchy. Furthermore, the need to address the primordial and irrational aspects of Man was recognised. Economic statecraft must include greater state control over important industries, strategic economic integration with other states, and preservation of gemeinschaft as cultural and spiritual rejuvenation produces economic prosperity.

Geoeconomic competition among Western allies is increasing. The development of a commonly advanced Western society requires the harmonisation of geoeconomic activities. During the Cold War, the US reaped geostrategic benefits from subsidising the development of successful economies on the front lines in Western Europe and East Asia. Rather than retaliating against geoeconomic efforts by its allies, the US prioritised collective strength against the communist world. This translated into the US accepting the funding of the security of its allies, and tolerating the geoeconomic policies of capitalist states that cannibalised US industries. Security dependency also had a mitigating effect as the US could build up large deficits, while its allies for a long time refrained from trading in their devaluing dollars for gold. Yet, political pressures could only maintain internal solidarity to a certain extent, as the Europeans gradually began abandoning their dollars, which resulted in the US closing the gold window and returning to a fiat currency in 1971.

Towards the end of the Cold War, the US became more reluctant to accept the geoeconomic policies of Europeans and East Asian allies. This shift was demonstrated by geoeconomic rivalry in the airline industry. Western European airlines received formidable support from their governments in terms of subsidies, which allowed them to operate at a loss to conquer the US market. European governments provided virtually interest-free loans to their airlines to develop new airliners until they became competitive with their counterparts. Airbus Industrie penetrated and rose in the US market by running deficits at the expense of the taxpayer, at one time leasing out 23 of its A300 airliners to US Eastern Air Lines at a price of $1 a year (Luttwak 1993b: 28). Luttwak (1993b: 34) used geoeconomic language to explain the European march against the US:

Just as in the past when young men were put in uniform to be marched off in pursuit of schemes of territorial conquest, today taxpayers are persuaded to subsidize schemes of industrial conquest. Instead of fighting each other, France, Germany and Britain now collaborate to fund Airbus Industrie's offensive against Boeing and McDonnell-Douglas. Instead of measuring progress by how far the fighting front has advanced on the map, it is worldwide shared for the targeted products that are the goal.

The cosmopolitan free-trade argument would suggest that the US was benefitting as the European taxpayer was effectively subsidising air travel for Americans and thus elevating their standard of living. Yet, such an assessment reduced American citizens to mere consumers rather than producers. The 'hidden hand' of the free market did not naturally reallocate the excess capital and labour to high-skilled professions in dominate positions on the global value-chain, rather industrial jobs were replaced with low-skilled and low-paid retail jobs. Within a relatively short period of time, European airliners had risen to the status of world leaders, while American airlines without government support were pushed towards bankruptcy. Germans then began to apply the same strategy to their car manufacturers, communication industry, superconductors, and other strategic industries (Luttwak 1993b: 34). However, the golden days of European economic statecraft appears to be in the past. After spending a fortune of taxpayers' money to acquire market share from Boeing, Airbus announced in 2017 it would establish its second global innovation centre in China, while the first is in the US (Airbus 2017).

Similar developments were evident with America's East Asian allies. The economic miracle of Japan and South Korea did not occur on the back of free-market capitalism, rather by developing large conglomerates based on personal relationships. The Japanese Keiretsu and South Korean Chaebol are referred to as guided capitalism as their governments support strategic industries. Funds were channelled from the government and favourable loans provided, while various means were used to keep foreign competitors out of the domestic market, while simultaneously subsidising an export-based development strategy. Consolidation of democracy from the 1980s therefore entailed less government control over key industries as the long-term planning by authoritarian governments rescinded, special interests disrupted economic bureaucrats, and democratic support for radical development declined once prosperity was established (Kim 2017: 459). The US could tolerate losing a market share as South Korea's prosperity delegitimised the communist North Korea, while the Japanese and Taiwanese success stood in stark contrast with the economic backwardness of China. The strictly controlled capitalism of South Korea, Taiwan, and Singapore guided the most successful post-war economic development.

While regional economic blocs are an imperative tool for harmonising geoeconomic power, they have also begun to falter thereby making the West more vulnerable to the rise of new geoeconomic powers. The North American Free Trade Agreement (NAFTA), the Transatlantic Trade and Investment Partnership (TTIP), and the Trans-Pacific Partnership (TPP) aimed to advance collective geoeconomic power for global leadership, yet they failed to protect American producers from its economic allies. The TPP created a dilemma as China's influence could be reduced, yet it would leave American manufacturing vulnerable to the competitive advantage of US allies. Once in power, Trump's 'America First' policy communicated that the US was prepared to forego international leadership to protect domestic industries. This translated into cancelling the TTP and possibly NAFTA. The TTIP, a similar economic partnership to control standards, legislations, and trade rules aims to unite the North Atlantic and marginalise Russia. A similar dilemma surfaces as TTIP offers geoeconomic power, yet within the economic bloc power is transferred from elected officials to intrusive and unelected international experts. The EU similarly facilitates collective geoeconomic power, however, internal rivalry is evident as German geoeconomics is weakening other member states.

While the EU developed its geoeconomic capabilities after the Cold War to gain greater autonomy from the US, it has been followed by geoeconomic conflict between EU members. More specifically, the EU facilitated collective power vis-à-vis external actors, yet the balance of power within the EU is unravelling due to structural flaws and Germany's own divisive geoeconomics. Berlin's relative power increased as the EU facilitated German economic expansion and its conversion into political capital. EU enlargements to the East disproportionately benefitted Germany, undermining the equilibrium upheld by parity with Britain and France. The Euro endowed Germany with a severely devalued currency that augmented existing efforts of wage suppression to maximise exports and minimise imports. The 2013 US Treasury Report recognised that Germany strengthened its economy at the expense of its neighbours (US Treasury 2013: 3). As Germany gradually cannibalised the productive power and wealth of the Mediterranean member states, its political power also rose as Berlin could 'save' its southern neighbours with 'bailouts'. However, the Euro is unlikely to survive due to its structural flaws – as the Euro's political purpose of federalising the Union undermines its economic function. The first chief economist of the European Central Bank, Otmar Issing, aptly described the Euro as a 'house of cards' destined to collapse (Evans-Pritchard 2016).

With fewer economic incentives for regional economic integration, Germany and the EU elites have become more reliant on authoritarian means, threats, and intimidation to keep the union together (Stiglitz 2016). Democratically elected and accountable representatives gradually cede power to experts and European technocrats to manage the integration project. The absence of consensus is evident by consecutive failed referendums, which are then brushed aside. Following the French and Dutch rejection of the 'Constitution for Europe' in the 2005 referendums, the constitution was simply redrafted as the Lisbon Treaty without requiring another referendum (Helm 2007). Ireland, the only country obliged to ratify the new 'constitution' with a referendum, rejected the Lisbon Treaty. Followed by an EU-sponsored information campaign, Ireland was asked to vote again, much like the additional referendum after the Nice Treaty. The Czech President even triggered a walkout in the European Parliament when he argued that 'neither the present status quo nor the assumption that the permanent deepening of the integration is a blessing or should be a dogma for a European democrat' (Taylor 2009). In 2011, the Eurocrats responded to the failure of Greece and Italy to fall in line by first ousting the Greek Prime Minster and substituted him with a former vice-president of the European Central Bank, and then had the Italian Prime Minister removed and replaced by a former European Commissioner. Berlin and Brussels are similarly under great pressure to deter Greece from abandoning austerity, or to punish the UK for leaving the EU to discourage other member states from following its path.

The harmonisation of German state-building and European region-building established after the Second World War has begun to unravel. Subsequently, the former German Foreign Minster, Joschka Fischer (2015), warned that the narrative and imagery of the 'ugly German' was resurfacing. While Germany is too powerful to maintain a balance of power within the EU, it is too weak to establish German hegemony in Europe. Nazi Germany attempted to develop moral legitimacy for its military conquests by nurturing the concept of a 'New Europe' and a 'European civilisation'. The common purpose was to unite against a common adversary, the barbaric 'Asiatic Bolshevism' in the east (Brydan 2016). Albeit, the weakness and failure of the shared European concept derived from sovereign inequality or hierarchical structure as the ideas of European solidarity conflicted with Germanic/ Nazi superiority, which alienated even Germany's closest allies (Brydan 2016). The rise and decline of the EU can be explained by similar contradictions. The EU largely ascended by claiming ownership and monopolising the concept of Europe and centuries of European history. Yet, the notion of European solidarity conflicts with the implicit idea of German moral superiority and 'normative leadership' by imposing 'European values' on other member states. From good governance, immigration, and post-modernist values, Germany increasingly asserts sovereign inequality under the guise of a teacher-student relationship.

To the ire of several EU member states, Germany has taken on the role as a socialiser to make the rest of Europe more like Germany. This stokes old fears that a powerful Germany anchored in Europe would make the continent a German Europe, rather than a European Germany. Europe resembles Orwell's 'Animal Farm' where 'all animals are equal, but some animals are more equal than others'. The Hungarian prime minister, Victor Orban, scorned liberal democracy and critiqued Germany for dictating to the rest of the continent how they should live. In Greece, Poland, and across the continent loathing has been on the rise as 'Europe' becomes synonymous with German rule. The self-proclaimed leader of the Brexit-movement, Nigel Farage, protested that 'we are now living in a German-dominated Europe, something that the European project was actually supposed to stop' (Todd 2016: 92). Across the Atlantic, President Trump scorned German geoeconomics by claiming that 'the Germans are bad, very bad'. German Chancellor, Angela Merkel, responded in May 2017 by suggesting that 'we Europeans must really take our destiny into our own hands' (Paravicini 2017).

Geoeconomic competition with former communist adversaries is also intensifying. Previously the international division of labour had been relatively peaceful as the main adversaries were communist states, who were not skilful at economic statecraft. American outsourcing to what is a de-facto capitalist China has exacerbated rapid de-industrialisation. This process was supported by the liberal delusion of economic interdependence with adversaries as an absolute gain. Lawrence Summer explained US-Chinese economic interdependence inaccurately by arguing that decoupling the relationship would lead to 'mutually assured financial destruction' as 'they need us as much as we need them' (Ferguson 2010). Yet, China does not consume but invest, and they buy strategic corporations and not merely exports. Interdependence was not symmetrical, as the partnership entailed China being reliant on the US as an export market, and US dependence on China to fund its trade deficits. The interdependence logic was evidently faulty as every year the Chinese were acquiring more US Treasuries until the partnership became a threat for both sides. The Americans grew wary of increasing Chinese geoeconomic influence over the US, while the Chinese were concerned they would not get back their investments as the US would either eventually default or devalue their currency. Following the global financial crisis, these concerns were justified, as China was effectively blackmailed. Washington requested Beijing to either fund more of the US deficit or have their current investment devalued as the US Federal Reserve would then have to print US dollars and thereby devalue the currency.

China subsequently began transitioning away from its former development strategy of a 'peaceful rise' that relied on building its strength without attracting unwanted attention by the US hegemon. The former development strategy was unavoidably temporary, as it would eventually become untenable for both China and the US. China conquered a growing share of strategic industries as it advanced technologically and ascended in global value-chains. Energy security and dependence on trade also made it necessary for China to assert control over transportation corridors. The Silk Road project, formally known as One Road One Belt (OBOR), consists of land-corridors and maritime corridors outside the control of the US. Competing mechanisms for economic cooperation was also established by developing China-led international investment banks, China-controlled international payment systems, and internationalising the use of its currency.

In contrast, the US has become increasingly reliant on military coercion to maintain its power, which exhausts its geoeconomic capabilities. Ambitions for prolonged unipolarity after the Soviet Union disintegrated encouraged excessive and expensive militarism instead of a return to durable economic statecraft. Following the September 11 attacks and the subsequent US invasion of Afghanistan, the US increased its efforts to establish land-corridors to the energy-rich Central Asian region. The invasion of Iraq would ideally have established Iraq as an American outpost to project influence in the Middle East, similar to Japan's role in East Asia and Germany's in Europe after the Second World War. The expansion of the US as a land-based army further diminished its competitive advantage as an offshore balancer. The offshore balancer can choose the opportune moment to enter a war after other powers have exhausted themselves, while the maritime power expends less cost in terms of treasury and blood (Mearsheimer and Walt 2016). The invasion of Afghanistan and Iraq largely replicated the mistake of the Vietnam War, which was to abandon the competitive advantage of a maritime offshore balancer in favour of a less competitive and expensive land-power strategy that drained its resources. Kennedy's (1987) 'imperial overstretch' appears to have been realised as the US drains the core for resources to fund the periphery of its empire.

The relative decline of the West's collective geoeconomic power and reduced solidarity is causing a return to history as Germany also becomes more dependent on traditional military force to maintain access to resources and transportation corridors. Horst Köhler, the Germany's president, argued in May 2010 that military deployments are required for securing free trade routes or preventing regional instabilities, which would negatively influence out trade, jobs, and incomes (Szabo 2015: 7). Germany's Defence Policy Guidelines of 2011 similarly recognised that 'free trade routes and a secure supply of raw materials are crucial for the future of Germany and Europe', which 'is why transport and energy security and related issues will play an increasingly important role for our security' (German Ministry of Defence 2011: 3). Efforts to expand the EU's sphere of influence in terms of controlling regional energy, transportation corridors, and trade regimes, manifested itself in support for toppling governments on its southern and eastern periphery, including Ukraine in 2004 and 2014. In 2015, Carl Bildt conceded that 'we wanted to build a ring of friends, and got a ring of fire' (Bordachev 2016).

Conclusion

The ideology of unfettered economic liberalism is decimating both the community and society, which will unavoidably give rise to unpredictable political forces offering alternatives. Increasing economic efficiency as a rational development is eviscerating the community that serves the irrational component of Man. The rapid development of global markets and new technology is driving creative destruction at an unprecedented scale. People are dislodged from interpersonal ties, they lack function as a lower percentage of people have the skills to function in a more complex society, and the concentration of wealth fuels economic inequality. The EU epitomises how excessive gesellschaft decimates gemeinschaft. The EU as a grand economic-political structure aimed to bring order to a diverse and chaotic Europe, increasing the distance between the political establishment at the top and the people at the bottom. The creative destruction from an economic deterministic society was temporarily mitigated by aspirations of perpetual global leadership, as globalisation meant 'Americanisation' or 'Westernisation'. However, the remedy to an identity crisis is rescinding with non-Western powers using geoeconomics to ascend in global value-chains and conquer an increasingly greater share of world markets. The assault on the nation-state in the name of economic efficiency and globalisation inevitably motivates a radical backlash from the defenders of the nation-state, who then have incentives to contest global warming and other challenges that cannot be resolved by the nation-state alone.

Du Bois and Luttwak aptly predicted that 'fascist political economy' is the wave of the future. The state will need greater control over the economic levers of power to remain competitive in the international system, and concurrently promote local culture and nationalism to balance materialism and economic determinism. It is however imperative to recognise that the rationalisation of the economy preceded the Nazi party, as extreme racism, militarisation, and violence must be evaded. While the demise of communism and the prospect of unipolarity incentivised unyielding globalisation, the relative decline of the West is putting in place motivations to embrace a new grand idea to unify and establish a moral compass consistent with geoeconomic interests. A starting point for political discussion should be based on the empirical fact that global markets and new technologies produce economic inequality and reduced social capital, which fuels instability in society. Systemic incentives are pushing the world towards a structure where civilisations become meta-strategic power entities based on strategic integration and regionalism to preserve cultural integrity and still enjoy collective bargaining power in international markets.

Part IV

Resurgence of Russia

Neomodernism and geoeconomics

7   The geography of Russia's gemeinschaft and gesellschaft

Introduction

Russia is inclined to be a gemeinschaft-based civilisation, yet its encounters with powerful Western adversaries has through history motivated Russia to radically purge its community to modernise. The traditions and spirituality of the community in Russia have been disposed to prosper due to its large, rural, and remote land-based territory with low physical connectivity. The need for a large military to defend its long borders created an inclination towards authoritarianism and a hierarchical structured society due to the asymmetrical balance between the government with a large standing army even during peacetime and the rural population. Russia subsequently fell behind the Western Europeans in terms of industrialisation and modernisation, which left the orthodoxies and spirituality of the Russian community in a better position to be preserved. Yet, Russia has been compelled to undergo periods of rapid modernisation and embrace burgeoning gesellschaft as a necessary response to threats emanating from the West. The Western modernisation initiatives by Peter the Great, Sergei Witte, and Pyotr Stolypin, all created counter-reactions in terms of fuelling Slavophile Eurasianism.

where is Catherine the Great?

Russia's geography makes its civilisation unique as gemeinschaft and gesellschaft manifest themselves as an East–West dilemma. The traditional and spiritual community is linked to the vastness of Eurasia, which is contrasted with the modernisation and rationalism of advanced society in Europe. Russia's rival political philosophies reflect this zero-sum dilemma between European modernism and Eurasian spirituality. The Slavophiles seek a distinct eastern identity and rival the pro-Westerners (zapadniki). Much like their American counterparts, Russian leaders viewed the moral decadence in Western European manufacturing societies with derision and sought to counter it by preserving traditional rural and agrarian communities. However, Russia concurrently admired the Western Europeans for the same reasons, the modernisation, affluence, and opportunities available in advanced society. Finding a balance between gemeinschaft and gesellschaft has largely depended on a national idea positioned between Europe and Eurasia. This geographical make-up has through history produced radical pendulum swings between the traditional and modern, which obstructs a middle ground that produces stability.

The purpose of this chapter is to assess Russia's historical strengths and weaknesses as a civilisation by exploring the tenuous balance between its community and society. This chapter will first survey how the East–West dynamics have historically pulled Russia in opposite directions. Russia has through its history been vulnerable to absolutism in terms of embracing either a modern European future or a traditional and spiritual Eurasian path, with each extreme creating an equally radical counter-position. Encounters with a more modern West has repeatedly prompted Russia to periodically play catch-up by implementing drastic changes at the peril of its community.

Second, the geoeconomics of Russia in the late 19th century is explored to assess the opportunities and perils of modernisation. After her humiliation in the Crimean War during the 1850s, Russia began to pursue rapid modernisation to catch up with Western Europe. Britain's control over the Eurasian continent from the maritime periphery was challenged by Russian power expanding from the core. Yet, Russia also displayed signs of imperial overstretch as it was unprepared to defend its new maritime borders, while simultaneously becoming excessively reliant on foreign finance. Meanwhile, the push towards modernisation fuelled Slavophile Eurasianism as a counter-reaction in defence of gemeinschaft.

Third, the communist and post-communist era displayed an atrocious neglect of gemeinschaft and economic statecraft due to the ideological delusion of transcending the imperishable. The radical universalism of the communists resulted in purging the community in an effort to eradicate nationhood, religion, and distinct ethno-cultural traditions. Gesellschaft was also undermined by ongoing crucial economic statecraft and demoted Eurasianism to a backward geopolitical project. Furthermore, the extreme authoritarianism and repudiation of liberal principles inflicted a humanitarian crisis on the Russian people. The post-communist era was a radical pendulum swing towards a delusional liberal ideology. Community and society were yet again neglected due to the endeavour to become more like the West. The traditional and spiritual were considered out-dated and replaced with radical individualism and materialism at a time when the country was undergoing social decay. Economic liberalism deprived Moscow of economic statecraft as a tool for modernisation, and therefore led to de-industrialisation and set the Russian economy on the path to colonial status. The subsequent civilisational decay made Russia vulnerable to Western expansionism towards its borders.

Last, the recovery of Russia under Putin entailed reasserting state control over strategic industries to improve domestic societal problems and rely more on economic statecraft in foreign policy. When economic statecraft is insufficient to balance Western expansionism, military power has been used to enforce Russia's red lines to maintain the status quo in Georgia, Ukraine, and Syria. The rise of Russia will nonetheless depend on modernising its society and reviving its community, while avoiding a foreign policy that exhausts its resources.

Russia and the West: political liberalism and geoeconomics

Russian civilisation sprouted from Europe, which sparks a reasonable debate about whether Russia is a separate civilisation or simply a European power that fell behind on political and economic modernisation. The two civilisations have their shared roots from the Roman Empire, before parting ways as it fragmented. Western European civilisation continued to evolve from Western Rome, while the Russian civilisation has more cultural heritage from the Byzantine Empire. Russia inherited liberal Enlightenment values from its shared civilisation with the West, such as equality, science, humanism, and even democracy. Albeit, its traditions, community and spirituality developed distinctively, contributed to Russia becoming a balance to Western liberalism.

Russian civilisation developed from the Slavs' interactions with the Vikings in the north and the Byzantine Empire in the south (Quigley 1966: 81). The Mongol invasion of Kievan Rus from the east also had a profound impact by separating Russia from the Byzantine Empire and Europe. Western Europe then rose from the 1500s as powerful maritime states with sea-based empires, while Russia established itself as primarily a land-based power. Russia's Western borders became most vulnerable to foreign invasions over the next 500 years. The Poles invaded in 1605, the Swedes in 1707, the French in 1812, the Germans in 1914 and in 1941, and the collective West armed with nuclear weapons under US leadership has since remained the principal threat to Russia's existence.

To survive in the European neighbourhood, it became imperative for Russia to establish itself as a modern great power. Efforts by Peter the Great to modernise Russia entailed drastic revisions imposed on culture and language to make Russia more European. Modernisation commenced prior to his reign; however, Peter the Great radically amplified these initiatives. St. Petersburg was constructed as Russia's 'window to Europe' and was made the capital in 1712 to cement Russia's status as a European power. As St. Petersburg was a port city full of foreigners, the commercial and political interactions with Europe increased. Peter the Great also constructed a powerful navy to develop Russia as a maritime power like its European counterparts. Besides economic and military development, the European Enlightenment movement and political liberalism also seduced Russia.

Following victory in the Napoleonic wars, Russia's status as a European great power was solidified (Neumann 2008: 138). The subsequent Concert of Europe, which would be in existence for the next hundred years, introduced a modern European international order that envisioned rule based on consensus instead of force. This established a conservative order in Europe as a balance of power became the foundation for the European order, while the violent expansion of the liberal ideals of the French Revolution and other revolutionary movements were curtailed. Yet, Western Europe gradually embraced more liberal forms of governance, while Russia held on to an autocratic form of governance that also stifled its economic development.

Russia's image as a great power was shattered in the Crimean War between 1853 and 1856. The humiliating and costly defeat in the Crimean War devastated the Russian economy and precipitated the need to swiftly industrialise and modernise Russia (Blackwell 2015: 184). It became evident to Russia that sustaining a prolonged war required modern infrastructure for logistical support, and an industrialised economy that could be converted to become an autonomous supplier for Russia's war efforts. During the war, Russia could not use commercial vessels to supplement the navy, competitive modern technologies were in deficit, supplies were short and delayed as armaments had to be imported, and even the transportation infrastructure was severely underdeveloped as railroads to Crimea were absent and there was a lack of horses. The underdeveloped society had made fighting a war problematic and brought the state to its knees. Reliance on the agricultural sector for grain exports was not sufficient in terms of income and it made Russia too reliant of weather conditions, which resulted in the large population becoming vulnerable to periodic famines.

Russian geoeconomics and gesellschaft

The lessons from the Crimean War had been learned and by the end of the 19th century, Russia was modernising by embracing geoeconomic policies consistent with economic nationalist philosophy. Russia's Finance Minister, Sergei Witte, even published a paper in 1889 translating the economic theories of Friedrich List that had been implemented in the US and Germany. Industries, transportation corridors, and new mechanisms for economic and financial cooperation were established. The principal risks derived from the reliance on foreign financing and the demise of gemeinschaft.

Industries were developed with social and economic reforms. Recognising the weakness of a feudal state, Russia had liberated the serfs from the landlords with the Emancipation Reform in 1861. The market economy was intended to strengthen the economy and thereby also the military. Economic policies aimed to develop a powerful manufacturing base by reducing imports and increasing exports, to liberate Russia from its low-ranking position in value-chains as an exporter of agricultural products and importer of manufactured goods. Witte largely continued the policies of his predecessor, Vyshnegradsky, by attempting to achieve greater symmetry in Russia's unequal trade relationship with Western powers. The Russian state intervened in the market to 'climb the ladder' in international economic value-chains. Tariffs were placed on manufactured imports to assist infant industries, such as the Tariff Act in 1891 that provided protection for Russian cotton, iron, and industrial machinery. Throughout the 1890s, Russia subsequently became the fastest growing major economy in the world.

Finance minister Pyotr Stolypin, Witte's successor, implemented successful agrarian reforms that further enhanced the rights and productivity of peasants. The reform laid the foundation for a market-based agricultural sector. Yet, the modernisation entailed weakening the communes and replacing them with a loyal class of wealthy middle class peasant farmers. The Peasant Land bank was established in 1906 to provide loans, indented to empower peasants to abandon the communes and establish independent farms. Communes were eventually broken up in 1910 and the booming population was encouraged to migrate towards the east along the path of the Trans-Siberian Railway. The right of private ownership and the agrarian bank was intended to develop a wealthy middle class of private landowners among the peasants. Within the decade from 1905 to 1915, land ownership among peasants grew from 20 percent to 50 percent. Yet, the dislodgements from the communes were widely resisted among the peasants, as the traditional community had been the source of collective security. The unprecedented concentration of power within the agricultural sector caused dismay, and the rich landowners would later be labelled by Bolsheviks as exploitative kulaks and were subsequently purged.

Transportation corridors were imperative for the development of Russia. The lack of roads and rail made Russia dependent on using its superb river systems. Though, connectivity would diminish when the rivers froze for several months a year. The various regions of Russia developed greater autonomy by producing and consuming locally, which strengthened the community but limited the productive potential of the society. While a source of regional economic autonomy and community, it stifled the power of the authorities. Russia developed initially as a quasi-colonial economy with the first railroads from 1857 and onwards being financed by French, British, and German corporations to extract Russian resources. The construction of railroads declined during the economic depression in Western Europe between the 1870s and 1890s. Once Witte came to power, railroads developed at an unprecedented rate. Russia developed more railway than any other state in the world to connect the vast territory, with positive synergy effects for energy extraction. Russia's 31,219 kilometres of rail in 1891 reached 53,234 kilometres in 1900 and 70,156 by 1913. New territories were accessible for economic activity, yet the wealth tended to concentrate as peasants in the rural areas gained less.

Having learned from the lack of logistical support during the Crimean War, this lesson was applied to expansion into Central Asia. Once Russia conquered new territory, roads and rail were constructed to cement the territory into the Russian empire and prepare the logistical support for conquering new threats at its periphery. The network of Russian railroads intensified the Anglo-Russian rivalry in Central Asia that had initially begun in 1815 and became known as the 'Great Game'. Britain emerged as a modern maritime power, wielding immense economic power by increasingly dominating the world and the Eurasian periphery from the seas. In contrast, Russia was a traditional large land-based military power with little economic strength. Napoleon had previously encouraged Russia to use its prerogative as a dominant Eurasian land-power to undermine the British port-based empire, which became increasingly feasible as Russia pushed south. Towards the end of the 1820s, Britain was alarmed by Russia's annexations of Ottoman and Persian territory, seemingly destined to also control the coastal regions. Concurrently, the growing ideological gap coincided with power interests as Britain began to implement democratic reforms in the 1830s, while Russia was reliant on authoritarian means to uphold its influence in Eastern Europe. Aspiring to establish a Eurasian North–South land-based transportation corridor, Russian railways were directed towards India. Fearing for its colonial control over India,

Britain invaded Afghanistan to create a buffer zone between the Russian Empire and the British India.

By the early 1900s, the trans-Siberian railway established an East–West land corridor as another front to challenge to British maritime power. The trans-Siberian Railway had the geoeconomic strategic intention of making Russia the principal intermediary between Europe and East Asia. Following Britain's victory over China in the Opium Wars, London established a strong presence in East Asia. Yet, China's subsequent weakness also enabled Russia to appropriate 1.5 million square kilometres of territory in the Far East from China, which gave Russia a long border along the Pacific Coast. Mackinder (1904: 434) cautioned that Russia was challenging the dominance of the maritime transportation corridor as the bedrock of British power:

> Steam and the Suez Canal appeared to have increased the mobility of sea-power relatively to land-power. Railways acted chiefly as feeders to ocean-going commerce. But transcontinental railways are now transmuting the conditions of land-power and nowhere can they have such effect as in the closed heartland of Euro-Asia.

However, while Russia appeared to prevail in the rivalry with Britain, the Mackinder's forecast was disrupted by the rise of new powers such as Germany, Japan, and the US. Russia failed to establish itself as a formidable naval power on the Pacific Coast when it tried to undermine the power of Japan. Russia's land-based connectivity was underdeveloped to adequately support a war with Japan, yet Russia was reluctant to reach a compromise with Tokyo to harmonise interests. Japan was alarmed by the growing influence of the Tsar in Manchuria and Korea, while the expectations of growing influence of Russia in the region incentivised Japan to declare war in 1904 when it still had an advantage. The miscalculation by Russia resulted in a costly defeat.

The lack of control over international economic and financial mechanisms for cooperation was also a profound weakness for Russia. The rapid industrialisation under the policies of Witte had made Russia excessively reliant on loans from foreign banks. By 1900, foreigners held close to half of the industrial capital in the country. The rapid industrialisation to catch up with Europe had required substantial foreign loans, culminating in excessive dependence on stability in Europe and Asia. This made Russia especially exposed due to instabilities in the early 1900s. Furthermore, the reliance on foreign loans continued an unequal partnership with the West and was detested by large parts of Russia, adding insult to the shift away from agriculture.

Slavophile Eurasianism to augment gemeinschaft

The debate between Slavophiles and Westernisers was greatly impacted by Russia's turn to economic statecraft. The Slavophiles had emerged as a protest to the westernisation initiated by Peter the Great. Slavophilism shared profound similarities with the theory of Tönnies (1957[1887]) regarding gemeinschaft and gesellschaft. The organic and spiritual Russian culture was contrasted with the moral decadence of industrial Europe. Slavophiles cautioned against being infected by following the modernising model of the Western Europeans, and the westernisers of Russia were largely seen as the embodiment of this modernisation virus that had to be contained and reversed. Following the fragmentation of the Roman Empire, the excessively individualistic Western Europeans were believed to have gone down a perilous road as they would have to face a dilemma: 'Rome kept unity at the expense of freedom. Protestants had freedom but lost unity' (Khomyakov 1895). For the westernisers, the Mongol invasion had split Russia from its native European civilisation and progress entailed returning to the European family. In contrast, Slavofile thinkers of the Eurasian movement, such as Savitsky and Trubetskoy, argued that the Mongols had protected the Orthodox Church and defended Russia from the decadence of the Roman-Germanic world (Mirsky 1927).

   With striking similarities to Thomas Jeffersons's idealised agrarian society, Khomyakov (1895) argued that Russians living in agrarian communities had higher moral standing, were better Christians, and were more united. Haxthausen (1856) similarly recognised the value of Russia's preservation of its traditional rural communities as a source for unity and cohesion. Haxthausen's fascination with rural Russia was largely a response to the declining community in his native Western Europe, where increasingly complex political and economic structures were adopted. Maritime powers were depicted to be imperialist by nature and had to be balanced by a strong Eurasian continental power. Writers such as Tolstoy, with international appeal, also celebrated the simple life and the spirituality of traditional Russian agrarian communities.

   The challenge for Russia has been to combine the advanced society of Western Europe, while preserving 'sobornost', the spiritual unity and religious communities of Russia (Khomyakov 1895). Suggestive of Plato's striving towards a middle ground or metaxy, Voegelin (1974) posits that Man moves between the material world and the emotional consciousness. Lossky (1952) likewise recognised the dichotomy between reawakening the spiritual community and developing complex society, and built on Hegel's dialectical approach by arguing in favour of recognising the contradictions in order to harmonise them.

   The push towards a romantic and spiritual gemeinschaft-based civilisation manifested itself as Eurasianism. The establishment of new frontiers by Russia's rapid eastern expansion in the late 19th century spurred the belief in a spiritual revival. Suvchinsky postulated that Russia's destiny in the vast East augmented its appealing mystical character (Mirsky 1952). A Eurasian orientation would therefore replenish the spiritual depth of traditional communities that had been eroded by cultural simplification in complex industrialised societies (Leontiev 1875). Dostoyevsky (1994[1881]: 1373) advocated for a Eurasian frontier, comparing it to the American frontier:

   When we turn to Asia, with our new view of her, something of the same sort may happen to us as happened to Europe when America was discovered. For, in truth, Asia for us is that same America which still have not been discovered. With our push towards Asia we will have a renewed upsurge of spirit and strength. Just as soon as we become more independent we'll at once find out what we have to do; but living with Europe for two centuries we've become unaccustomed to any kind of activity and have become windbags and idlers.

The instability in the early 1900s that eventually culminated in the revolution in 1917 was indicative of the failure to reach a balance. The failure to embrace liberal reforms in the political sphere made Russia incapable of responding to social challenges emanating from rapid industrialisation over the past 25 years (Neumann 2008). The shift away from agriculture dislodged people from the traditional rural communities that Russian traditions and spirituality had rested upon. The geoeconomic rise and decline of the community was not compensated by the increasing affluence and standard of living for average Russians. The loss of autonomy of the worker was compounded by the growing economic and social inequalities. The rapid growth and industrialisation had concentrated the wealth in the upper class, while the influx of labourers into the cities had resulted in poor living conditions as the populations of Moscow and St. Petersburg doubled within the span of a few years. The poor planning of cities to accommodate people caused discontent. The unions crumbled, which left workers without legal protection and subsequently exposed to exploitation. As the affluence of the rich rose and the wealth of the workers stagnated, economic growth skewed the balance of power and enabled the upper class to increasingly dominate the working class. Subsequently, the flaws in Russia's economic statecraft were interpreted by the Marxists as a failure of capitalism.

Communist and post-communist neglect of gemeinschaft and gesellschaft

Communism did not create a new Man by transcending gemeinschaft and gesellschaft, instead the maintenance of the community and advancement of society was neglected. Russian economic statecraft for the following decades and Eurasianism was demoted to a backward geopolitical project, resulting in domestic underdevelopment and excessive reliance on the military in foreign policy. Soviet Eurasianism lacked the economic statecraft that had made Eurasian geoeconomics a modernising project, and it failed to reproduce the traditional. The communists were extremely hostile to nationhood, religion, and culture. The Russian Orthodox Church was purged, which had exercised an essential role in developing the national identity, culture, and spirituality of Russian character and community. Uspenskii, a former Red Army commander, lambasted the Left for betraying Russian spirituality:

Everything connected with the people, its way of life, its faith and religion, all of this is alien to our left-wingers. Not only do they not accept the faith of the people, but they are also hostile to the most sublime manifestations of the people's national spirit. To them Tolstoi is a religious fool, Dostoevskii an obscurantist, even Pushkin expresses the culture of the nobility. And this is without even mentioning their hatred for all Russian philosophers, from Khomiakov to Bulgakov. For them the Russian historical experience is merely foul soil which has to be cleared away, and that's where their historical intolerance, lack of moderation, and desire to create a social miracle comes from. So where do little kids and old men and women come in? We'll just create history as fast as possible according to our own plan. At the moment people believe in it, and if anyone doesn't we'll make them.

(Gillespie 1989: 202)

[handwritten margin notes: "Today in NS / NYTimes Putin's "Creating own reality""]

The ideological and military frontiers of the Soviet Union functioned as a temporary remedy for the decline of community. Yet, Lenin's promise of an unattainable Marxist utopia imperilled the legitimacy of the authorities and the state. The absence of economic statecraft undermined economic development, while political authoritarianism made Moscow incapable of responding adequately to stagnation. Albeit, it is a common misperception in the West that the legitimacy of the Soviet authorities was predominantly challenged by liberal pro-Western political forces. The Slavophiles became a formidable opponent to communist authorities as they had perverted the collective ethos of Eurasianism.

Civilisational disorientation ensued in the post-Soviet era. Following the economic and moral bankruptcy of institutions in the illiberal Soviet system, the pendulum swung to the embrace of neo-liberalism as another dangerous extreme. Russia was in dire need of replenishing its community after more than seven decades of communism, followed by the loss of its state, ideology, and much of its territory. Instead, the objective of becoming more like the West entailed denouncing traditional Russian values as out-dated and instead celebrating radical individualism and materialism. Russia in the 1990s appeared to be vulnerable to its own identity politics. Following the demise of the Soviet Union, the possible disintegration of the Russian Federation became a distinct possibility, from the Urals, Tatarstan, and most violently in Chechnya. The challenge was to cement a national identity for a multi-ethnic Russia, which had been supressed during the Soviet Union. A Russian general commented on the situation in the region of Tatarstan in Russia: 'half the population is building mosques, the other half is building churches. And the bosses are building big brick houses for themselves' (Mann 2005: 23–24).

Adopting the neo-liberal economic policies of the West was even more destructive to communities in post-communist states, which were ill prepared for the radically different societal dynamics due to the absence of the long-standing individualist ethos and political culture. A dying community was evident by low birth rates, sparking assumptions in the West that Russians were 'voting with the womb' to end their own existence, while life expectancy also plummeted to horrific levels. Russians experienced the loss of a country and ideals, dislodged communities, and broken families. Putin (2005) framed the challenges of the new Russia by referring to its dramatic birth:

Let me remind you again of how modern Russian history began. First of all, it should be acknowledged, and I have spoken of this before, that the collapse of the Soviet Union was the greatest geopolitical catastrophe of the century. And for the Russian people, it was a real drama. Tens of millions of our citizens and fellow-countrymen found themselves outside the Russian Federation. Moreover, the epidemic of disintegration spread to Russia itself. Citizens' savings lost their value. The old ideals were destroyed. Many institutions were disbanded or simply hastily reformed . . . With unrestricted control over information flows, groups of oligarchs served exclusively their own corporate interests. Mass poverty started to be accepted as the norm. All this evolved against a background of the most severe economic recession, unstable finances and paralysis in the social sphere. It seemed to many at the time that our young democracy was not the continuation of Russian statehood, but its final collapse, the prolonged death throes of the Soviet system.

Gorbachev ✓
? Conned
by the
West
?

Yeltsin operated under the false premise that economic liberalism and unambiguous commitment to the West would culminate in affluence within a Greater Europe. Instead, the domestic disunity became an existential threat to the Russian Federation, while the West ensured that the main institutions of Europe would maximise collective bargaining power to enhance asymmetrical interdependence vis-à-vis Russia. Neoliberal economic reforms stripped the Russian state of control over strategic markets. By privatising the vast natural resources, Moscow could not use economic statecraft as a tool to improve the dilapidating social conditions at home or use energy to obtain a voice in international affairs. Instead, in what became known as a 'criminal revolution', the resources were concentrated in the hands of a few oligarchs who would use these resources to exert their influence over the state. Chaos ensued, expressed economically as mass poverty, financial paralyse, crime, and corruption, while oligarchs pillaged the country for their own personal interests. Russia was set to return to a quasi-colonised economy akin to what it had been in the mid-19th century by merely supplying natural resources to the West. With the West gradually courting the oligarchs that were taking control over the country, the political independence of Russia was also at stake.

Imperial overstretch had collapsed the Russian state for a second time in the 20th century as resources were transferred from the core to the periphery, in the process acquiring more adversaries. Revival of the Russian community and society required stability along its borders to focus on domestic development. Putin (2011) expressed this sentiment as he quoted Pyotr Stolypin: 'Give Russia 20 years of internal and external peace and quiet and it will change beyond recognition.' A popular 'Island Russia' theory emerged similar to the idea that the US prospered as an island defended by the Atlantic and Pacific Ocean. A much more passive foreign policy that would allow for resources to be directed to domestic development could exist by ensuring its periphery was surrounded by a 'sea' of space free from geopolitical rivalry (Tsymbursky 1993). In the north is the Arctic Ocean; in the south there are deserts and mountain regions; in the east vast uninhabited spaces; and without the Soviet territories in the West, Russia had also disconnected itself from Europe and yet again become an 'island'. Russia could maintain its island status as the source of security if it resisted imperial ambitions and avoided constructing an anti-Western coalition (Tsymbursky 1993).

The main challenge would be to prevent incursion by rival civilisations into its adjacent 'waters' by creating buffers and this became Russia's main challenge. Russian security was contingent on ensuring that there were Russian-friendly governments on its borders, rather than annexing the territory as borders further to the west would move Island Russia closer to Europe. If Western expansionism would end Ukraine's buffer status, Tsymbursky (1993) advocated that Russia should intervene and establish the regions east of the Dnieper as independent states. Russia's policy towards the buffer regions appears to promote Russian-friendly independent states as opposed to merely moving its borders closer to the West. Crimea should be the exception due to the military, economic, and cultural significance of the peninsula. Eastern Ukraine should be treated in accordance with the Island Russian thesis. As Karaganov (2017a) argued:

> Russia should press for undelayed broad autonomy for Donbass within Ukraine. Later, Russia should work towards the emergence of a neutral, independent and Russia-friendly Ukraine or many Ukraines, if Kiev fails to retain control over the entire territory of the country. The only way for Ukraine to survive is to turn from an object of rivalry into a bridge and a buffer.

Huntington's (1993a) *Clash of Civilizations* likewise advocated for clearly delineating the civilisational borders to avoid skirmishes. Between Europe and Russia, especially the Ukraine, Georgia, and Moldova stand out as the populations that are divided between the gravitational pull towards the West and Russia. There are fewer divisions within the Baltic States, yet the political oppression of the Russian-speaking population was necessary to convert the region from a bridge to a bulwark. The shared civilisational space of the former territory of the Soviet Union and the Russian Empire was unravelled. Russia's former fellow citizens were also in need of cementing statehood and sovereignty by rediscovering a distinct identity, which was manifested in de-Russification policies to marginalise ethnic Russians and purge the Russian language and culture. In the international sphere, Russia was incapable of upholding its red lines to preserve its security.

Russia was unable to resists continuous waves of NATO enlargements, the development of missile defence systems, support for the colour revolutions in Georgia and Ukraine in 2003 and 2004, military force against Yugoslavia, Iraq and Libya, and re-drawing borders in Europe with the de facto NATO annexation of Kosovo. Transportation corridors were similarly severed as physical infrastructure, regulations, and laws that were previously unified in a common Soviet system split along the new sovereign borders. NATO expansion placed further limitations on Russian freedom of navigation by advancing US influence and presence in the Baltic Sea and the Black Sea. The West pushed for new energy pipelines through the Georgia-Azerbaijan energy corridor to push back Russian influence. This pipeline mimicked the Batumi-Baku railroad transportation corridor that Mackinder had advocated to assert control over almost a century earlier as a geoeconomic tool of an anti-Russian alliance. To firmly establish this anti-Russian bulwark, the US funded and trained the Georgian military, which increased more than 10-fold in the five years from the Western-backed 'Rose Revolution' in 2003 to the Georgian attack on South Ossetia in 2008 (Stalenheim, Perdomo and Skons 2008). Supporting the ethno-cultural nationalists in Ukraine against the Eastern Slavic nationalists was similarly instrumental in converting Ukraine into an anti-Russian bastion.

The return of Russia?

The rise of Russia is disputable, which is contested in the West. The portrayal of Russia by Western politicians, media, and academia is contradictory as both a backward declining power, and as a menace growing in power. The imminent political, economic, and social collapse of Russia has been predicted for almost three decades, while concurrently making dire forecasts about Russia re-establishing the Soviet Empire, undermining the West's liberal democratic order, and invading NATO members. Russia is labelled a weak regional power, and still blamed for grand conspiracies by pulling strings behind most of the West's most pressing problems. These inconsistent depictions derive from Russia continuing its spectacular rise from the ashes of the devastating 1990s, while it remains uncertain if the lingering internal and external challenges can be overcome.

Once in power, the Putin administration instantaneously embraced geoeconomic principles for state-building and region-building, and forcefully repudiated its nascent colonial status. Natural resources were nationalised to develop a strong middle class and scale back the intrusive influence of oligarchs who were increasingly courted by the West. The development of large national corporations within the energy sphere made Russia competitive in international markets, provided an indispensable revenue stream, and political influence. Economic incentives were used to promote friendly governments along its periphery. Case in point, Russia's energy discounts were traded with Ukraine in return for extending the lease of the strategic port in Sevastopol.

Yet, Russia's continued geoeconomic development requires a drastic diversification of strategic industries, substantial investments in new competitive physical transportation corridors, and the development of new mechanisms for international economic and financial cooperation. The geoeconomic revival of Russia has severe flaws to be resolved. The dark side of the impressive recovery in the 2000s was the energy curse, as easy money made from exporting natural resources made it easier to import of manufactured goods rather than embrace painful reforms. Furthermore, Europe's increasing reliance on Russian energy did not culminate in a post-Cold War settlement that reformed the zero-sum structures. Russia did not achieve the required asymmetrical advantage as Europe's reliance on Russian energy supplies was balanced by Russia's excessive dependence on Europe for demand (Diesen 2017).

Russia's resurgent military power makes it possible to enforce red lines, and it has made its foreign policy increasingly influential in international affairs. In Georgia in 2008, Ukraine in 2014, and Syria from 2015, Russia demonstrated its ability to balance Western-backed revision and maintain the status quo by military force. To have its voice in international affairs, Moscow must establish itself as a great power, an indispensable security guarantor along its periphery from Europe, the Middle East, Central Asia, East Asia, and the Arctic. However, military successes can paradoxically undermine the long-term standing of Russia by elevating individuals in the government who view the military rather than geoeconomics as the preferable tool. The costs of an expensive military must be balanced with additional revenue by for example increasing its weapons sales, expanding economic connectivity, or other geoeconomic synergy effects. Furthermore, Moscow must ensure that its growing role as a security provider endows it with more allies than adversaries.

Socio-politically, Russia has not yet developed a coherent civilisational idea to unite the country and offer an alternative to the West. Political stability in Russia excessively relies on Putin's popularity and political legitimacy, which resulted from saving the Russia from the perilous 1990s and delivering prosperity and stability. Eventually, political legitimacy and stability must be transferred to strong institutions rooted in grand unifying ideas. The absence of a civilisational idea is evident by the lack of sufficient continuity from the past, and attractive forward-looking ideas. Russia enjoys post-communist pragmatism, yet a clear ideological foundation is required for unity and soft power in the wider world.

Efforts to develop cultural influence or soft power have been a long-standing objective. The Soviets initially attempted to build an empire through culture and ideology as soft power to obtain support for the post-war order (Babiracki 2015). The victory of fascism became a cornerstone of Soviet attractiveness, which remains crucial in the national identity. As a strong advocate of de-colonisation, Moscow's communist ideology became attractive across the third world and evoked sympathies among various groups in the West. The inspiring virtues of social equality compelled the US to shift its ideological narrative from capitalism versus communism to democracy versus authoritarianism. However, over the following years Europe de-colonised and thereby weakened the ties between capitalism and imperialism. Concurrently, the Soviet Union introduced new forms of oppression. The soft power achieved from defeating fascism and saving Europe had already been undermined from the 1950s and 1960s when hard power was used against Hungary and Czechoslovakia (Nye 2004: 9). The US was also successful in propagandising 'totalitarianism' by exaggerating the similarities between Nazi Germany and Soviet Russia and neglecting the differences (Adler and Paterson 1970). The Soviets' ideological inconsistency became more evident as repression and misuse of military force undermined its role as the guardian of human freedoms (Rutland and Kazantsev 2016: 399).

Moscow's renewed efforts to develop a positive imagery of Russia throughout the 2000s were not directly contrasted with a decaying Western culture. Russia's pursuit of soft power has mostly focused on taking ownership over communicating the imagery and narratives of Russia, as opposed to developing alternative political and economic ideas. Yet, the Soviet ideas about soft power still lingers in Russia's conception of soft power, which centres on social progress and justice (Lukyanov 2013). These ideas are promoted though Russian culture, the media, and groups of 'Russia's friends' (Lukyanov 2013). The concept of 'cultural diplomacy' was introduced by President Medvedev. Putin (2012) defined soft power as:

> The promotion of one's own interests and approaches through persuasion and attraction of empathy towards one's own country, based on its achievements not only in the material sphere but also in the spheres of intellect and culture . . . Russia's image abroad is not formed by us, because it is often distorted and does not represent the real situation in our country nor our contribution to global civilization, science, culture, and the position of our country in international affairs. Those who are shooting and sending out rocket attacks left and right are praised, while those who warn about the need for a restrained dialog are somehow guilty. And we are guilty for having failed to explain our position.

Soft power then made its way into the Foreign Policy Concept in 2013, defined as 'a comprehensive toolkit for achieving foreign policy objectives building on civil society potential, information, cultural and other methods and technologies alternative to traditional diplomacy'. The exclusive focus on a 'golden past' omits the forward-looking component. The anti-imperial solidarity movement has been recreated to a lesser extent by resisting Western expansionism, yet Russia was not a real obstruction to the West and de-colonialism has become out-dated (Lukyanov 2013). The mere label of the 'post-Soviet space' is as ambiguous as the 'post-Cold War era', a mere reference to what it used to be but that no longer exists.

Conclusion

Russia is at a civilisational crossroads as it grows in strength at a time when a post-Western world is emerging. Yet, Russia concurrently needs to rejuvenate its weakened community and prepare its society for an increasingly complex world. A grand civilisational idea and identity that incorporates a socio-economic and military role in a rapidly changing world is imperative. The history of Russia from the Crimean War, the Bolshevik Revolution, and the neoliberal policies under the Yeltsin era should stand as a warning to avoid radical shifts between the traditional and modern. Russia has the formidable task of not reducing the zero-sum domestic rivalry between traditionalists/nationalists who demand economic statecraft, and cosmopolitans/globalists who seek laissez-faire capitalism. Moscow must embrace political pluralism in terms of accommodating both socio-economic conservativism and liberalism to experiment towards a balance, and avoid radical swings caused by the inclination in human nature to seek absolute truths. Finding a middle ground or metaxy requires Russia to embrace its ethno-cultural and civic distinctiveness, and concurrently modernise and develop a competitive society to become an influencer rather than a mere recipient of globalisation. The relative decline of the West and identity crisis will likely produce instability and erratic behaviour, while a bourgeoning and confident Asia presents new Eurasian threats and opportunities.

8 Russia's Eurasian resurgence

Neomodernism and geoeconomics

Introduction

Neomodernism and geoeconomics offer a more viable alternative to the Western-centric order based on liberal democracy and free-market capitalism. The neomodernist and geoeconomic tenets built into Russia's new Eurasianism is not a clearly articulated policy of Russia. The purpose of this chapter is to explore the rational systemic incentives to embrace this approach and compare it to the indications of Russia gradually pursuing these inducements. Decision-makers are not always rational and, much like in the past, a shock to the system caused by economic collapse, war, or a revolutionary movement could easily derail Russia from its current trajectory.

Russia's aspirations to integrate into a Western-centric world or a 'Greater Europe' after the Cold War were reasonable at the time. The economic and moral bankruptcy of the Soviet system contrasted with a more attractive model, and seemingly the only alternative – the modern European welfare state with free trade and liberal political liberalism as the instrument for prosperity and organising society. The destiny of the new Russia appeared to be a conservative capitalist European nation state with its roots in Christianity, family values, and European traditions. However, the foundations for a Greater Europe quickly diminished as the West rejected the inclusion of Russia in the European family, and then Europe began to abandon the qualities that had made it attractive. Initially, Moscow focused on the West's efforts to create a new Europe without Russia as NATO and the EU became the principal organisations to represent the continent. These institutions continued until the Cold War division of Europe by facilitating collective bargaining and asymmetrical interdependence. Moscow is engaged by NATO and the EU, but only in 28+1 formats (member states versus Russia) to create 'interdependence' that minimise Russia's autonomy and influence. Later, Moscow's desire to be part of the new 'Europe' also diminished as the West gradually began to lose its geoeconomic prowess, while excessive liberalism decimated the previous balance with conservativism.

With relative power rapidly shifting from the West to the East, Russia's efforts to both modernise and preserve the traditional will undergo fundamental change. The geographic dilemma of choosing the West to modernise or a Eurasian orientation to reproduce the traditional is now waning after more than 500 years of Western dominance. The new international distribution of power warrants a reconceptualisation of Eurasianism due to the geoeconomic rationale of pivoting to the East, and feasibility of a neomodern philosophy as an alternative to returning to modernism or following the West's tragic experimentation with postmodernism.

Eurasianism offers a strand of neomodernism and geoeconomics that can balance gemeinschaft and gesellschaft. The new Eurasianism builds on classical Slavophile conceptions of Eurasia that embrace the traditional and modern, while offering geoeconomic competitiveness and a new frontier. There are still competing conceptions of Eurasianism, and the strand of neomodernism and geoeconomics to be pursued by Russia will be contingent on domestic and international influences. The purpose of this chapter is to assess the systemic pressures towards which Russia appears to be gravitating. Still, unforeseen disruptions to the domestic or international system could result in a different path. The dramatic shift of geoeconomic power from the West to the East radically changes the concept of Eurasia for Russia. The dichotomy between Western modernity and Eastern spirituality diminishes. Russia's economic prowess is advanced by pivoting to the East, while the ability to preserve the community is also easier due to the vast geographical expanse.

This chapter first explores the rising political neomodernism in Russia. Neomodernism attempts to balance and bridge the traditional with the advanced by restoring the equilibrium between liberalism and conservativism. Neomodernism calls for a resurgence in romanticist nationalism due to the central role of the state to replicate the community. Russia needs to develop as an entity of power with strengthened collective identity and shared spirituality, with the capability to pursue shared interests to advance society. Neomodernism requires grand narratives that emphasise historical continuity and greater truths. Moscow will engage the international system on the principle of restoring the balance between the distinctive and the universal, by reproducing Russia's own culture and developing universal, rules-based and pragmatic formats for international collaboration. Russia is drawn towards neomodernist ideas for both domestic and international reasons. Domestically, it is imperative to restore the community and society that was suppressed by the communists. Internationally, Russia benefits from establishing common cause with classical conservatives in the West who also aim to preserve shared traditions and Christian heritage. Eurasianism can negate the radical shifts between a modern European identity and a traditional/ spiritual Eurasian identity by facilitating the middle ground.

Second, Russia's inclinations towards Eurasian geoeconomics will be surveyed. The gravitation towards Eurasian geoeconomics can elevate Russia in global value-chains to create more favourable symmetry in the economically interdependent world. Russia's Western-centric foreign policy and initiative to create a 'Greater Europe' condemned Russia to the margins of a geoeconomic constellation hostile to Russian influence. Eurasian geoeconomics presents Russia with greater capacity to use its territory to skew the balance of dependence by diversifying partnerships and fostering reliance on Russia. Eurasia offers greater prospects for Russia to assert its influence over strategic industries, transportation, and energy corridors, and new mechanisms for international cooperation where Russia has a seat at the table and can create a more favourable format for globalisation. It will be concluded that neomodernism and geoeconomics can make Russian society more competitive and its community more durable.

What is neomodernism?

Neomodernism responds to the failures of postmodernism. Postmodernist rejection of truths and 'grand narratives' produced radical elusiveness of knowledge and meaning, while even common language is deconstructed. The subsequent cultural and moral relativism has eroded shared and unifying ideas to the extent that it impedes internal cohesion and the ability to organise domestic and international relations. Neomodernism represents a cyclical development between chaos and order. The postmodern introduced chaos by deconstructing all walls that brought order by defining us and the other. The neomodern represents the return of order by erecting walls. A return to the utopianism, absolutism, and excessive rationalism of modernism is also not attractive as unconstrained political liberalism is destined to follow the path of communism and fascism. An even further return to premodernism is also not possible or desirable since the excessive embrace of the irrational undermines the ability to advance society to obtain opportunities for the populace and competitiveness for the state. Rather than following the postmodernist criticism of European post-enlightenment modernity as a social construction to mask oppressive power relations, neomodernism suggests that modernity without the premodern eviscerates social capital.

Neomodernism revives the philosophies of the 19th century that recognised and embraced the contradictory impulses of Man. Eschewing the premise of a possible and pending utopia, neomodernism instead recognises that the evolutionary biology has destined human beings to an imperishable struggle between community and society, the rational and irrational, the modern and traditional, and order and chaos. It is difficult to balance these contradictions due to what Plato recognised to be a human trait, the inclination to use strong contrasts to express truths, which spurs radical and absolutist behaviour. Recognising that Man is flawed, political pluralism is necessary to accommodate opposing beliefs about human nature. Rather than finding a balance between the ideas of liberalism, socialism, and nationalism, the rivalry between the modernist ideologies in the 20th century made each more radical.

Neomodernism recognises the primacy of the nation-state as the ideal vehicle to balance the traditional and modern. The nation-state has proven its ability to construct collective identity and spirituality, define shared interests, mobilise resources to achieve economic prosperity and advance human freedoms, and reduce chaos in the international system as sovereignty diminished overlapping authorities. The homogenising nation-state ideally functions as a melting pot by ironing out internal differences to enhance unity, and delineating distinctive external conceptual borders. National unity derives from a strong ethno-cultural core and civic ideals that offer transcendent grand narratives and truths that all of society can gravitate towards. Some sub-groups and communities who seek to reproduce their distinct identity and traditions will almost unavoidably resist the melting pot process. This could produce a societal security dilemma as sub-groups develop the identity of 'we' in opposition to the dominant group and the state as the 'other'. Conversely, without a gravitational pull towards the centre, the state is likely to become divided and 'immoral' due to a lack of internal cohesion and a sense of shared fate. The neomodernist solution is to embrace benign hierarchies, as the culture of distinct indigenous peoples of Russia are nurtured. However, identity of sub-groups in society must be positioned beneath an overarching and dominant Russian culture and patriotism.

Globalisation based on the neoliberal consensus after the Cold War presents an obvious threat to political pluralism. Much like biodiversity, political diversity allows better handling of crisis: 'Universalism, if realized, would result in a sharp decline of the complexity of the global society as a while and the international system in particular. Reducing complexity, in turn, would dramatically increase the level of systemic risks and challenges' (Kortunov 2017a). Neomodernism draws on romanticism to restore collective identities and religion as the source of meaning, spirituality, and morality. Civilisations are only durable when modernisation and advancement of society is balanced by the reproducing the traditional. The inner soul or culture of a civilisation is balanced with pragmatic and calculative ways of engaging with external actors.

Neomodernism builds a balance between the distinctive and the universal to engage with the world with a common rule-based system, rather than ambiguous 'common values' that can be applied inconsistently. Neomodernism advocates the state to function as a 'melting pot' that homogenises towards one shared identity. In contrast, the global community should be structured as a 'salad bowl' to preserve the distinctiveness of states. The state has the important role of conserving national identity, traditional values, and the sacred in community. The concept of 'glocalisation' recognises the need to harmonise the distinctiveness of the local with global conformity, as opposed to allowing globalisation to cause cultural homogenisation (Robertson 2012). The profound challenge for the state is to engage with the international community to ensure a seat at the table, which is instrumental in strengthening and defending one's own identity and culture as opposed to conforming to the identities of others. As the proverb goes: 'without a seat at the table, you are likely to be on the menu'.

The West: from a role model to a cautionary tale

Russian gravitation towards neomodernism is largely a response to the failure of Western postmodernism to organise domestic and international affairs. Russia's experimentation and rejection of communism is imperative as postmodernism also attempts to develop a new Man by deconstructing the class relations of the past. Marxist political economy divides the world into class warfare between the oppressive bourgeois and the oppressed proletariat. Cultural postmodernism similarly interprets the tensions in society as a class conflict between the narratives of the privileged and the marginalised.

The Russian nation and the traditional community suffered greatly under the onslaught of communism, and the absence of capitalist tools resulted in insufficient modernisation of society. The decline of Russia's status as a gemeinschaft-based civilisation due to the fragmentation of community and reduced social capital has been the source of its most pressing social problems. The breakdown of the family unit, rise of single-mother parenthood, low birth rates, high mortality and abortion rates, emigration, alcohol and drug abuse, violence, crime, and incarceration are some of the social problems burdening Russia. Furthermore, the absence of a unifying national identity that instils meaning with ideals, tradition, and spirituality can lead to the rise of nihilism, rival loyalties, radicalism, and even secessionism.

Initially, the failure of the Soviet system was contrasted with the success of the West, implying that there were no alternatives to emulating the West. Yet, from the early 1990s, the West began to lose its attractiveness as the state, traditional family values, religion, and gender roles were gradually deconstructed. The embrace of multiculturalism, third-wave feminism, and identity politics were all symptoms of postmodernism gradually deconstructing Western civilisation. Karagnov, a prominent scholar and presidential advisor, submitted that Russia and 'the majority of Europeans' wanted to be part of the Europe of Konrad Adenauer and Charles de Gaulle that valued European Christian heritage, and therefore 'for the next decades, Europe will not be a model that is attractive to Russia' (Neef 2016).

Embracing postmodernism threatens to deconstruct and destroy Russian civilisation (Dugin 2012). While taking a distinctively different approach from Dugin, Putin has made similar remarks concerning his opposition to postmodernism. Putin (2013a) posited:

> We see that many Euro-Atlantic states have taken the way where they deny or reject their own roots, including their Christian roots which form the basis of Western civilization. In these countries, the moral basis and any traditional identity are being denied – national, religious, cultural, and even gender identities are being denied or relativised. There, politics treats a family with many children as juridically equal to a homosexual partnership; faith in God is equal to faith in Satan. The excesses and exaggerations of political correctness in these countries indeed leads to serious consideration for the legitimization of parties that promote the propaganda of paedophilia. The people in many European states are actually ashamed of their religious affiliations and are indeed frightened to speak about them. Christian holidays and celebrations are abolished or "neutrally" renamed, as if one were ashamed of those Christian holidays. With this method one hides away the deeper moral value of those celebrations. And these countries try to force this model onto other nations, globally. I am deeply convinced that this is a direct way to the degradation and primitivization of culture. This leads to deeper demographic and moral crisis in the West. What can be better evidence for the moral crisis of human society in the West than the loss of its reproductive

function? And today nearly all 'developed' Western countries cannot survive reproductively, not even with the help of migrants.

Putin (2013b) later also criticised cultural and moral relativism as a threat to distinctive and transcendent identities:

> Today, many nations are revising their moral values and ethical norms, eroding ethnic traditions and differences between peoples and cultures. Society is now required not only to recognise everyone's right to the freedom of consciousness, political views and privacy, but also to accept without question the equality of good and evil, strange as it seems, concepts that are opposite in meaning.

Russia also has international systemic incentives to formulate a coherent alternative ideology to the liberal democratic order that underpins the Western-centric world order. After the collapse of the Soviet Union, the West replaced the capitalist-communist demarcation with a liberal democracy-authoritarianism divide. Redrawing the ideological boundaries in Europe by focusing on 'common values' rather than compatible values provided support for the new power configuration as NATO and the EU pushed eastwards. George Kennan argued in 1998 in response to NATO expansion to Poland, Hungary, and the Czech Republic: 'Russia's democracy is as far advanced, if not farther, as any of these countries we've just signed up to defend from Russia' (Friedman 1998). Kennan predicted NATO expansionism would compel Russia to respond and thereby spark another Cold War. What Kennan missed was that by using ideology or 'normative leadership' to justify Western collective hegemony and the marginalisation of Russia, Russia's eventual response would likely also include the development of a competing political philosophy.

Moscow scorns 'democractic messianism' as a global Brezhnev doctrine of limited sovereignty by legitimising Western interference across the world in a new civilising mission to shape the world according to its own image (Karaganov 2006). Committing to develop liberal democracy implies endeavouring to become more like its rival powers in the West, which would diminish Russian soft power in the shared neighbourhood and legitimise the West cultivating sovereign inequality by intruding into Russia's domestic affairs under the auspices of socialisation in a teacher-student relationship. Similarly, Russia cannot define its identity as European and simultaneously resist the 'shared neighbourhood' gravitating to Europe (Mezhuyev 2017). Russia's concept of 'sovereign democracy' was an early attempt to counter the West's new Brezhnev doctrine with the idea that democracy cannot exist without sovereignty. Sovereignty is the main principle of international law in the Westphalian system, which suggests that states accept less flexibility in foreign policy in return for more predictability.

Sovereign democracy has evolved towards a more cohesive neomodernist philosophy that aims to reinvent the role of the state and reshape interactions in the international system. The collapse of the Soviet Union freed Russia from ideological commitments and made it more pragmatic, albeit Moscow yearns for an ideology to harmonise its ideas with power interests. Pragmatism towards pursuing national interests and the absence of a political ideology has reduced the prospect of soft power (Rutland and Kazantsev 2016: 400). International competition also creates systemic pressures to drift towards a neomodernism political ideology. The proliferation of neomodernism redraws the battle lines of international competition from the democracy-authoritarian binary divide, towards a traditionalist versus cosmopolitan divide.

Eurasian neomodernism: reviving romantic nationalism and 'grand narratives'

The binary ideological division during the Cold War, mirroring the bipolar power distribution, diluted policy makers to believe there was no alternatives to liberal democracy. Huntington (1993b: 191) posited that:

'deluded'

> There is the argument that the collapse of Soviet communism means the end of history and the universal victory of liberal democracy throughout the world. This argument suffers from the Single Alternative Fallacy. It is rooted in the Cold War assumption that the only alternative to communism is liberal democracy and that the demise of the first produces the universality of the second.

The simple binary ideological divide of the Cold War also blinded both sides to the fact that they were modernist ideologies, which tore away at gemeinschaft. Solzhenitsyn, widely popular in the West for authoring *The Gulag Archipelago* and as a human rights advocate during the era of the Soviet Union, recognised similarities in both liberalism and communism as modern political philosophies. When Solzhenitsyn was invited to Harvard University to receive an honorary degree and give a speech, he surprised the audience by criticising both communism and capitalism for failing to preserve the traditional. Solzhenitsyn (1978: 26) argued that Western civilisation had turned its back on:

> the spirit and embraced all that is material with excessive and unwarranted zeal . . . [Our spiritual life] is destroyed by the dealings and machinations of the ruling party. In the West, commercial interests tend to suffocate it. This is the real crisis. The split in the worlds is less terrible than the similarity of the disease plaguing its main sections.

Solzhenitsyn later became an ardent supporter of Vladimir Putin, arguing against unlimited rights as it would eventually unravel order rather than promote freedom, and that Russia therefore had to find its own democratic path (Horvath 2011).

Liberalism can be constrained as Russia has not philosophically or ideologically committed itself to either the neoliberalism consensus or a postmodernist repudiation of tradition and spirituality. While a nascent individualistic and materialistic culture has emerged, especially among the younger generation, conservative values and pride in traditional culture remain strong and enjoy high legitimacy. The lack of moral authority for political liberalism and without previous successes of economic liberalism, make it feasible to make a reversal to defend traditional culture and build a Eurasian geoeconomic strategy.

It is a risk that Moscow will reject, as opposed to moderate, liberal impulses. Putin (2005) recognised in the past the value of liberal European traditions for modernisation as an important component of Russian civilisation:

> For centuries, the ideals of freedom, human rights, justice and democracy that were gained through suffering and won by European culture, have been a determining value and a guiding principle for us. For three centuries, together with other European nations, hand in hand with them, we have gone through a process of enlightenment and experienced difficulties in setting up parliamentary rule, municipal and judicial power and forming similar legal systems.

Yet, Putin has also been explicit that 'Our society, including the liberals, must understand that there must be order' (Elder 2010). Putin (2013b) claimed that Russian conservativism was not intended to obstruct society from elevating, but prevent it from descending 'into chaotic darkness and a return to a primitive state'. These ideas eventually manifested themselves in Russia's document on the *Foundations of the State Cultural Policy* of 2014, which stated that 'Russia must be viewed as a unique and original civilization' and therefore advocated 'the rejection of such principles as multiculturalism and tolerance' for those 'imposing alien values on society'.

Grand narratives of the Russian soul and identity have been reintroduced to overcome the civilisational disarray left behind after the collapse of the Soviet Union. Historical continuity is imperative in developing a grand narrative, which harmonises the past with a forward-looking vision for the future. Surveying Russia's turbulent history, the memory of the Soviet Union is divided and a consensus shapes around taking pride in the achievement of the people, while condemning the structures of government. Without a past, Russia risks an identity crisis and thus being without a future. Moscow instead distances itself from and condemns Stalinist crimes, such as the Katyn massacre, while proudly claiming ownership over achievements because Russia is the principal successor of the Soviet Union. The educational system recognises the dual role of historical textbooks – to accurately educate about the past and instil patriotism. The refusal to level a blanket condemnation of all Soviet history is usually portrayed in the West as efforts to whitewash Stalin. Ironically, the Russian authorities frequently condemn the crimes of Stalin, and instead seek to rehabilitate the public image of the Tsars that was tarnished by the communists.

The Kremlin has actively collaborated with the Orthodox Church to restore its status and spiritual role within Russia. Putin (2013a) argued that 'without the values embedded in Christianity and other world religions, without standards of morality that have taken shape over millennia, people will inevitably lose their human dignity'. Religion has rapidly recovered from communism and regained its foothold in Russian society. Religion has been important for societal cohesion and unity since Prince Vladimir adopted Orthodox Christianity for his nation. Vladimir allegedly chose Orthodoxy because of the beautiful worship that called on the past, and because the faith was shared by the prosperous and enlightened Byzantine Empire. Mirroring the ideas of Nietzsche, Uspenskii linked morality intrinsically to religion:

> The whole trouble stems from the fact that we look for causes not in ourselves, but outside; in the social environment, in ideology and so on. We don't take into account human nature, that's the trouble, you see . . . And it's exactly human nature, with its unbridled passions, that was the major factor in Ivan the Terrible's oprichnina and in Stepan Razin's dictatorial rule over his outlaw followers. Formally Stepan Razin's men were all equal, but they were still governed by fear, arbitrariness, denunciation, torture and execution. And why? Because the chains of Christian restraint fell away, and everything became permitted.
>
> (Gillespie 1989: 204)

Eurasian neomodernism

Eurasia offers a more convincing path towards neomodernism. Russia's promotion of the 'Russian world' (Russkij Mir) envisions culture not only as the foundation for state-building but also region-building. The Russian world represents the revival of a foundational myth of an ancient civilisational space encompassing primarily the successor states of Kievan Rus, and secondary the other former Soviet Republics. Connecting culturally with the ethno-cultural compatriots in the Russian world is important to restore the ties that broke with the fall of the Soviet Union and thereby augment Russian soft power. Beyond the Russian world, East Asia is today the home of traditional conservative values and economic prosperity. The family and other social institutions in East Asia have demonstrated great capacity to sustain stable communities under pressures from the complex and rapidly evolving economic structures.

Russia's inclinations towards neomodernism bear many similarities to China's nascent neo-Confucianism, an effort to rediscover traditional values, culture, ethics, and social harmony of traditional Confucianism in the face of drastic modernisation. Neo-Confucianism embraces modernisation, yet recognises it must be built on a pre-modern foundation. With rapid economic development and an aversion to utopianism, there were incentives to revive Confucianism to ensure morality and harmony do not become the price of modernisation (Bell 2008). Cultural relativism and universalism, central in communism and Western postmodernism, is threatening the foundation of Chinese civilisation. Consistent with civilisational studies, culture is central in neo-Confucianism as civilisation cannot advance and be reborn without firm roots in cultural continuity.

Gemeinschaft is explicitly referenced in Chinese literature, with frequent citations of Carl Schmidt and Martin Heidegger.

A common view in both Moscow and Beijing is that modernisation entails adopting Western culture. Globalisation introduced powerful market forces that disrupted local communities, as modernisation in the unipolar era equated to accepting Westernisation. The negative effects of globalisation are sought to be balanced by actively reproducing the cultural identity to protect the traditional and ensure globalisation does not become Westernisation. Neo-Confucianism was largely born in the 1920s as a reaction to the excessive rationalism by intellectuals who advocated disposing of Chinese traditionalism and moving towards the more developed West. The anti-Westernism in China and resistance to the destructive power of capitalism eventually manifested itself under communism. More so than in Russia, communism in China was very hostile to traditional community and society. The Cultural Revolution represented the most extreme form of purging to prevent it from contaminating the communist future and the new Man. In the 1980s, ironically when traditional conservativism was abandoned in the West, a new cultural conservativism arose in China (Cha 2003: 482). While the rise of gesellschaft occurred in both the West and China, only in the West did moral legitimisation of gesellschaft occur to combat the leanings toward gemeinschaft. In contrast, China considered gesellchaft as the downfall of morality.

Asia also offers a more attractive democratisation model. The Asian model for democratisation appeals to Moscow for three reasons. First, the priority devoted to national unity as an end is considered a necessity after the collapse and disintegration of the Russian Empire in 1917, the Soviet Union in 1991, and then almost the Russian Federation at the end of the 1990s. Second, democratisation remains a sovereign project by rejecting the emulation of the West as it repudiates the self-proclaimed 'normative leadership' of the West. In the West, it is common to accuse Moscow of being hostile to NATO and the EU due to fears that democracies along Russian borders will eventually challenge the legitimacy of its authorities. However, Russia has excellent relations with Asian democracies, suggesting the concern is about bloc-politics rather than democracy. Third, embracing focus on the collective restrains radical individualism and provides historical continuity for Russia's socialist past.

Asian democracies are commonly argued to sustain 'Asian values' and paternalistic tendencies such as harmony of the collective, community, consensus, and family (Tanji and Lawson 1997; Bell 2007). It is disputed whether an alternative 'Asian model' for democratisation exists due to the pluralism of values, identities, and democratic models across Asia. Furthermore, the authoritarian tendencies in several Asian democracies can be characterised as undemocratic or indications of an underdeveloped democratic consolidation (Hood 1998). Some commonality among Asian democracies are however evident in terms of democratisation being treated to some extent as a means to an end, rather than embodying an inherent good (Reilly 2007). Considering democracy as a means to an end implies that when democracy weakens order and produces social problems, it no longer serves the objective of organising society (Fukuyama 1995).

(handwritten top margin: Sun, am Election Day: Japan Today front page concedes election to ABE vs. female mayor of Tokyo — before the vote! early)

East Asian democracies gradually introduced political freedoms and pluralism to promote national unity, government stability, reduce political fragmentation, and prevent dissatisfaction among the population (Reilly 2007). Newly democratised countries, such as Japan and Taiwan, also centralised power in the early stages of democratisation. Political groups that did not adhere to the established path were purged, while the authorities cultivated an acceptable opposition by engaging in pacts. Economic development is imperative as it restrains radical alternatives and strengthens national unity as a precondition for democratic transition and consolidation. Furthermore, several Asian countries remain persistent that their democracies will not follow the Western model (Fukuyama 1995). Yet, illiberal democracies can struggle to sustain harmony if they descend to mere tyranny of the majority (Zakaria 1997).

The Asian or Eurasian approach to democratisation is consistent with the theories on democratisation by the leading academics in the field. National unity is widely argued to be a fundamental requirement for democracy (Lijphart 1969; Rustow 1970; Diamond 1990; Gill 1995). National unity requires a shared identity and common purpose to define the long-term interests of a country and how to achieve them. National unity is developed among the political elites by negotiating a basic 'cross-party unity', and within the population by cultivating 'social unity' that enhances the sense of belonging to a shared political community. National unity implies that 'the vast majority of citizens in a democracy-to-be must have no doubt or mental reservations as to which political community they belong to' (Rustow 1970: 350). National unity must therefore take priority and precede all other stages of democratisation as political pluralism is unstable when elites are not united (Rustow 1970: 351). Democracy is a paradox as it is based on the notion that political pluralism develops unity, however, this pluralism must be confined within 'accepted boundaries' as 'cleavage must be tempered by consensus' (Diamond 1990: 49). This consensus entails defining what constitutes national interests and what the acceptable means are towards these ends. If the political culture is severely fragmented 'the pressures towards moderate middle-of-the-road attitudes are absent' (Lijphart 1969: 208–209).

In a polarised society, authorities have incentives to limit the scope of political pluralism by constraining disruptive forces that further divide the state. Lijphart (1969: 216) defines 'consociational democracies' as a 'government by elite cartel designed to turn a democracy with a fragmented political culture into a stable democracy'. The role of the elites is to 'make deliberate efforts to counteract the immobilising and unstabilising effects of cultural fragmentation' (Lijphart 1969: 212). A consociational democracy constitutes a long-term development as it strengthens over time by socialising political elites and making cooperation among the elites habitual. Furthermore, time allows the elites to develop a convincible model for development, a national idea and shared interests can create societal and cross-party consensus on fundamental issues. The only time unity among the elite is not essential for democratisation is when the segments of the elite that favour democratic reform are so powerful that they can neglect the others (Gill 1995).

(handwritten left margin: the in US log come to mean the profiteering + power of the elites – short of the people or return as a whole)

(handwritten bottom margin: Who's going to socialize the political elites? "Big Brother" or "The father in Heaven"?)

Putin is criticised at great length in the literature, with accusations of 'hollowing out' democratic institutions and creating a 'patron regime' that prevents a potent and independent opposition from emerging (Hale 2010; Mendras 2012). However, the motivation for centralising power tends to be neglected or simply explained as Putin being self-serving in terms of pursuing grand Tsarist power ambitions. The point of departure in the discourse is not the challenge of developing national unity to consolidate democracy, supported by the historical precedents of states centralising power in the early stages of democratisation. When Putin took over the presidency the country was pulled in all directions from within by incompatible political forces: the oligarchs, nationalists, communist, secessionists, and liberals. By the end of the 20th century it was common and reasonable to predict that the Russian state would collapse.

After taking the presidency, Putin famously announced he would develop a 'dictatorship of law'. This was to be achieved by continuing to centralise power to constrain what was considered a radical and criminal opposition (Gill 2006). The democratic infrastructure has not yet matured, and the leadership perceives it to be unfeasible to change a system they are constrained by. A parallel system has therefore developed where the leadership employs undemocratic and arbitrary means to strengthen democracy and the rule of law. These two competing political orders exist in parallel and in contradiction with each other, and are labelled 'the dual state in Russia' (Sakwa 2010a). The first system is referred to as the 'normative state' or constitutional state that is 'regulated by law and enshrining the normative values of the democratic movement'. The second system is coined the 'administrative regime' that uses para-constitutional powers that subvert the constitutional spirit, though while not renouncing or deviating from its institutional constraints (Sakwa 2010a: 185). The informal powers are not in the constitution, but consist of informal networks that amount to high-level corruption (Fish 2005). The coexistence between these two systems is informal as 'post-communist Russia has been in a permanent state of exception, exercised not through constitutional provisions of some sort defining a state of emergency, but though an informal and undeclared derogation from constitutional principles' (Sakwa 2010a: 199). Most of the post-Soviet states inherited and replicated these Soviet-era political mechanisms in which an informal politburo of political elites makes the key decisions (Cheterian 2009).

While Putin placing himself at the centre of Russian politics was at the expense of developing strong institutions, he demonstrated an aptitude for developing the foundations for national unity. Following the fragmentation of society and lack of a political consensus after the calamitous 1990s, political cohesion has been to some extent restored. Developing national unity depends on the ability to offer a successful economic model that enhances the standard of living. Rustow (1970: 351) argued that people are unlikely to adopt loyalty to a political community unless it can 'achieve some considerable degree of modernity in its social and economic life'.

Russia largely follows the Asian democratisation model by marginalising radical alternatives and cultivating an acceptable opposition. While Western commentators tend to fetishise and depict insignificant political figures such as Nemtsov or Navalny as the principal opposition, it is the anti-Western Communist Party that represents the main opposition. While harbouring some extreme positions, the Communist Party owes much of its popularity to not involving itself with the oligarchs in the 1990s. Behind the communists is the extreme right wing, nationalist, and neo-imperial 'Liberal Democratic Party' led by Vladimir Zhirinovsky. Putin's United Russia realised the threat of having the Communist Party as the main opposition, and one of its strategies appears to have been to create opposition parties that can siphon off the protest votes that would otherwise have gone to the communists. Most noteworthy, the Kremlin supported the establishment of 'A Just Russia' in 2006 as an acceptable alternative that could absorb some of the protest votes. The party supports a 'New Socialism' as a moderate leftist alternative to United Russia to displace the Communist Party (Sakwa 2010b). Following the 2012 elections, 'A Just Russia' gained more seats in the State Duma than Zhirinovsky's Liberal Democratic Party. A peculiar democratisation process appears to be taking shape as 'A Just Russia' gains momentum and takes on a life of its own by opposing United Russia on various issues. The party nonetheless appears to abide by a 'pact' with the Kremlin by banning its members from participating in protests and not accepting funding from 'non-governmental organisations' financed by foreign governments.

President Medvedev (2009) argued in a lengthy article outlining his vision of Russia's future that changes 'will be gradual, thought-through, and step-by-step'. The rejection of a revolutionary rubric is based on painful historical lessons. Accelerating the democratisation process with revolutionary approaches could cause a return to the 'paralysing' 1990s: 'We will not rush. Hasty and ill-considered political reforms have led to tragic consequences more than once in our history' (Medvedev 2009). Medvedev refers to the need to establish a basic 'cross-party consensus' on the direction of Russia, which includes democratising 'by harmonising the interests of the individual, society and government'. Such a cross-party consensus is not envisioned to be a limitation on democracy, but rather a condition:

> The political system will be renewed and improved via the free competition of open political associations. There will be a cross-party consensus on strategic foreign policy issues, social stability, national security, the foundations of the constitutional order, the protection of the nation's sovereignty, the rights and freedoms of citizens, the protection of property rights, the rejection of extremism, support for civil society, all forms of self-organisation and self-government. A similar consensus exists in all modern democracies.
>
> (Medvedev 2009)

The political leadership suggests that the next step in Russia's democratisation and development of the rule of law is to dismantle the 'administrative state' by eliminating informal powers and corruption at the highest level. Medvedev (2009) criticised the legal nihilism in Russia and argued that the challenge was now to bring the leadership under the rule of law to construct a true constitutional state. A key tenet of the argument was that the progression of Russia is dependent on the ability of political leaders to replace each other in power, as in other democratic countries. Medvedev (2009) suggested that this process was already ongoing and Russia is becoming increasingly transparent 'even if the ruling class does not necessarily like this'. With the reduced potency of extreme revolutionary alternatives, Medvedev (2009) argued that a new system is emerging that consists of 'free competition and open political associations'. Putin appears to be continuing the path as outlined by Medvedev. Putin's policies of combatting corruption at the top level aims to eradicate the 'informal powers' in Russian politics. Much effort has also been made by Putin to strengthen the judiciary and the legal system (Sakwa 2010a: 199).

Eurasian geoeconomics

Developing a Eurasian geoeconomic configuration enables Russia to create more favourable symmetry in the economically interdependent world. Excessive dependence on the West demoted Russia to a peripheral position, vulnerable to Western institutions that facilitate collective bargaining power to minimise Russian autonomy and influence. In contrast, repositioning Russia to the heart of a Eurasian geoeconomic constellation as the successor of the Mongol Empire can increase dependence on Russia by other states. Furthermore, developing economic connectivity with the entire Eurasian landmass enables Russia to reduce its reliance on any one state or region. However, Russia cannot independently create a rival Eurasian geoeconomic format capable of challenging the Western-centric order. Establishing Eurasian partnerships is required to develop the optimal 'balance of dependence', mimicking the geopolitical balance of power.

The first component in a developing a geoeconomic strategy for a greater Eurasia entails integrating a Russian-centric Eurasian core in the post-Soviet space. The Eurasian Economic Union is intended to facilitate collective bargaining power, increase trade between member states, develop shared strategic industries, harmonise physical transportation corridors, and establish common investment banks and trade regimes that determine standards and legislation. The Eurasian Economic Union has to date fallen short on its intended and desired function due to divergent interests, unclear function, and concerns among weaker member states that Russia will absorb their sovereignty.

The second element of Eurasian geoeconomics is to construct an East–West economic corridor. China is evidently the principal partner due to its ability and preparedness to challenge the Western-centric geoeconomic system by conquering more strategic industries, developing new transportation corridors with One Road One Belt initiative (OBOR), and launching new financial banks and trade regimes to alter the formats for international cooperation. After the Western-supported coup in Ukraine in 2014, Russia swiftly signed agreements with China for increased connectivity with gas pipelines, transportation corridors, investment banks, and use of national currencies. Yet, China's bilateral economic superiority vis-à-vis Russia threatens to replicate the same asymmetrical relationship Moscow has with the West. A durable partnership with China therefore requires Russia to diversify its economic ties with more multilateralism to ensure that while China may be the more powerful state in the region, it will not be able to dominate.

The third component of the new Eurasian configuration entails making the East–West economic corridor more durable by diversifying ties in Northeast Asia. This is an important region due to geographical proximity as Russia can develop its economic activity on its Pacific coast, while highly developed and energy-hungry states such as Japan and South Korea are potential partners for modernising the Russian Far East. Russia's Eurasian integration strategy is strikingly similar to the South Korean 'Eurasian Initiative' that aspires to harmonise Korean integration, Northeast Asian integration, and broader Eurasian integration. Russia is attempting to connect South Korea to the Eurasian landmass with common industries, shared transportation and energy infrastructure by land through North Korea, and by sea with modernised Russian ports. Japan evidently has more interests vested in maintaining regional leadership in a maritime partnership with the US to contain China. Yet, as China-centric Eurasian connectivity initiatives progress, Japan has a strategic interest to diversify Russian dependence to ensure that Moscow's somewhat neutral position in Northeast Asia is not compromised.

The last essential part of Russian geoeconomics in Eurasia is to develop a North–South economic corridor to diversify away from excessive reliance on the East–West corridor. The North–South corridor primarily links Russia with Iran and India. The former enjoys growing influence in the Middle East, while the latter is expected to have higher economic growth than China in 2018. Iran has expressed interest in developing a more autonomous Eurasian geoeconomic model due to its experience with Western sanctions and even being suspended from Society for Worldwide Interbank Financial Telecommunication (SWIFT), which is the main messaging network that enables financial institutions to issue orders for global financial transactions. The China–Pakistan Economic Corridor (CPEC) and its possible extension to Iran has incentivised India to augment its own Eurasian connectivity projects by strengthening its ties to Iran and Russia. The recent inclusion of India and Pakistan into the Chinese-Russian-led Shanghai Cooperation Organisation, and the potential offer to Iran, will support a multilateral Eurasia that is less reliant on the West, yet without being dominated by the more powerful China.

Strategic markets developed within the Eurasian model attempt to reverse the energy curse by instead using the revenue from the energy sector to fund temporary subsidies and tariffs to support infant industries until they become competitive in international markets. As Putin emphasised, protectionism is a temporary tool to become competitive rather than isolating Russia from global markets:

> The import replacement programme's aim is not to close our market and isolate ourselves from the global economy. We need to learn how to produce quality, competitive goods that will be in demand not just here in Russia, but on the global markets too.

(Russian Federation 2015)

Many projects have fallen short of their expectations, yet advances have been made. Nine out of ten new cars sold in Russia are now domestically produced, with similar initiatives being put in place to provide incentives for airplanes to be constructed domestically. Putin also indicated that only Russian-flagged ships would be permitted to sail along the Arctic Northern Route in the future (De Bacci 2017). Russia has become an agricultural leader largely due to import substitution (Connolly 2016). Import substitution also increased productivity in other key industries such as engineering, pharmaceuticals, light industry, and petrochemicals (Werner 2015). Tariffs and subsidies are aimed towards innovation and technological leaps with initiatives such as the high-tech Skolkovo project and science hubs to elevate Russia in global value-chains. Leadership in high-end and innovative technologies is important since merely playing catch-up is insufficient as the world is undergoing a new industrial revolution with automation and robotics. Staying ahead of the curve with new technologies in energy production, robotics, and other strategic industries will result in indispensable economic and political power (Karaganov 2016: 461). Besides advancing with high-technological innovations, the National Technology Initiative of 2014 should also be directed towards enhancing existing technologies and offering essential state support without disrupting market forces. Furthermore, larger state-supported systemic changes are imperative since the absence of a domestic infrastructure results in Russian technology being sold to foreign corporations.

Transportation and energy infrastructure has gradually been diversified to reduce the excessive reliance on the West. The ESPO oil pipeline signified the initial pivot to the East, while the following Power of Siberia gas pipeline intensified Russia's ambitions to develop its market share by supplying its neighbours in the Far East. Funds have been allocated to projects such as upgrading the rail network in the Russian Far East and a high-speed railway to China. The North–South corridor includes an upgrade of land-based transportation at the east and west of the Caspian Sea, in addition to the construction and modernisation of ports on the Pacific Coast, the Caspian Sea, the Baltic Sea, and the Black Sea.

Mechanisms for economic and financial cooperation have been developed that respond to the failure of Russia in the late 19th and early 20th centuries. Projects include institutions such as the Eurasian Economic Union, the BRICS Development Bank, and support for the Shanghai Cooperation Organisation to take on geoeconomic competencies. In concert with China, Russia has also embarked on a de-dollarisation programme and accumulated vast amounts of gold. Energy agreements between Russia and China denominated in local currencies is expected to grow when dealing outside of the dollar and to snowball into other markets. In 2017, China announced it would sell oil in yuans, which would be backed by gold. Russia announced it would ban the use of dollars at its ports.

Morality and gemeinschaft are aimed to be protected with Eurasian economic statecraft. As wealth and economic activity continues to rapidly shift from the West to the East, Russia has increased geoeconomic incentives to embrace a Eurasian identity that includes its traditional values and spirituality. Russia's radical and destructive pendulum swings between Western modernism and Eastern traditionalism has to a large extent been the result of the proximity to Europe. Linking modernisation to adopting a European identity has eroded the preparedness to preserve the distinctiveness of Russian civilisation. Other great civilisations in the East undergoing modernisation, such as China, Japan and India, have been more confident in their uniqueness. This has translated into modernising by borrowing from the West, while balancing these efforts by concurrently asserting their traditional values and institutions. Linking modernisation to a Eurasian identity harmonises the societal make-up of Russia with economic interests. Furthermore, the civilisational pluralism in the East can make Russian distinctiveness an asset, as opposed to being chastised by the West for failing to conform to 'common values' and institutions that do not adequately include Russia.

Geoeconomics requires embracing a mixed economy that is based on embracing the benefits of capitalism, coupled with awareness and acceptance that economic inefficiencies of state intervention are required to some extent to preserve the community. While geoeconomic competitiveness is taking centre stage in Russia, Putin (2013a) cautioned against economic determinism as Russia must remain a state with an economy rather than an economy with a state:

> After all, in the end economic growth, prosperity and geopolitical influence are all derived from societal conditions. They depend on whether the citizens of a given country consider themselves a nation, to what extent they identify with their own history, values and traditions, and whether they are united by common goals and responsibilities. In this sense, the question of finding and strengthening national identity really is fundamental for Russia.

Conclusion: a victorious Eurasian Russia

It is concluded in this chapter that the systemic pressures for embracing neomodernism and geoeconomics harmonise with a Eurasian strategy and identity. Russia has emerged victorious by rejecting the Western imposed neo-Weimar policy and instead of succumbing to vengeful politics, Moscow began:

> emphasizing not post-modern, but modern or post-post-modern values: national sovereignty, freedom of political and cultural choice for all countries and peoples, personal and national dignity and normal millenniums – old human values. Also it turned itself from a peripheral European country into a great Asian-Pacific Eurasian one.
>
> (Karaganov 2017b)

Neomodernism offers a philosophical foundation to respond to the failures of postmodernism, by constraining both political liberalism and excessive Slavophile traditionalism. Geoeconomics endows the state with the required influence in the market to augment the effectiveness of society, and protect social capital in the community. Eurasianism decouples Russia from the historical inclination to link modernisation to a rational European identity at the expense of the civilisational distinctiveness of Russia's Eurasian make-up, which has throughout history caused destructive shifts between the modern and traditional, and the rational and irrational. Furthermore, Eurasian geoeconomics repositions Russia from the excessive dependence at the periphery of Europe to the centre of Eurasia, where Russia can reduce its dependence on other and concurrently increase it value to its partners.

It is imperative to recognise that neomodernism and geoeconomics should alter the formats and symmetry of interdependence with the West, rather than isolate and immunise Russia from foreign influence. In other words, Moscow benefits from drawing Europe into a Eurasian constellation that instils more cordial relations. Promoting neomodernism as an international conservative movement in the West and developing favourable symmetry in economic interdependence can be converted into political capital to promote a mutually acceptable post-Cold War settlement in Europe.

9   The rise of 'populists' in the West and their affinity towards Russia

Introduction

Great civilisations first develop a strong order and culture based on physical and conceptual walls to defend 'us' from 'them'. When order and safety have been established, there is an incentive to bring walls down as engagement with the chaos beyond the borders is required to advance. Yet, as civilisation advances on the material and rational, and seemingly reaches its height, the distinctive cultural order that defined and sustained civilisation becomes unsustainable. The terminal stage is characterised when a civilisation is no longer willing to defend itself. Secularism degrades into contempt for religion, multiculturalism produces hostility towards one's own culture, and feminism is reduced to mere demonisation of men. Civilisation splits between the cosmopolitan elites who construe demise of the past as progress and morality, and the 'internal proletariat' who seeks to rejuvenate in-group loyalty, authority, and order of the community as a moral imperative. As there are fewer and fewer traditions to preserve, conservatives gravitate towards romantic nationalism and authoritarianism in an effort to restore the past. Toynbee (1946) recognised that at this critical juncture of civilisation the 'internal proletariat' have through history reached out to an 'external proletariat', a rival gemeinschaft-based civilisation at the periphery that offers a rebirth of civilisation.

Great civilisations have throughout history been challenged by civilisations with less advanced societies at their periphery. The gemeinschaft-based civilisation at the periphery, historically belittled as barbarians, provides a frontier to augment internal solidarity and to distract from internal decay caused by a declining community. Yet, when the advancement of the more powerful civilisation begins to completely devour the traditional and spiritual, polarisation ensues due to the loss of common purpose between the elites and the internal proletariat. The urbanised cosmopolitan elites are committed to the advancement of society and increasingly display contempt for the traditional as relics of a bygone era. The more rural proletariat aims to defend and restore the traditional, as they attain fewer benefits from the complexity of advanced society and carry most of the burden for the loss of community. When the cosmopolitan elite is perceived as the greatest threat to meaning by undermining the ability to reproduce the past, the traditionalist or nationalist looks towards the gemeinschaft-based civilisation at the periphery as an ally.

At the periphery of European civilisation there are mainly the American, Islamic, and Russian civilisations that could provide renewal for a dying European civilisation. These civilisations have shared much with European civilisation, yet they were also established as the 'other' and have at various points in history almost consumed European civilisation. Following the destruction of Europe in the Second World War, European civilisation had an extension of life and renewed spirit as American civilisation asserted its influence over Western Europe Yet, this renewal would be temporary. Much like Solzhenitsyn, Toynbee considered the Cold War a conflict between two tyrannies, the communist from the East and the capitalist society from the West, with Europe stuck in the centre.

The transition from the ethno-cultural nation-state to globalism exemplifies the radical advancement of liberalism and rationalism that unavoidably erodes the community and the traditional order. Liberalism developed within the physical and conceptual walls of the nation-state, which ensured order and safety. Liberalism's repudiation of such walls as immoral undermines the viability of liberalism itself. The Right and Left have subsequently manifested themselves as a rivalry between nationalism and globalism. The ability to offer renewal of European civilisation diminishes as American culture goes the way of the dodo as religion and tradition decline, while the vulgarity of its popular culture loses its ability to distract from decadence. The decline of Europe is now more aptly defined as the decline of the West. Islamic civilisation has growing influence in Europe due to mass migration into the continent, yet it has little capacity to offer renewal of culture as the Islamic faith is particularly dominant in their culture. The lack of commonality or cultural harmonisation undermines the ability for renewal and integration as the incompatible culture is reproduced and remains resilient within Europe.

This chapter first explores the rise and fall of former Western civilisations to demonstrate the inclination towards continuity. Once a civilisation perishes, a civilisation at the periphery with shared roots takes leadership and thus offers rebirth. When the Soviet Union disintegrated and communism was dismantled, the West effectively established a liberal 'universal empire'. Seemingly at the height of its existence, the West had lost the frontier that provided a remedy for decadence, while the absence of alternative ideologies opened the floodgates to unfettered liberalism. Unwillingness to defend and reproduce Western civilisation could be masked as progression until reaching a critical breaking point, when the elites and the people drift apart. While liberalism has exhausted itself, a crisis of the West is delayed until an alternative emerges (Deneen 2018).

The second part of the chapter addresses Russia's dual role in history as an adversary and role model. The inclination towards being a gemeinschaft-based civilisation has earned Russia both scorn and admiration. Russia has simultaneously been perceived as a barbarian at the gates that resist modernity, and revered for the possibility of it infusing Western civilisation with renewed vitality. During an identity crisis in the West, Russia's attractiveness has increased.

The third section of the chapter surveys the rise of 'populists' as a romantic nationalist backlash to the unwillingness of the elites to defend civilisation. Moral panic is inflicted on large sections of the population when the definition of 'we' is perceived to collapse, and the political leadership is unable to address challenges as its legitimacy and authority rested on perpetual economic growth. The elites, no longer capable of responding to challenges, are eventually unable to use imagery and personalities as a distraction. Last, the populists in the US and Europe and their favourable attitude towards Russia will be assessed. The populists tend to see Russia as a powerful ally in what has essentially become a globally integrated movement against the liberal authoritarian elites as the dividing lines in the world transition from the liberal democratic-authoritarian divide to a nationalist-globalist divide. For the populists, Moscow transitions from being a chief adversary to become an ally due to its unapologetic advocacy for the traditional, spiritual, and the nation-state.

It is concluded that the attractiveness of Russia in the West will be contingent on its genuine intentions and ability to restore the nation-state as the main agent of conserving the traditional. Russia will need to develop a convincing geoeconomic model that can deliver prosperity to its population, preserve the community, and shift political interests of the West towards the East.

The death and rebirth of Western civilisations

Great Western civilisations have in the past exhausted themselves and faltered, and on their ruins new Western civilisations were born. Rather than developing independently, 'each [civilisation] has been linked in the closest fashion with those that preceded it, and has in turn brought influences of many kinds to bear on those that arose subsequently' (Cunningham 1900: 1). The foundation of Hellenistic society has continuously been reproduced after the collapse of Greece and then Rome. Ancient Greece is recognised as the cradle of Western civilisation, which grew in power based on geoeconomic principles and an identity balanced between the distinctive and universal. Greek power largely relied on controlling maritime corridors, which enabled troop movements and trade. Concurrently, open democratic society was conducive to growth and augmented their appeal abroad. Ancient Greece was also the earliest recorded use of the East as the 'other' to the West. Aeschylus' play 'The Persians' was one of the earliest works castigating the 'other' in the East as the 'barbarian' in opposition to the civilised Greeks in the West (Bisaha 2004: 45). Greek pride and culture was instrumental for the expansion of Hellenistic civilisation to the east: 'The development of Greek Civilisation was followed by its diffusion through the conquests of Alexander and his generals' (Cunningham 1900: 9). Alexander the Great pursued land-based expansion to the east as the frontier of Western civilisation, and differed from the Romans as land-corridors were used to eliminate Persian seaports and support bases. Even after the rise of the Republic of Rome and the Roman Empire, Greek language and philosophy spread across the civilisations that filled the vacuum in the territories previously conquered by Alexander the Great.

While the Romans inherited much of Greek ideals and traditions, they were less divisive in terms of 'us' versus 'them' divide in terms of castigating other cultures as barbaric (Bisaha 2004: 47). The term 'West' is widely recognised to have originated with the partition of the Roman Empire into a western and eastern part. Rome's rivalry with Carthage over trade in the Mediterranean included the use of military power to advance commercial competitiveness. Rome was largely unique by allowing foreigners to settle as citizens. Forming a more complex society, living under Roman law became synonymous with being 'civilised', in opposition to the barbarians living outside Rome. Universality allowed greater absorption and expansion, yet it also made the internal solidarity more fragile. As the Roman Empire expanded, the accommodation of the people on the conquered land diluted homogeneity and thus internal cohesion. Heather (2005: xi) describes how victory at the periphery led to defeat at the core:

> In 376 a large band of Gothic refugees arrived at the Empire's Danube frontier, asking for asylum. In a complete break with established Roman policy, they were allowed in, unsubdued. They revolted, and within two years had defeated and killed the emperor Valens – the one who had received them – along with two-thirds of his army, at the battle of Hadrianople.

At what appeared to be the height of Roman power, the demise of the core meant that Rome could not defend its frontiers, morality declined, the economy fell, loyalty to the political system dropped, the social system declined, and an overconfident army began serving local interests.

The demise of the Roman Empire and lack of a successor led to cultural and economic regression during the Middle Ages. The vacuum left by the Roman Empire was eventually filled by the Carolingian empire in 800AD, which encompassed much of Western Europe and is often described by historians as the first 'Europe'. A shared civilisational task was to uphold the civilised order during the Middle Ages. The Romans paved the road to the spread of Christianity. Christianity filled much of the vacuum of authority left behind after the Roman Empire. While the split with Orthodox Christians in the South and East marked a division, the principal 'other' became Muslims and was reinvigorated with the Crusades. The birth of modern Europe required the demise of the Roman Empire as its predecessor (Gibbon 1776). The patchwork of municipals and people left behind following the demise of the Roman Empire was filled by the Church, and Germanic warlords claiming hereditary rule – contrasting with the Romans who saw liberty in purely civic and political terms, while the barbarians outside Rome deemed liberty to be the result of their individuality (Guizot 2013[1828]). The combination and harmonisation of this paradox produced conservation of strong municipals and imperial traditions, coupled with the individualism of the Germanic barbarians. European civilisation became more adaptable by embracing pluralism. The danger derived from the possibility that Europe would abandon pluralism and succumb to the fate of former civilisations (Guizot 2013[1828]).

Arthur Balfour suggested that European civilisation may not be as fortunate as the Roman Empire, as there were no external sources that could renew the ideas and ethos of Europe. Much like the Hellenic culture spread to Asia faded, so would Western European culture disappear by barbaric forces. Albeit, on an optimistic note, Balfour (1908: 58–59) argued:

> The influence which a superior civilisation, whether acting by example or imposed by force, may have in advancing an inferior one, though often beneficent, is not likely to be self supporting; its withdrawal will be followed by decadence, unless the character of the civilisation be in harmony both with the acquired temperament and the innate capabilities of those who have been induced to accept it: that as regards those nations which still advance in virtue of their own inherent energies, though time has brought perhaps new causes of disquiet, it has brought also new grounds of hope; and that whatever be the perils in front of us, there are, so far, no symptoms either of pause or regression in the onward movement which for more than a thousand years has been characteristic of Western civilisation.

Without external adversaries, the populace becomes more aware of its internal differences and begins to fragment. The Roman historian Sallust wrote that following the victory and destruction of the adversary Carthage that the Roman republic turned on itself as groups within began to become rivals. Georgy Arbatov, a Soviet political scientist and advisor, similarly proclaimed at the end of the Cold War in 1988: 'We are going to do a terrible thing to you. We are going to deprive you of an enemy.'

Death of gemeinschaft: the West's unwillingness to defend itself

The unipolarity and economic expansionism that followed in the post-Cold War era temporarily brushed over intensifying decadence. Yet, Fukuyama's (1989) exuberant optimism about the 'end of history' was quickly confronted with more pessimistic predictions. As the external adversary was gone, there was growing evidence of internal challenges such as a rising underclass, racial fragmentation, moral anxiety, romanticisation of anti-social behaviour, and a culture of entitlement at the expense of individual responsibility. It was feared that democracy could become 'synonymous with a helpless hedonism' and prove incapable of addressing the tensions related to global challenges, race, economic inequality, and morality (Fuller 1992: 125). Alluding to the decay of gemeinschaft, Fuller (1992) proposed a greater need for government to revive morality by imposing 'sin taxes'. Friedman and Mandelbaum (2012) also warned of a possible gloomy future in the absence of an adversary to incentivise internal unity within the US and the advancement of civilisation. Economic, political, and social decay was expected due to difficulties in education, immigration, climate change, and infrastructure, while new technology and global markets siphoned off jobs. Debt, deficits, and political polarisation were expected to endure, with fears that democracy would regress due to political incentives for lobbying (Friedman and Mandelbaum 2012).

The apparent unwillingness of Western civilisation to defend itself is usually expressed by increasing hostility within the West over its own legacy. The critique of Western civilisation and pessimism about Western community/culture is commonly found on the Left. Yet, across society there is a growing rejection of degenerate mass culture, mass consumerism, media functioning as entertainment, capitalism undermining tradition, de-humanising government institutions, tech- nocratic police state, scorning the inevitable racism domestically and imperialism internationally as efforts to avert the decline of the West (Herman 1997: 365). Radicalism found in religions and cults is usually based on extreme nihilism and a belief that the world is beyond repair and the old order must be burned to the ground before a new a better alternative can emerge. Religion becomes a cultural refuge for a community in decline, as people rediscover faith as a defence against gesellschaft. Sam Harris (2011) expressed his concern that 'nearly half of the American population is eagerly anticipating the end of the world. This dewy-eyed nihilism provides absolutely no incentive to build a sustainable civilisation'. Toynbee recognised that he was inclined to welcome the end of Western civilisation:

> I am conscious of having a certain "down" on Western civilization and have often tried to think out why I have it . . . Partly it is the feeling that the Ancient World is the real home of the human spirit, and that what came after is rather a pity.

(cited in Merry 2005: 32)

Across the Atlantic, the old continent faces similar challenges. The days when Europe towered over the world in terms culture and civilisation are long gone, and Europe is presently in systemic decline. Economic stagnation, unemployment, cultural and spiritual decay, and a population facing plummeting birth rates are temporarily brushed over with rapid immigration of migrants from the Islamic world (Laqueur 2007; Thornton 2008). While the growing Islamic population in Europe threatens to dilute national identities and cultures, and the pernicious lure to solely blame Muslims for civilisational decay is also a threat. Much like the Jews being depicted as the source of the decline of civilisation in the 1930s, the simplistic portrayal can induce excitement in the masses to be given an achievable solution to a complex and imperishable condition. Yet, the ideological commitment to multiculturalism is indicative of a civilisation unwilling to reproduce its own culture and existence. Having abandoned religion and ideologies that Men were willing to kill for, Europe has succumbed to nihilism as it also shed what is worth living and dying for. While money has been elevated to the primary indicator of value, the vicious irony is that the Europe and the broader West is in relative economic decline as well. At the current impasse, the ideal policy for the US and Europe to move forward would be debt defaults, protectionism, and retreat into autarchy (Moyo 2011).

Ferguson (2011: 325) speculates that 'maybe the real threat is posed not by the rise of China, Islam or CO2 emissions, but by our own loss of faith in the civilisation we inherited from our ancestors'. Historically, the civilisation is 'no longer able to defend itself because it is no longer willing to defend itself' (Quigley: 1961: 160). Mass immigration and rapidly changing demographics deconstruct the nation-state, overwhelm the cultural identity and spark a crisis. Europe's death is strange as its cultural demise is not resisted (Murray 2017). As the ethno-cultural core weakens, the political leadership largely rejects any challenge to societal security by expressions of self-loathing and nihilistic unwillingness to reproduce the native culture. The hostility towards one's own culture and traditions was best summarised in a statement by Sweden's Prime Minster in 2006: 'Only barbarism is genuinely Swedish. All further development has been brought from outside.' In 2004, the Swedish Minister of Integration had similarly announced to a Kurdish audience that Swedes were jealous of them because, unlike Swedes, they have a culture (Murray 2017: 107). Likewise, the German Integration Commissioner argued that there is no such thing as 'specific German culture' and it was offensive to expect immigrants to assimilate a shared set of cultural values (FT 2017). In the Netherlands, the Justice Minister was open for introducing Sharia Law if the country's growing Muslim population achieved it by democratic means.

Systemic incentives encourage the establishment to dismiss concerns about societal security as xenophobia, sovereignty and nationalism with racism, native religion with fundamentalism, cultural homogeneity with totalitarianism. Rather than address the concerns about the inability to reproduce the culture and traditions of the country, the elites rely increasingly on attractive personalities, image-building, and branding. Morality was gradually perverted and replaced with virtue-signalling. On the left, the elites began conflating reality and entertainment. Hollywood became actively engaged in the election campaign of Bill Clinton, movie stars appeared as political pundits, and news anchors replaced reporting the news with broadcasting opinions. Bill Clinton's saxophone debut at the Arsenio Hall Show indicated legitimacy being built upon personal charisma to make him relatable and likable. Obama followed the same tactics by appearing on TV shows and even performing with dance, surrounding himself with celebrities, and becoming the first candidate to develop his own political brand/trademark. The conservatives' mantra of preserving the community is ideologically inconstant as they simultaneously commit themselves to unremitting free-trade and globalism. The Republicans therefore also shifted to culture to become more relatable, which is reminiscent of Plato's description of the affluent seeking legitimacy by pretending to be poor. President G.W. Bush, a Texan oilman and son of a former president, established himself as an anti-elitist and anti-intellectual to project the image of the underdog.

The 2016 US presidential election perfectly displayed the detachment of the elites and the imagery in response. The result was a historic polarisation of America between gemeinschaft and gesellschaft as urban America and rural America were culturally mobilised against each other. Both candidates represented the elites. Hillary Clinton, the wife of a former president, is renowned for being a war hawk and intimately connected with Wall Street. Donald Trump, a billionaire living in a tower in New York, became the spokesperson for the people against the rich elites. The contempt for the elites had been used against Trump during the republican primary, with Ted Cruz accusing Trump of having 'New York values' rather than being committed to traditional rural America.

Basing her election campaign on identity politics, Clinton positioned herself as the self-proclaimed spokesperson of the marginalised: women, ethnic/religious minorities, and the LGBT community. Unlike Obama, she was unable to reach out to the white working class who had suffered economically as their political currency was diminished. After all, white working men were on top of the dominance hierarchy in accordance with identity politics. Clinton infamously expressed her disdain for Trump supporters by describing them as a 'basket of deplorables' and promised to 'put a lot of coal miners and coal companies out of business'. The inability of Hillary Clinton to recognise the economic hardship of white men in the rustbelt states, due to their 'privileged' race and gender in the intersectional hierarchy, opened a large vacuum that Trump could seize upon. Furthermore, the irony became evident as the self-declared spokesperson for the oppressed appeared to reinforce harmful stereotypes by depicting women and minorities as one-dimensional by obsessing solely on misogyny or racism, as opposed to having a wide array of priorities ranging from economics to security policies. Women were expected to vote with their vaginas by electing the potential first female president, while Hispanics were all expected to be outraged by having limited immigration. Her pandering was also focused on group identities by for example putting on a fake accent when campaigning in Middle America, while pretending to always carry hot sauce in her purse when she appeared on a radio station targeting African Americans. Following her defeat, Clinton (2017) argued in her post-election book, *What Happened*, that her loss was partly caused by white husbands and boyfriends convincing their partners not to vote for her, and partly due to angry white Americans being afraid of losing their white privilege in society. While a majority of the population elected a black president in the two previous elections, voting for a white woman was supposedly where racist America drew its line in the sand.

The postmodernist division of society into oppressors and victims eventually spurs a revolt by the identity groups punished for allegedly having unearned privilege. Rorty (1998) defined liberal democracy as giving birth to 'a more evolved form of humanity'. Yet, the excesses of social justice polarise as 'the cultural Left has a vision of an America in which the white patriarchs have stopped voting and have left all the voting to be done by members of previously victimised groups' (Rorty 1998). The subsequent rise of neo-gemeinschaft was therefore to be expected as 'Americans still want to feel patriotic. They still want to feel part of a nation which can take control of its destiny and make itself a better place' (Rorty 1999: 99). Eventually, 'when liberals insist that only fascists will defend borders, then voters will hire fascists to do the job liberals won't do' (Frum 2017).

The return of romantic nationalism

In his renowned essay, *Why Fascism is the Wave of the Future*, Luttwak (1993a) predicted that a more fascist form of government was awaiting. Luttwak, (1993a) observed that 'the moderate right has little to offer philosophically, except more free trade and globalisation', while the moderate left can only offer more distribution of wealth to groups that successfully obtain victimhood status. Protectionism and other interventionism in the market is depicted by both the Right and Left as a betrayal of the moral and virtues of consumer choice – the alleged foundation of Western civilisation. The flexibility required for making an economy more efficient enhances economic insecurity for the middle class, which previously had primarily plagued the lower working-class. Furthermore, the 'state with an economy' incrementally degrades to an 'economy with a state' as economic growth becomes the principal indicator of performance.

The two principal values of the Right, global free-market capitalism and traditional family values, are incompatible and the former rapidly degrades the latter. Subsequently, conservatism is left hollowed as complaining has almost become the sole tool for guarding traditional life and family values. The loss in authority of key institutions has been the source of cultural decline:

> Everything about modern life works against community and trust. Globalization and urbanization put people in touch with the different and the novel. Our economy rewards initiative over conformity, so that the weight of convention and tradition doesn't squelch the latest gizmo from coming to the attention of the next Bill Gates. Whereas parents in the 1920s said it was most important for their children to be obedient, that quality has declined in importance, replaced by a desire for independence and autonomy.
>
> (Bishop 2017)

The lack of authority and the inability of Western civilisation to defend itself has fuelled support for a pendulum swing towards a New Romanticism by again reaching out to restore what the instinctive demands. It is a human disposition to demand the authoritarianism and reject tolerance when it is believed that the moral and normative order that define 'us' is threatened (Stenner 2005). A rapid shift in sentiment and morality occurs as the populace instinctively feels the need to restore the conceptual and physical walls that define 'us'. A 'normative threat' develops, defined as the feeling:

> that the integrity of the moral order is endangered and the perceived 'we' is falling apart. It is a fear that the moral order is collapsing, rather than his concrete situation, that triggers his turn against foreigners and any others whom he sees as a threat.
>
> (Stenner 2005)

Authoritarianism is usually understood as being negative, yet it is also a moral virtue. Authority is required to sustain hierarchies that maintain order and morality (Haidt 2012). Liberal challenges to the authority in key institutions has often been the source of cultural decline:

The urge to help the inner-city poor led to welfare programs in the 1960s that reduced the value of marriage, increased out-of-wedlock births, and weakened African American families. The urge to empower students by giving them the right to sue their teachers and schools in the 1970s has eroded the authority and moral capital in schools, creating disorderly environments that harm the poor above all. The urge to help Hispanic immigrants in the 1980s led to multicultural education programs that emphasized the differences among Americans rather than their shared values and identity.

(Haidt 2012: 309)

People instinctively seek to restore the authority of political leadership as their legitimacy dwindles. The legitimacy of the political leadership has since the Second World War rested almost solely on the impossibility of perpetual economic growth. This requires ever-more deregulation, worker mobility, and reduced constraints by the family and community. A dual crisis becomes unavoidable: first, diminished legitimacy of authority as the real wages of people stagnates, and the relative economic power of the West subsides. Second, social and political upheaval ensues as economic insecurity increases and the interpersonal connection with the family and community dwindles. With increasing economic insecurity and the absence of community for refuge, voters become more hostile to the political establishment that are seen to safeguard a corrupt system. Reminiscent of Plato's argument in *The Republic*, the voters will look for a strongman to rewrite the rules and dispose of the establishment, even with the risk of the strongman becoming a tyrant. Rorty (1998) predicted excessive economic liberalism to be followed by increased political radicalism:

Members of labor unions, and unorganized and unskilled workers, will sooner or later realize that their government is not even trying to prevent wages from sinking or to prevent jobs from being exported. Around the same time, they will realize that suburban white-collar workers – themselves desperately afraid of being downsized – are not going to let themselves be taxed to provide social benefits for anyone else. At that point, something will crack. The nonsuburban electorate will decide that the system has failed and start looking around for a strongman to vote for – someone willing to assure them that, once he is elected, the smug bureaucrats, tricky lawyers, overpaid bond salesmen, and postmodernist professors will no longer be calling the shots . . . Once the strongman takes office, no one can predict what will happen.

The 'populists' represent the new Romanticists, who seek to de-throne a detached establishment that has made its legitimacy and continuity contingent upon loyalty to cosmopolitism and globalism. Huntington (2004: 5), argued that ordinary citizens prioritise the preservation of traditional values, national identity, culture, and manufacturing jobs as the source for national unity. In contrast:

for many elites, these concerns are secondary to participating in the global economy, supporting international trade and migration, strengthening international institutions, promoting American values abroad, and encouraging minority identities and cultures at home. The central distinction between the public and elites is not isolationism versus internationalism, but nationalism versus cosmopolitanism.

While the populists are united in their instinctive gravitation towards reproducing the traditional, they emerge in various and often contradicting strands. In contrast to outlining a rationalist position, the Romanticists are faced with the formidable task of theorising, articulating, and comprehending the complex irrationality of the human consciousness. The recognition of a dying community leads to people seeking meaning in something new and restoring the human soul with alternatives, which entails the pendulum swinging back with detrimental effects on society. Pessimism about the path of Western civilisation encourages people to seek refuge in failed and morally disreputable political ideologies of the past or embrace new forms of radical tribalism. In the past, even Heidlegger and his contemporaries embraced Hitler's National Socialism to harmonise the preservation of the German soul with the development of an advanced domineering German intellect and power. Rather than seeking a new concept for civilisation, others may revert into smaller sub-groups for a meaning that castigates the 'other' based on their 'identity'. Society therefore also experiences an increase in radical ecologists, feminists, ethnic-minorities, religious fundamentalists, and other ways of rediscovering community.

With the demise of traditional institutions and structures, traditional conservatism has less to preserve and instead revives the past. The project for cultural and religious fundamentalism to rediscover a lost past usually leads down a dangerous path. Even reviving the central role of the family is dangerous and entails an assault on existing Western norms, such as female participation in the workforce by rolling back equality and self-determination. Culture as a shared inheritance will have to accommodate the new changes and recognise that all cultures change over time and there is no going back.

Russia as the historical 'other': barbarians at the gates or successor of the West?

The inclination to be a gemeinschaft-based civilisation has made Russia the West's 'other' for the past 500 years. Russia has been either been depicted as backward and standing in the way of liberal progress and modernisation, or revered for preserving the traditional. Already from the eve of Sorokin's sensate/material era in the West from the early 16th century, it became common to portray Russia as an authoritarian and brutal country that stood in opposition to the rational and rule of law in Western Europe.

During the Romantic age, what had previously been depicted as backward and alien in Russia was viewed by many as exotic traits of a country in touch with the ideational and spiritual. The societal hardship of the industrial revolution in Western Europe produced nostalgia for a lost past, which was believed to remain intact in a less modernised Russia. German, British, and French writers and philosophers romanticised the spirituality of the vast Russian steppes and contrasted it with the emptiness of the manufacturing societies of modern Europe. In the late 19th century, English and Russian churches began developing closer connections and improving religious ties between two branches of a common Christian European civilisation, which was intended to improve mutual understanding following the hostilities that had derived from the Great Game (Hughes 2004). Spengler (1922) identified the spiritual impulses from Russia as the possible source of renewal when the materialistic and spiritually deprived Europe would eventually fall. Russia was defined as primitive and religious, though unlike his Russophobic contemporaries, this definition was not derogatory as he defined this condition as being a civilisation in its youth in contrast to the aging and decaying West (Spengler 1922). De Maistre, a French philosopher, diplomat, and prominent figure of the Counter-Enlightenment movement, blamed excessive rationalism and rejection of Christianity for the chaos in post-revolutionary France. Yet, it is uncertain whether Russia has the ability or intent to act as a partner to revitalise traditionalism and spirituality in the West. While de Maistre sought to reach out to Russia as an intact culture untarnished by modernity, he found that the Russians were rapidly emulating decaying French culture. Furthermore, irrespective of their faults, the Western elites appeared capable of overcoming the challenges of modernisation.

The October Revolution completely altered Russia as the 'other' in terms of its attractiveness and threat. Communism purged Russia's attractiveness as a gemeinschaft-based civilisation by attempting to transcend tradition and spirituality. Russian attractiveness was contingent on another form of modernity, the ambition to create a new Man by transcending its capitalist past. Following the revolution, the impressive industrial progress and scientific triumphs of the Soviets presented attractive rival political and economic ideas (Rutland and Kazantsev 2016: 399). The Soviet rise gave momentum to Western socialist movements that pushed to advance the welfare state, and more radical communist movements to replicate the Russian social experiment. The Soviet Union also incentivised Western states to embrace fascism or liberalism as counter-ideologies in response to and in opposition to communism.

Following the Second World War, the power struggle continued between the two remaining modernist ideologies. The Soviet Union peaked in the 1970s, at a time when the creative minority in the West seemed incapable of responding to economic stagnation. Moscow's success compared to the West's struggles appeared to discredit both capitalism and democracy. The ideological rivalry with the Soviet Union encouraged the US and UK to double down on free-market capitalism in the 1980s by removing constraining protection for the community and thereby abandoning traditional conservativism. Yet, the West's Christian heritage and nationhood was instrumental in elevating its moral superiority in contrast with the atheist/godless East that prevented 'captive nations' from organising as sovereign states based on distinct ethno-cultural characteristics.

Russian civilisation lost much of its attractiveness in the West following the fall of the Soviet Union. The community had been purged and social cohesion unravelled, leaving traditions and spirituality in tatters. The society was underdeveloped in terms of a dysfunctional economy, collapsing financial system, outdated technologies, and an inability to deliver opportunity or prosperity. The economic collapse and the rise of the oligarchs justly fomented the imagery of a criminal revolution without a viable economic development model or perhaps even a future. Without an ideological frontier to distract from the contemporary dismay with the promise of a glorious future, nihilism and civilisational decay appeared unavoidable. While the favourable imagery of the Soviet Union faded, the negative was preserved. The decisions by Russian leaders are consistently construed through pre-existing cognitive frameworks that depict Russia as an unkind place and its foreign policy as antagonistic. Russia still enjoyed some soft power from the Soviet era amongst the far Left and anti-colonialist groups. Yet, Russia's cultural standing within its civilisational space declined rapidly as the nation-building initiatives in neighbouring states led to politicising the Russian language and culture in a de-russification campaign.

Russia's new conservative ethos became especially profound under Putin's third term, which filled a much-need ideological vacuum within Russia and as an alternative for competition in the conservative 'shared neighbourhood' between the West and Russia. Lastly, the new conservatism has also had a profound impact within the West, where the postmodernist rejection of the traditional has caused a fierce backlash. In a report with the title *Putin is a New World Conservative Leader*, Abzalov argued that adherence to traditional values and consistency on his position has made Russian conservativism influential around the world (RBK 2013). As Putin asserts the Western assault on national culture and traditions is a top-down imposition, Russian conservativism is also implicit in the defence of democracy. According to the Russian President, Europe has become morally degenerate by abandoning 'their roots, including Christian values that constitute the basis of Western civilisation' (Putin 2013a).

Putin (2013b) insinuates that Russia's reaction to the erosion of traditions and moral decay creates a common cause with political forces around the world:

> We know that there are more and more people in the world who support our position on defending traditional values that have made up the spiritual and moral foundation of civilisation in every nation for thousands of years: the values of traditional families, real human life, including religious life, not just material existence but also spirituality, the values of humanism and global diversity. Of course, this is a conservative position. But speaking in the words of Nikolai Berdyaev, the point of conservatism is not that it prevents movement forward and upward, but that it prevents movement backward and downward, into chaotic darkness and a return to a primitive state.

Rise of the American romantic nationalists

The rift between the 'internal proletariat' and the elites has been growing for years in the US. The cosmopolitan elites detached from community could continue for a long period by drawing on an urbanised voter base in New York and California that benefits disproportionately from globalisation. The 'petulant, self-righteous, intolerant' liberal elites become contemptuous for the 'those who stubbornly refuse to see the light' (Lasch 1996: 28). For the liberal elites, Middle America 'has come to symbolise everything that stands in the way of progress: "family values", mindless patriotism, religious fundamentalism, racism, homophobia, retrograde views of women' (Lasch 1996: 28–29).

Trump was a populist presidential candidate who infiltrated the Republican Party and broke with the failed orthodoxies of the conservatives, unable to address the problems of globalism. The fervent opposition and panic within the Republican Party only fuelled his credentials as a true outsider and anti-elitist. Trump unapologetically rejected the entire narrative of America's ills deriving from privileged white men oppressing minorities, and instead portrayed it as a ploy by unpatriotic cosmopolitan elites. The more 'outrageous' Trump was during the campaign, the more validity he built as a patriot by rejecting political correctness. The passion of Trump appeared genuine in his opposition against globalism. He has been a consistent vocal critic since the 1970s concerning the US paying for its allies' military, which allowed these allies to spend the money on geoeconomic subsidies that were eroding the economic core of the US. In his inauguration speech, rather than evoking the traditional rhetoric about being the leader of the free world in terms of the liberal democratic-authoritarian divide and globalist ambitions, he announced his intention to 'unite the civilised world' and declared 'the right of all nations to put their own interests first'. Once in power, Trump dispensed with free-trade rhetoric and replaced it with 'fair trade'.

Steve Bannon represented Trump's ideological foundation of economic nationalism and preserving American traditional culture. Bannon defines himself as an 'economic nationalist' and called for returning to Hamilton's American System since 'the globalists gutted the American working class and created a middle class in Asia' (Feder 2016). Bannon largely identified the crisis in the US as declining gemeinschaft and gesellschaft:

> Capitalism really generated tremendous wealth. And that wealth was really distributed among a middle class, a rising middle class, people who come from really working-class environments and created what we really call a Pax Americana. It was many, many years and decades of peace. And I believe we've come partly offtrack in the years since the fall of the Soviet Union and we're starting now in the 21st century, which I believe, strongly, is a crisis both of our church, a crisis of our faith, a crisis of the West, a crisis of capitalism.
>
> (Feder 2016)

The subsequent three pillars of the Trump administration according to Bannon were therefore security through sovereignty, economic nationalism rather than unremitting free-trade, and de-construction of the administrative state as it perpetuates the tyranny of the status quo.

Many American conservatives or romantic nationalists, dismayed by the decline of traditional values, have begun to survey foreign powers by their commitment to national culture and Christianity. This entails reconsidering their relationship with Russia. Pat Buchanan, an American conservative, presidential advisor, and former presidential candidate, hailed Russia as an ally in the new world. In an article with the title *Is Putin One of Us?*, Buchanan (2013) posited that:

> As the decisive struggle in the second half of the 20th century was vertical, East vs. West, the 21st century struggle may be horizontal, with conservatives and traditionalists in every country arrayed against the militant secularism of a multicultural and transnational elite . . . [Putin] is seeking to redefine the 'Us vs. Them' world conflict of the future as one in which conservatives, traditionalists, and nationalists of all continents and countries stand up against the cultural and ideological imperialism of what he sees as a decadent west.

" *The Great White Patriarch* "

Buchanan (2014) suggested that in contrast to the Cold War, Russia was on the right side of history, on the side of God, in the struggle of the 21st century:

> Putin is plugging into some of the modern world's most powerful currents. Not only in his defiance of what much of the world sees as America's arrogant drive for global hegemony. Not only in his tribal defense of lost Russians left behind when the USSR disintegrated. He is also tapping into the worldwide revulsion of and resistance to the sewage of a hedonistic secular and social revolution coming out of the West. In the culture war for the future of mankind, Putin is planting Russia's flag firmly on the side of traditional Christianity.

how scary!?

Roy Moore, who won the Republican primary for the Republican Senate with campaign support from Bannon and Farage, also expressed certain affinity for Russian conservatism. Moore argued that America 'promote[s] a lot of bad things' with reference to same-sex marriage, and 'maybe Putin is right' and 'maybe he's more akin to me than I know' (Delk 2017). Bannon considers traditionalist states like Russia to be a necessary ally, yet he cautioned that the Kremlin could merely have expansionist ambitions concealed as traditionalism. Nonetheless, Bannon argued that traditionalists gravitate towards Putin because:

> They believe that at least Putin is standing up for traditional institutions, and he's trying to do it in a form of nationalism – and I think that people, particularly in certain countries, want to see the sovereignty for their country, they want to see nationalism for their country. They don't believe in this kind of pan-European Union or they don't believe in the centralized government in the United States. They'd rather see more of a states-based entity that the founders originally set up where freedoms were controlled at the local level.
>
> (Feder 2016)

While 51 percent of Republicans regarded the Russian President 'very unfavourably' in 2014, this number had reduced to 14 percent only two years later. By January 2017, 75 percent of Republicans answered that Trump had the 'right approach' towards Russia (Foer 2017). Obama expressed his frustration with the polarisation of American politics impacting the ability to act as a unitary actor, and encouraged a return to embracing a shared enemy under the auspices of dividing the world along liberal democracy and authoritarianism:

> Over a third of Republican voters approve of Vladimir Putin, the former head of the KGB. Ronald Reagan would roll over in his grave. And how did that happen? ... Because for too long, everything that happens in this town, everything that's said, is through the prism of, does this help or hurt us relative to Democrats? Relative to president Obama?

While Daddy Bush was head of the CIA (McCarthy 2016)

The European populists

For Romanticists or 'populists' across Europe, the EU embodies the assault on national identities and traditional values. Anti-establishment parties across Europe tend to depict Russia as upholding the conservative virtues and representing a possible salvation from 'Merkel's Europe of the banks' (Braghiroli and Makarychev 2016: 219). The ambition of EU federalists to concentrate power in Brussels is scorned for undermining national identities, democracy, and economic competitiveness. Chancellor Merkel's announcement that German borders were open for refugees resulting from the destruction of Libya and Syria, without consulting its European counterparts, caused a refugee/migrant crisis that would also challenge the ability of European societies to reproduce their cultures and traditions. The liberal commitment to accept staggering numbers of refugees and migrants ran counter to public sentiments, with the majority in almost every European country favouring a slow down or completely halt to Muslim migration to Europe (Goodwin and Raines 2017). The EU countered public opinion by threatening economic sanctions against member states refusing to accept refugees and migrants.

The NATO Destruction of Libya, Syria, Iraq, Afghanistan Palestine etc etc

The UK's relationship with Brussels has been defined by an attraction towards the EU's geoeconomic power and the shared political space, and an aversion to EU political power and identity due to the desire to remain English. After the UK signed the Maastricht Treaty in 1992 as a sign of abandoning classical conservative values and the centrality of state, Nigel Farage and other disgruntled conservatives left the Conservative Party and became founding members of the populist UK Independence Party (UKIP). UKIP was largely constructed as a single-issue party seeking a referendum on EU membership. Under the leadership of Farage, UKIP rose from obscurity and became the British party with the largest representation in the European Parliament in 2014. The Conservative Party under the leadership of Prime Minister Cameron, attempted to oust UKIP from British politics by accepting a referendum on British membership in the EU, which was expected to fail. After leading Britain out of the EU, Farage hinted at global aspirations by offering support to other European states to free themselves from the EU, and participated actively in the election of Trump.

Farage's favourable views of Russia largely reflects similar British concerns of the EU monopolising on representing Europe and undermining the nation-state. Following the Russian intervention in Georgia, Farage criticised 'NATO and the EU [for] encroaching upon Russia', which was 'provocative' and 'wrong' (BBC 2008). After the EU support for the 2014 coup in Kiev, Farage lambasted the EU for having 'blood on its hands' due to its 'imperialist, expansionist' actions (BBC 2014). With a detached political establishment, the British Left has moved further to the left. Despite fierce opposition from his own party, Jeremy Corbyn took over leadership of the Labour Party in 2015. Much like Farage, he also accused NATO of provoking Russia into responding in Ukraine.

garbled

In France, Le Pen led the corresponding populist branch of French politics. She took National Front from unelectable obscurity, to become one of the two final presidential candidates before ultimately losing the election to Macron. Domestic politics was not framed in the traditional manner, rather Le Pen posited that 'the divide is no longer between the right and the left, but between the patriots and the globalists . . . It's a choice of civilisation. I will be the president of those French who want to continue living in France as the French do' (Noack and Birnbaum 2017). In international politics, Le Pen scorns the EU, NATO, and globalist elites for undermining traditional culture. In contrast, Le Pen portrays Putin as the defender of 'the Christian heritage of European civilization' (Polyakova 2014). Much like Farage, Le Pen depicted the National Front as part of a global movement of cooperation between independent nation-states: 'A new world has emerged in these past years . . . It's the world of Vladimir Putin, it's the world of Donald Trump in the US. I share with these great nations a vision of cooperation, not of submission' (Henley 2017).

In the Netherlands, the rise of the Freedom Party under the nationalist leadership of Geert Wilder is indicative of the paradox of liberal progressiveness producing illiberal regression. Wilder is renowned for his fierce critique of both Islam and the EU as threatening Dutch identity. From being an unelectable party in the past, the Freedom Party came in second place in the 2017 elections. The Netherlands, the most liberal and progressive country in Europe, is an important case study for excessive liberalism and postmodernism causing a pendulum swing. Progressive liberalism tore away at religious parties in the 1960 that had **s** previously been dominant in terms of influencing identity and structuring society. With pressures rising for new sources of shared identity, the monarchy and orange sports teams provided insufficient succour. Unlimited freedoms were incrementally embraced in the form of a new identity, most famous abroad for a liberal approach to gays, drugs, and prostitution. A welcoming approach to immigrants atoned for the colonial past and created a European liberalism diametrically opposed to the painful memories of Nazi occupation. The Netherlands began to embrace a civic identity that required the rejection of its ethnic identity as exclusionary. The immigrants entering in large numbers from predominantly conservative Muslim countries creates a challenge for both the ethno-cultural and civic identity.

In Hungary, the very vocal rejection of liberal democracy and critique of the EU has been linked to both gemeinschaft and gesellschaft. Advocating illiberal democracy, Prime Minister Victor Orbán (2014) posited that liberal democracies 'will not be able to sustain their world-competitiveness in the following years' and 'today, the stars of international analyses are Singapore, China, India, Turkey, Russia'. The issue of gemeinschaft became more prominent during the refugee/migrant crisis. Orbán accused the EU elites of betraying the cultural and religious traditions of Europe, and offered instead asylum to Europeans oppressed by liberal authoritarianism (DW 2017).

In the Czech Republic, former President Václav Klaus accused the EU elites of attempting to eviscerate traditional society to transition beyond the nation-state. Klaus argued (2017) that 'behind Germany's (and the whole Western Europe's) policies stand the irrational ideologies of multiculturalism, of Europeanism, of humanrightism supplemented by plans to create a new European society and a new European man'. The new Prime Minister, Andrej Babis, also known as the Czech Trump, won the 2017 election by warning against the identity crisis caused by the EU's hostility towards the nation-state and migrants destroying the ethno-cultural make-up of the continent.

In Poland, the right-wing Law and Justice opposition party took power in 2015 on a platform of increasing wages and preserving traditional Catholic values. Rescinding on former pledges to take in refugees, Prime Minister Beata Szydlo decried the 'madness of the Brussels elite' for creating a 'utopia of open borders' and betraying the continent's Christian roots. While in the past it would be impossible for a Polish government to stay in power with such fierce criticism from the EU elites, the Law and Justice party gets its legitimacy from its defence of the traditional and the nation-state (Adekoya 2017).

Germany has remained the main pocket of resistance in Europe to the demise of postmodernism, yet without having anything new to offer as its policies cause apprehension. Merkel's difficulties in establishing a government in 2017 and 2018 could indicate that the bastion of a post-national EU is faltering. The right-wing party, AfD, became the third largest party in the 2017 election on an anti-EU and anti-immigration platform. The shift to the Right resembles the outcome of the 2017 election in Austria, which placed Kurz in power on an anti-immigration platform.

However, the rise of the populist in the US and Europe has compelled the elites to reconsider their stance. The President of the European Council, Donald Tusk (2016) recommended slowing down the assault on the nation-state:

> It is us who today are responsible for confronting reality with all kinds of utopias. A utopia of Europe without nation states, a utopia of Europe without conflicting interests and ambitions, a utopia of Europe imposing its own values on the external world. A utopia of a Euro-Asian unity. Obsessed with the idea of instant and total integration, we failed to notice that ordinary

people, the citizens of Europe do not share our Euro-enthusiasm. Disillusioned with the great visions of the future, they demand that we cope with the present reality better than we have been doing until now.

Summers, Obama's former economic advisor and chief economist for the World Bank, advocated embracing 'responsible nationalism' to counter the rise of populism following Brexit and the rise of Trump. The ability to make meaningful changes to policy is however doubtful as the opposition to the radical liberal philosophy is not deemed to be legitimate, and represents a mere bump in the road that can be transcended.

Conclusion

As Western societies continue to polarise, new 'populist' political groups combatting their own cosmopolitan elites are gradually discovering and establishing a common cause with Russia. Moscow can position itself in a leadership position of an international conservative movement, due to its bold ambition to replenish its gemeinschaft-based civilisation by championing social conservativism and economic nationalism. Russia's attractiveness in the West will be contingent upon clearly establishing itself as a unified state with a dynamic economy, as a model for the West where there are increasingly economies with states. Yet, Russia also suffers from a fragmented community and less competitive society; a principled international conservative movement could denigrate into philosophical cover for an opportunistic and kleptocratic elite.

Conclusion

Cooperation and competition in the post-Western world

The crisis in the Enlightenment project, liberalism, and subsequently Western civilisation is caused by their success rather than their failure. Success led to excesses as the advancement of humanity is measured by ever-increasing rationality and radical individualism that eventually eviscerate the culture that sustains civilisation. A revolt is subsequently unfolding to defend and reproduce Western civilisation. The populists can be conceptualised as classical conservatives that seek to rejuvenate what is lost rather than conserve what still exists. While their instincts push them towards rebalancing the modern and traditional, the ability to articulate and implement a cohesive policy is unlikely. With Russia being seen as an ally to embrace, the question to be asked is: what is the intention and ability to wield its newfound influence?

Liberalism and rationalism are key components of Western civilisation, which have through political pluralism coexisted with the equally important aspects of Western civilisation such as culture, tradition, religion, family, and other distinct institutions. Liberalism is a virtue by freeing the individual from arbitrary authority. Yet, excessive liberalism becomes a vice by liberating the individual from the arbitrary authority of the family, community, religion, the nation-state, and other hierarchical relationships that human beings require for meaning and to organise society. Rationality is similarly a virtue by liberating Man from premodern superstition and elevating the potential of humanity. Albeit, human beings are not completely rational creatures, and excessive rationality corrupts the understanding of human advancement by construing it as the gradual elimination of the irrational. This culminates in growing animosity towards common spirituality, religion, and culture that humans instinctively depend upon. Hence, Western civilisation prospered by embracing liberalism and rationalism, yet condemned itself to decay by self-identifying solely by these values.

Western civilisation flourished with the Enlightenment project and liberal advancements of society, which was balanced by the homogenous ethno-cultural nation-state. Similarly, the benefits of economic liberalism could be enjoyed after establishing geoeconomic dominance by using state intervention to assert control over strategic industries, transportation corridors, and mechanisms for international economic and financial cooperation. Western civilisation advanced due to a balance between conservativism and liberalism. The German rationalisation movement of the economy after the First World War radically altered the organisation of the state and society, which was implemented by the collective West after the Second World War. Political pluralism then began its descent, which intensified further when classical conservativism unravelled in the 1980s. In its place, a bipartisan commitment to neoliberalism policies, unfettered capitalism, and civic identities was established. The demise of communism as the 'end of history' became the victory for liberalism as the last modernist ideology standing. In victory came defeat as liberalism transitioned from an ideology to an uncontested truth, which further radicalised unfettered liberalism under the auspices of globalisation. The protection of traditional values and culture has since become an empty slogan, and economic protectionism naughty words. The postmodernist deconstruction of social structures that provided meaning and order unavoidably fuelled nihilism as a domineering threat, while eroding the foundation for competitiveness in international affairs.

Unconstrained neo-liberalism has decimated classical conservativism to the point there is little to conserve, which gives rise to a new populist political class determined to recreate the past. The family unit cannot be restored by revoking the emancipation of women, and ethno-cultural homogeneity should not be replenished by repression and ethnic cleansing. Western civilisation is therefore at a crossroads as the status quo is untenable, while efforts to bring back a lost past has been the mission of some of the worst regimes in history. The traditional ethos on the liberal Left has been to tear down physical and conceptual walls that divide 'us' and 'them' to promote justice, which has manifested in the flawed morality of globalism and cosmopolitanism. The traditional ethos of the conservative right has been to maintain walls to preserve in-group loyalty, traditions, and respect for authority, which has manifested itself in the morality of nationalism and patriotism.

Understanding the challenges of civilisation requires a renewed exploration of the imperishable and contradictory impulses of human beings that was central in 19th-century European philosophy. These important lessons were replaced by the pernicious ideological modernist absolutism of the 20th century in an attempt to create a new Man liberated from his past. Political and socio-economic policies to advance a rational, calculative, and liberal society must be built on a foundation that recognises the evolutionary 'irrational' instincts that human beings relied on for survival for thousands of years and are represented by the community. Rather than aspiring for an equilibrium between the instinctive and rational, modernist, and postmodern ideology has fostered absolutist extremes that incentivised the mobilisation of an equally radical counter-position. Much like unfettered free trade produces an inclination towards socialism, so will purely civic identities give rise to excessively ethno-cultural identities. In the past the excesses of the Enlightenment produced the counter-Enlightenment movement, while today liberal authoritarianism and postmodernism are fuelling a new class of populists seeking to rediscover romantic nationalism and economic nationalism.

The populist movements sweeping across the West are symptomatic of communities decimated from excessive political and economic liberalism, and declining competitiveness of societies as the geoeconomic foundations for the

West's primacy for the past 500 years is ending. While populist groups instinctively recognise the real crisis in Western civilisation, they do not necessarily have the appropriate response. How do political leaders reach out to what the voters intuitively desire and need, by only employing a language committed solely to the rational? The innate, instinctive, and irrational component of Man is obscure and not easily articulated, which leaves a vacuum that can be easily filled by demagogic and morally disreputable actors. Efforts by the elites to demonise populist movements as inherently xenophobic will inadvertently give a powerful political platform to destabilising and dangerous bigots. When only fascists appear to be willing to defend physical and virtual borders, much of the population will instinctively gravitate towards the fascists.

The West will undergo a turbulent and unpredictable period as it addresses its identity crisis and geoeconomic decline. Sorokin (1941) predicted that the West would undergo a civilisation shift as the sensate era was ending, which organised society on the principle that only the rational and material world is real. The rise of populists introduces the opportunity to return to Sorokin's idealistic/integral culture that harmonises the ideational/spiritual and the sensate/material. However, the populists could also advance ethno-cultural and religious fundamentalism (ideational), or continue down the path of excessive materialism and nihilism (sensate), due to the lack of philosophical depth and the lure a radical counter-positions.

Portraying the neomodernist position of Russia as being shrewdly strategic in order to become a leader for a new ideology and an international conservative movement discounts the domestic problems and historical continuity that are behind Moscow's motivations. The emergence of Putin as a global brand and 'a symbol of an ideological and political alternative to the liberal world order . . . should surely flatter the Russian leader, whose ambitions have never gone so far (Lukyanov 2016). Nonetheless, Russia's response to its domestic challenges has inadvertently made Moscow tap into some very powerful undercurrents raging in the West.

Russia needs to respond to new opportunities and threats in relations with the West. The new political forces emerging can present an opportunity to normalise relations and finally reach a mutually acceptable post-Cold War settlement by ending the division of Europe. For example, Trump's election elevated hopes about redefining relations with the US. Trump expressed great reluctance to finance a global empire, criticised divisive Cold War institutions like NATO as obsolete, and appeared ready to strike a great power bargain with Moscow. Yet, the rise of the populists also brings threats due to unpredictability and instability. The romantic nationalists tend to lack a clear and cohesive philosophical alternative to the elites. It is easy to lose control over the masses as radical and morally questionable political forces can easily corrupt the populist base due to the difficulties of articulating the innate and primordial instincts of Man. It is paradoxical to frame a rational approach to the irrational in human nature that cannot be control. As Haidt argued: 'it's as though some people have a button on their foreheads, and when the button is pushed, they suddenly become intensely focused on defending their in-group, kicking out foreigners and non-conformists, and stamping out dissidents within the group' (Haidt 2016). The populists recognise the need to tear down the existing order, although they are not always clear about what should replace it. Trump's disorderly and inconsistent foreign policy is indicative of the disorder that follows when the former global hegemon comes to terms with its new role in the world. Furthermore, the establishment will fight the populists and consider an equal partnership with Russia to be a betrayal of liberal democratic values. The sabotage of the Trump administration by the intelligence services and military suggests that the deep state that underpins the establishment has enough autonomy to be considered a fourth branch of power.

The main question that should be asked in the West is how Russia will exercise its new influence as an aspiring gemeinschaft-based civilisation? What are Russia's intentions? Will Western decadence result in completely eviscerating the West as a civilisation as Balfour (1908: 58–59) warned, or does Russia intend to assist in rejuvenating the traditional and spiritual in the West? Furthermore, what are Russia's capabilities? Efforts through history to modernise were extremely destructive towards the community, with communism's efforts to industrialise without capitalism especially leading to a purge of nationhood and spirituality. Russia's societal problems are today in many ways worse than the West. Yet, there are indications of Russia moving in the right direction by addressing the root problem rather than succumbing to democratic messianism. Russia's ability to develop a 21st-century Eurasian character will be important to answer these questions. Eurasianism must embrace the opposing impulses of human nature by recognising that the Russian character was not the product of market activity, yet concurrently use the Eurasian geographical expanse to take control over key instruments of geoeconomic power. Russian Eurasianism, much like Chinese neo-Confucianism, would also need to harmonise differences rather than promote global conformity. This entails transitioning Europe from the heart of a Western-centric world peaching liberal democratic universalism, to a distinct civilisation at the inner Western periphery of a Greater Eurasia.

Bibliography

Abbott, L 1902. 'The Rights of Man', *New York Tribune*, 17 January.

Adams, B 1897. *The Law of Civilisation and Decay*, The Macmillian Company, London.

Adams, B 1947[1900]. *America's Economic Supremacy*, Macmillan, New York.

Adams, H 1919. *The Degradation of the Democratic Dogma*, The Macmillian Company, New York.

Adams, J 1814. 'From John Adams to John Taylor, 17 December 1814', *National Archives*, https://founders.archives.gov/documents/Adams/99-02-02-6371 [accessed 4 October 2017].

Adekoya, R 2017. 'Why Poland's Law and Justice Party Remains So Popular', *Foreign Affairs*, 3 November.

Adler, LK and Paterson, TG 1970. 'Red fascism: the merger of Nazi Germany and Soviet Russia in the American image of totalitarianism, 1930's–1950's', *The American Historical Review*, Vol.75, No.4, pp.1046–1064.

Agnew, J and Corbridge, S 2002. *Mastering Space: Hegemony, Territory and International Political Economy*, Routledge, New York.

Airbus 2017. 'Airbus selects Shenzhen for its China Innovation Centre', *Airbus*, 17 November.

Al-Azmeh, A 2012. 'Civilization as a political disposition', *Economy and Society*, Vol.41, No.4, pp.501–512.

Albrechtsen, J 2009. 'Move over, multiculturalism, your time is past', *The Australian*, 22 September.

Alesina, A and Glaeser, EL 2004. *Fighting poverty in the US and Europe: A World of Difference*, Oxford University Press, Oxford.

Alter, C 2015. 'U.N. Says Cyber Violence Is Equivalent to Physical Violence Against Women', *Time*, 25 September.

Andersen, M and Collins, PH 2015. *Race, Class, & Gender: An Anthology*, Nelson Education, New York.

Atlantic Monthly Press, 1921. 'William James to Henry Lee Higginson', *Atlantic Monthly Press*, Boston.

Babiracki, P 2015. *Soviet Soft Power in Poland: Culture and the Making of Stalin's New Empire, 1943–1957*, The University of North Carolina Press, North Carolina.

Babones, S 2018. *The New Authoritarianism: Trump, Populism, and the Tyranny of the Expert Class*, Polity, Oxford. Forthcoming.

Baldwin, DA 1985. *Economic Statecraft*, Princeton University Press, Princeton.

Balfour, A 1908. *Decadence*, Cambridge University Press, London.

Barrett, LF 2017. 'When is Speech Violence?', *The New York Times*, 14 July.

Bartholomew, J 2015. 'I invented "virtue signalling". Now it's taking over the world', *The Spectator*, 10 October.

Baru, S 2012. 'Geo-economics and Strategy', *Survival*, Vol.54, No.3, pp.47–58.

Baumeister, RF 1999. *Evil: Inside human violence and cruelty*, Macmillan, New York.

BBC 2008, 'Emily Maitlis interviewed Nigel Farage MEP', *BBC*, 31 August.

BBC 2014, 'Farage: EU does have "blood on its hands" over Ukraine', *BBC*, 27 March.

Bell, D 1975. 'Ethnicity and Social Change', in Nathan Glazer and Daniel P Moynihan (eds.) *Ethnicity: Theory and Experience*, Harvard University Press, Cambridge.

Bell, D 1976. *The Cultural Contradictions of Capitalism*, Basic Books, New York.

Bell, D 2008. *China's New Confucianism: Politics and Everyday Life in a Changing Society*, Princeton University Press, Princeton.

Bell, D 2009. *Beyond liberal democracy: Political thinking for an East Asian context*, Princeton University Press, Princeton.

Bergsten, CF 2012. 'Why the Euro Will Survive Completing the Continent's Half-Built House', *Foreign Affairs*, Vol.91, No.5, pp.16–22.

Bertalanffy, L 1975. *Perspectives on General System Theory Scientific-Philosophical Studies*, John Wiley & Sons, New York.

Bisaha, N 2004. *Creating East and West: Renaissance Humanists and the Ottoman Turks*, University of Pennsylvania Press, Pennsylvania.

Bishop, B 2017. 'Americans have lost faith in institutions. That's not because of Trump or "fake news" ', *The Washington Post*, 3 March.

Blackwell, WL 2015. *Beginnings of Russian Industrialization, 1800–1860*, Princeton University Press, Princeton.

Bloom, A 2008. *The Closing of the American Mind*, Simon & Schuster, New York.

Bordachev, T 2016. 'Fate of Europe: Return to Reality', *Valdai Discussion Club*, 27 June.

Bowers, CG 1932. *Beveridge and the Progressive Era*, The Literary Guild, Boston.

Bradford, A 2012, 'The Brussels Effect', *Northwestern University Law Review*, Vol.107, No.1, pp.1–67.

Braghiroli, S and Makarychev, A 2016. 'Russia and its supporters in Europe: trans-ideology a la carte', *Southeast European and Black Sea Studies*, Vol.16, No.2, pp.213–233.

Brydan, D 2016. 'Hard right, soft power: fascist regimes and the battle for hearts and mind', *The Conversation*, 20 September.

Buchanan, PJ 2010. *The Death of the West: How Dying Populations and Immigrant Invasions Imperil Our Country and Civilization*, Macmillan, New York.

Buchanan, P 2013. 'Is Putin One of Us?', *Official Website of Patrick J Buchanan*, 17 December.

Buchanan, P 2014. 'Whose Side is God on Now', *Official Website of Patrick J Buchanan*, 4 April.

Buchanan, PJ 2017. 'The US-Saudi Starvation Blockade', *The American Conservative*, 24 November.

Bundesbank 1978. 'EMS: Bundesbank Council meeting with Chancellor Schmidt (assurances on operation of EMS) [declassified 2008]', Bundesbank Archives N2/267, 30 November.

Burckhardt, J 2010[1878]. *The Civilisation of the Renaissance in Italy*, Dover Publications, New York.

Burckhardt, J 1959. *Judgements on history and historians*, George Allen and Unwon, Suffolk.

Burke, E 2012[1790]. *Reflections on the Revolution in France*, Dover Publications, New York.

Burke, E 2012[1796]. *Letters on Regicide Peace*, Liberty Fund, Indianapolis.

Cameron, D 2011. 'PM's speech at Munich Security Conference', *Gov.UK*, 5 February.

Campbell, B and Manning, J 2014. 'Microaggression and Moral Cultures', *Comparative sociology*, Vol.13, No.6, pp.692–726.

Cha, SH 2003. 'Modern Chinese Confucianism: The Contemporary Neo-Confusian Movement and its Cultural Significance', Social *Compass*, Vol.50, No.4, pp.481–491.

Chait, J 2015. 'Not a Very P.C. Thing to Say: How the language police are perverting liberalism', *New York Magazine*, 27 January.

Chang, J, Rynhart, G, and Huynh P 2016. 'ASEAN in Transformation', *International Labour Organisation*, July.

Cheterian, V 2009. 'From reform and transition to "Coloured Revolutions"', *Journal of Communist Studies and Transition Politics*, Vol.25, No.2–3, pp.136–160.

Cillizza, C 2014. 'Watch Americans' trust in each other erode over the last four decades', *The Washington Post*, 31 May.

Clinton, W 1998. 'Commencement Address at Portland State University in Portland', Oregon, The American Presidency Project, 13 June.

Clinton, HR 2017. *What Happened*, Simon and Schuster, New York.

Cohen, BJ 1991. *Crossing Frontiers: Explorations in International Political Economy*, Westview Press, Boulder.

Connolly, C 2008[1948]. *Enemies of Promise*, University of Chicago Press, Chicago.

Connolly, R 2016. 'The Empire Strikes Back: Economic Statecraft and the Securitisation of Political Economy in Russia', *Europe-Asia Studies*, Vol.68, No.4, pp.750–773.

Conrad, J 1996[1899]. *Heart of darkness*, Palgrave Macmillan, London.

Conway, M 2016. 'Obama dismisses Russia as a "weaker country"', *Politico*, 16 December.

Costa, DL and Kahn, ME, 2003. 'Cowards and heroes: Group loyalty in the American Civil War', *The Quarterly Journal of Economics*, Vol.118, No.2, pp.519–548.

Crenshaw, K 1991. 'Mapping the Margins: Intersectionality, Identity Politics, and Violence against Women of Color', *Stanford Law Review*, Vol.43, No.6, pp.1241–1299.

Cunningham, W 1900. *An Essay on Western Civilization in Its Economic Aspects*, Cambridge University Press, Cambridge.

Cunningham, W 2008[1905]. *The Rise and Decline of the Free Trade Movement*, Cosimo Classics, New York.

Davidson, G and Davidson, P 1988. *Economics for A civilized society*, Norton, New York.

Dawkins, R 2004. *A Devil's Chaplain*, Houghton Mifflin Company, New York.

De Bacci, A 2017. 'Vladimir Putin: Only Russian-flagged ships will be allowed to sail future Arctic "Northern Route"', *Russiafeed*, November.

Delk, J 2017. 'Alabama Senate hopeful: "You could say that" America today is evil', *The Hill*, 10 August.

Deneen, PJ 2018. *Why Liberalism Failed*, Yale University Press, London.

Diamond, LJ 1990. 'Three paradoxes of democracy', *Journal of democracy*, Vol.1, No.3, pp.48–60.

Diesen, G 2017. *Russia's Geoeconomic Strategy for a Greater Eurasia*, Routledge, London.

Dostoyevsky, F 1994[1881]. A Writer's Diary: Volume 2 – 1877–1881 [translated by Kenneth Lantz], Northwestern University Press, Illinois.

Dostoyevsky, F 2009[1864]. *Notes From Underground*, translated by Constance Garnett, Hackett Publishing Company, Cambridge.

Du Bois, WEB 1941. 'Neuropa: Hitler's New World Order', *The Journal of Negro Education*, Vol.10, No.3, pp.380–386.

Dugin, A 2012. *The fourth political theory*, Arktos, London.

DW 2017. 'Europeans oppressed by liberalism "welcome" to seek asylum in Hungary', *Deutsche Welt*, 10 February.

Dyer, TG 1992. *Theodore Roosevelt and the Idea of Race*, Louisiana State University Press, Louisiana.

Earle, EM 1943. 'Friedrich List, forerunner of pan-Germanism', *The American Scholar*, Vol.12, No.4, pp.430–443.

Eberlein, B and Grande, E 2005. 'Beyond delegation: transnational regulatory regimes and the EU regulatory state', *Journal of European Public Policy*, Vol.12, No.1, pp.89–112.

Eckes AE 1999. *Opening America's Market: US Foreign Trade Policy since 1776*, University of North Carolina Press, North Carolina.

Elder, M 2010. 'Vladimir Putin's warning shot to liberals: society must have order', *The Guardian*, 16 December.

European Commission, 2010. 'Europe 2020: A Strategy for Smart, Sustainable and Inclusive Growth', *European Commission*, Brussels, 3 March.

Evans-Pritchard, A 2016. 'Euro "house of cards" to collapse, warns ECB prophet', *The Telegraph*, 16 October.

Fagan P 1995. 'The Real Root Causes of Violent Crime: The Breakdown of Marriage, Family, and Community', *The Heritage Foundation*, 17 March.

Feder, JL 2016. 'This is How Steve Bannon Sees The Entire World', *BuzzFeed News*, 16 November.

Ferguson, N 2010. 'In China's Orbit', *The Wall Street Journal*, 18 November.

Ferguson, N 2011. *Civilization: The West and the Rest*, Penguin Books, London.

Fischer, J 2015. 'The Return of the Ugly German', *Project Syndicate*, 23 July.

Fish, MS 2005. *Democracy derailed in Russia: The failure of open politics*, Cambridge University Press, Cambridge.

Foer, F 2017. 'It's Putin's World', *The Atlantic*, March.

Ford, M 2015. *Rise of the Robots: Technology and the Threat of a Jobless Future*, Basic Books, New York.

Freud, S 1963. 'Reflections upon War and Death', in *Character and Culture*, Collier Books, New York.

Freud, S 2015[1930]. *Civilization and Its Discontents*, Broadview Press, Calgary.

Friedman, TL 1998. 'Foreign Affairs; Now a Word from X', *The New York Times*, 2 May.

Friedman, TL and Mandelbaum, M 2012. *That used to be us: How America fell behind in the world it invented and how we can come back*, Picador, New York.

Frum, D 2017. 'The Roots of a Counterproductive Immigration Policy', *The Atlantic*, 28 January.

FT 2017. 'German elections: how the right returned', *Financial Times*, 7 September.

Fukuyama, F 1992. *The End of History and the Last Man*, Hamish Hamilton, London.

Fukuyama, F 1995. 'Confucianism and democracy', *Journal of Democracy*, Vol.6, No.2, pp.20–33.

Fuller, GE 1992. *The democracy trap: the perils of the post-Cold War world*, Penguin Books, New York.

Gadamer, HG 1976. *Philosophical hermeneutics*, University of California Press, Berkeley.

Garrett, G 1961. *Rise of Empire*, Caxton Printers, Idaho.

[handwritten margin note: Where is coming he from?]

German Federal Ministry of Defence, 2011. 'Defence Policy Guidelines: Safeguarding National Interests – Assuming International Responsibility – Shaping Security Together', *German Ministry of Defence*, Berlin, 27 May.

Gibbon, E 1776. *The History of the Decline and Fall of the Roman Empire*, Penguin Books, London.

Gill, G 1995. 'Liberalization and Democratization in the Soviet Union and Russia', *Democratization*, Vol.2, No.3, pp.313–336.

Gill, G 2006. 'A new turn to authoritarian Rule in Russia?', *Democratization*, Vol.13, No.1, pp.58–77.

Gillespie, DC 1989. 'History, Politics, and the Russian Peasant: Boris Mozhaev and the Collectivization of Agriculture', *The Slavonic and East European Review*, Vol.67, No.2, pp. 183–210.

Gilpin, R 2011. *Global Political Economy: Understanding the International Economic Order*, Princeton University Press, Princeton.

Glazer, N 1983. *Ethnic Dilemmas: 1964–82*, Harvard University Press, Cambridge.

Glazer, N 1993. 'Is Assimilation Dead?', *The Annals of the American Academy of Political and Social Science*, Vol.530, pp.122–136.

Glazer, N, Moynihan, DP and Schelling, CS 1975. *Ethnicity: Theory and experience*, Harvard University Press, Cambridge.

Glazer, N and Moynihan, DP 1963. *Beyond the Melting Pot: The Negroes, Puerto Ricans, Jews, Italians, and Irish of New York City*, MIT Press, Cambridge.

Gleason, P 1980. *American Identity and Americanization, in Harvard Encyclopedia of American Ethnic Groups*, Harvard University Press, Cambridge.

Glubb, J 1976. *The Fate of Empires and Search for Survival*, William Blackwood & Sons Ltd, Edinburgh.

Gore, A 2013. *Earth in the balance: forging a new common purpose*, Routledge, New York.

Goodwin, M and Raines, T 2017. 'What Do Europeans Think About Muslim Immigration?', *Chatham House*, 7 February.

Gray, J 1995. *Enlightenment's Wake: Politics and Culture at the Close of the Modern Age*, Routledge, London.

Greenhouse, S 2016. 'Autonomous vehicles could cost America 5 million jobs. What should we do about it?', *LA Times*, 22 September.

Griswold, AW 1946. 'The Agrarian Democracy of Thomas Jefferson', *American Political Science Review*, Vol.40, No.4, pp.657–681.

Guizot, F 2013[1828]. *The History of Civilisation in Europe*, D. Appleton, New York.

Habermas, J 1998. 'Die postnationale Konstellation und die Zukunft der Demokratie', *Blätter für deutsche und internationale Politik*, Vol.7, No.98, pp.804–817.

Habermas, J 2015. *The Philosophical Discourse of Modernity*, Polity Press, Cambridge.

Haidt, J 2012. *The righteous mind: Why good people are divided by politics and religion*, Penguin Books, London.

Haidt, J 2016. 'When and Why Nationalism Beats Globalism', *The American Interest*, 7 October.

Hale, H 2010. 'Eurasian polities as hybrid regimes: The case of Putin's Russia', *Journal of Eurasian studies*, Vol.1, No.1, pp.33–41.

Hannan, D 2013. *Inventing freedom: How the English-speaking peoples made the modern world*, Harper Collins, New York.

Harman, O 2010. *The price of altruism: George Price and the search for the origins of kindness*, W.W. Norton, New York.

Harris, S 2011. 'Jewcy's Big Question: Why Are Atheists So Angry?', *Huffington Post*, 25 May.

Hartz, L 1955. *The Liberal Tradition in America*, Harcourt, New York.

Hawkins, M 1997. *Social Darwinism in European and American thought, 1860–1945: nature as model and nature as threat*, Cambridge University Press, Cambridge.

Haxthausen, B 1856. *The Russian Empire: Its People, Institutions and Resources*, Frank Cass and Company Limited, Oxon.

Heather, P 2005. *The fall of the Roman Empire: A New History of Rome and the Barbarians*, Oxford University Press, Oxford.

Heckscher, E 1955. *Mercantilism*, George Allen and Unwin, London.

Heidegger, M 2010[1927]. *Being and time*, State University of New York Press, Albany.

Heidegger, M 2014[1953]. *Introduction to metaphysics*, Yale University Press, London.

Helm, T 2007. 'Giscard: EU Treaty is the constitution rewritten', *The Telegraph*, 29 October.

Henley, J 2017. 'Le Pen, Putin, Trump: a disturbing axis, or just a mutual admiration society?', *The Guardian*, 29 April.

Herder, JG 2002[1772]. *Philosophical writings* [translated and edited by Michael N Forster], Cambridge University Press, Cambridge.

Herder, JG 1966[1800]. *Ideas upon Philosophy and the History of Mankind*, Bergman Publishers, New York.

Herman, A 1997. *The Idea of Decline in Western History*, The Free Press, New York.

Herman, E 2016. 'Amazon's Grocery Would Eliminate Thousands Of Jobs', *Forbes*, 7 December.

Hirschman, A 1945. *National power and the structure of foreign trade*, University of California Press, Berkeley.

Hobsbawm, E 1996. 'Identity Politics and the Left', *Institute of Education*, London, 2 May.

Hobsbawm, E 2007. *Globalisation, Democracy and Terrorism*, Little Brown, London.

Hont, I 2015. *Politics in Commercial Society*, Harvard University Press, London.

Hood, SJ 1998. 'The myth of Asian-style democracy', *Asian Survey*, Vol.38, No.9, pp.853–866.

Hoover, H 1963. *Addresses upon the American Road, 1950–1955*, Stanford University Press, Stanford.

Horvath, R 2011. 'Apologist of Putinism? Solzhenitsyn, the Oligarchs, and the Specter of Orange Revolution', *The Russian Review*, Vol.70, No.2, pp.300–318.

Hsu, H 2009. 'The End of White America', *The Atlantic*, January/February.

Hughes, M 2004. 'The English Slavophile: WJ Birkbeck and Russia', *The Slavonic and East European Review*, Vol.82, No.3, pp.680–706.

Huntington, SP 1993a. 'The clash of civilizations?', *Foreign affairs*, Vol.72, No.3, pp.22–49.

Huntington, SP 1993b. 'If not civilizations, what? Paradigms of the post-cold war world', *Foreign affairs*, Vol.72, No.5, pp.186–194.

Huntington, SP 1993c. 'Why international primacy matters', *International security*, Vol.17, No.4, pp.68–83.

Huntington, SP 2004. 'Dead Souls: The Denationalization of the American Elite', *The National Interest*, 1 March.

Jung, CG 1969. *Psychology and Religion: West and East*, Pantheon Books, New York.

Jung, CG 1973. *Letters Volume 1*, Routledge, London.

Kaczynski, T 1995. 'Industrial society and its future', *Washington Post*, 19 September.

Karaganov, S 2006. 'Dangerous Relapses', *Russia in Global Affairs*, 8 May.

Karaganov, S 2016. 'Global Challenges and Russia's Foreign Policy', Strategic Analysis, Vol.40, No.6, pp.461–473.

Karaganov, S 2017a. '2016 – A Victory of Conservative Realism', *Russia in Global Affairs*, 13 February.

Karaganov, S 2017b. 'Russia's Victory, new Concert of Nations', *Russia in Global Affairs*, 31 March.

Kaufmann, E 2000. 'Ethnic or civic nation? Theorizing the American case', *Canadian Review of Studies in Nationalism*, Vol.27, No.1/2, pp.133–155.

Kaufmann, E 2004. *The Rise and Fall of Anglo-America: The Decline of Dominant Ethnicity in the United States*, Harvard University Press, Cambridge.

Kaviraj, S and Khilnani, S 2001. *Civil society: history and possibilities*, Cambridge University Press, Cambridge.

Keating, D 2012. 'Commissioner Urges EU to face down Russia on energy', *Politico*, 10 October.

Kendall, TD and Tamura, R 2010. 'Unmarried fertility, crime, and social stigma', *The Journal of Law and Economics*, Vol.53, No.1, pp.185–221.

Kennan, GF 1993. *Around the Cragged Hill: A Personal and Political Philosophy*, Norton, New York.

Kennan, GF 2014. *The Kennan Diaries*, W. W. Norton & Company, New York.

Kennedy, P 1987. *The rise and fall of the great powers*, Random House, New York.

Kennedy, C 2013. 'The Manichean temptation: Moralising rhetoric and the invocation of evil in US foreign policy', *International Politics*, Vol.50, No.5, pp.623–638.

Khomyakov, A 1895. *Russia and the English church during the last fifty years*, Rivington, London.

Kim, SY 2017. 'Whither Developmentalism after Democratisation?', in TJ Cheng and YH Chu, *Routledge Handbook on Democratization in East Asia*, Routledge, London, pp.457–470.

King, D 2009. *Making Americans: Immigration, race, and the origins of the diverse democracy*, Harvard University Press, Cambridge.

Kissinger, HA 1968. 'The White Revolutionary: Reflections on Bismarck', *Daedalus*, Vol.77, No.3, pp.888–924.

Klages, L 1981[1929]. *Der Geist als Widersacher der Seele*, Bouvier Verlag Herbert Grundmann, Bonn.

Klaus, V 2017. 'EU elites aim to destroy European society as we know it', *Valdai Discussion Club*, 23 January.

Kortunov, A 2017a. 'False Conflict: Universalism and Identity', *Valdai Discussion Club*, 11 October.

Kortunov, A. 2017b. From Post-Modernism to Neo-Modernism, Russia in Global Affairs, 13 February.

Krastev, I 2017. *After Europe*, University of Pennsylvania Press, Philadelphia.

Krugman, P 2007. 'Trouble With Trade', *The New York Times*, 28 December.

Kukathas, C and Pettit, P 1990. *Rawls: a theory of justice and its critics*. Stanford University Press, Stanford.

Kuzio, T 2002. 'The myth of the civic state: a critical survey of Hans Kohn's framework for understanding nationalism', *Ethnic and Racial studies*, Vol.25, No.1, pp.20–39.

Kymlicka, W 1996. *Multicultural citizenship: A liberal theory of minority rights*, Clarendon Press, Oxford.

Kymlicka, W 2002. *Contemporary Political Philosophy: An Introduction*, Oxford University Press, Oxford.

Laqueur, W 2007. *The last days of Europe: Epitaph for an old continent*, Macmillan, New York.

Lasch, C 1979. *The culture of narcissism: American life in an age of diminishing expectations*, WW Norton, New York.

Lasch, C 1996. *The Revolt of the Elites and the Betrayal of Democracy*, W.W. Norton & Company, New York.

Lavrov, S 2012. 'Russia in the 21st-Century World of Power', *Russia in Global Affairs*, 27 December.

Leontiev, K 2014[1885]. *East, Russia and the Slavs [Vostok, Rossiya i slavyanstvo]*, T.1, Moscow.

Lijphart, A 1969. 'Consociational Democracy', *World Politics*, Vol.21, No.2, pp.207–225.

Lind, M 1995. *The Next American Nation: The New Nationalism and the Fourth American Revolution*, The Free Press, New York.

Lindsay, T 2016. 'A Marxist Education In "Hypersensitivity" As A Cause Of Violence On American Campuses', *Forbes*, 27 December.

Lippman, W 2008[1915]. *The Stakes of Diplomacy*, Transaction, New Brunswick.

Lipset, SM 1996. *American Exceptionalism: A Double-Edged Sword*, W.W. Norton & Co, New York.

List, F 1827. *Outlines of American Political Economy*, Samuel Parker, Philadelphia.

List, F 1885. *The National System of Political Economy*, Longmans, Green & Company, London.

Lossky, N 1952. *History of Russian Philosophy*, George Allen and Unwin, London.

Lukyanov, F 2013. 'Why Russia's Soft Power is Too Soft', *Russia in Global Affairs*, 1 February.

Lukyanov, F 2016. 'Putin is Giving America a Taste of its Own Medicine', *Russia in Global Affairs*, 19 December,

Lundestad, G 2003. *The United States and Western Europe since 1945: from "empire" by invitation to transatlantic drift*, Oxford University Press, Oxford.

Luttwak, E 1990. 'From Geopolitics to Geo-economics: Logic of Conflict, Grammar of Commerce', *National Interest*, No.20, pp.17–23.

Luttwak, E 1993a. 'Why Fascism is the Wave of the Future', *London Review of Books*, Vol.16, No.7, pp.3–6.

Luttwak, E 1993b. *Endangered American Dream*, Simon and Schuster, New York.

Luttwak, E 1995. 'The National Prospect', *Commentary Magazine*, 1 November.

Luttwak, E 1999. *Turbo capitalism*, HarperCollins Publishers, New York.

Lyotard, JF 1984. *The postmodern condition: A Report on Knowledge*, University of Minnesota Press, Minneapolis.

Machiavelli, N 2015[1532]. *The Prince*, Oxford University Press, Oxford.

Mackinder, H 1904. 'The Geographical Pivot of History', *The Geographical Journal*, Vol.170, No.4, pp.421–444.

Mann, M 2005. *The dark side of democracy: explaining ethnic cleansing*, Cambridge University Press, Cambridge.

Marcuse, H 1965. *A Critique of Pure Tolerance*, Beacon Press, Boston.

Matthias, P et.al. 1943. *The Cambridge Economic History of Europe*, Cambridge University Press, Cambridge.

May, T 2016. 'Theresa May's conference speech', *The Telegraph*, 5 October.

McCarthy, T 2016. 'Obama press conference: Russia hacks, US election, China and Syria addressed – as it happened', *The Guardian*, 17 December.

McDougall, WA 1998. 'Religion in Diplomatic History', *Foreign Policy Research Institute*, 2 March.

Mearshheimer J 2009. 'Reckless States and Realism', *International Relations*, Vol.23, No.2, pp.241–256.

Mearsheimer, JJ and Walt, SM 2016. 'The Case for Offshore Balancing', *Foreign Affairs*, Vol.95, No.4, pp.70–83.

Medvedev, D 2009. 'Go Russia!' [Rossiya Vpered!], *Gazeta*, 10 September.

Mendras, M 2012. *Russian Politics: The Paradox of a Weak State*, Columbia University Press, California.

Merry, RW 2005. *Sands of Empire*, Simon & Schuster, New York.

Mezhuyev, B 2017. ' "Island Russia" and Russia's Identity Politics', *Russia in Global Affairs*, 6 June.

Mills, CW 1951. *White collar: The American Middle Classes*, Oxford University Press, Oxford.

Mirsky, DS 1927. 'The Eurasian Movement', *The Slavonic Review*, Vol.6, No.17, pp.311–320.

Moses, AD 2004. *Genocide and Settler Society: Frontier violence and stolen indigenous children in Australian history*, Berghahn Books, New York.

Mott, WH 1997. *The Economic Basis of Peace: Linkages Between Economic Growth and International Conflict*, Greenwood Publishing Group, Westport.

Moyo, D 2011. *How the West was Lost: Fifty Years of Economic Folly – and the Stark Choices Ahead*, Penguin, London.

Murray, C 2012. *Coming Apart: The State of White America, 1960–2010*, Crown Forum, New York.

Murray, D 2017. *The Strange Death of Europe: Immigration, Identity, Islam*, Bloomsbury Publishing, London.

Neef, C 2016. 'We Are Smarter, Stronger and More Determined', *Spiegel*, 13 July.

Neumann, IB 2008. 'Russia as a great power, 1815–2007', *Journal of International Relations and Development*, Vol.11, No.2, pp.128–151.

Nietzsche, F 1967. *The Will to Power*, Random House, New York.

Noack, R and Birnbaum, M 2017, 'The leading French presidential candidates Emmanuel Macron and Marine Le Pen, in their own words', *The Washington Post*, 23 April.

Nolan Jr, JL 2016. *What They Saw in America*, Cambridge University Press, Cambridge.

Nowicki, A 2013. *Lost Violent Souls*, Counter-Currents Publishing, San Francisco.

NPR 2007. Political Scientist: Does Diversity Really Work?, *National Public Radio*, 15 August.

Nye, J 1990. 'Think Again: Soft Power', *Foreign Policy*, 23 February.

Nye, JS 2004. 'Soft Power: The Means to Success in World Politics', Public Affairs, New York.

Obama, B 2016. 'The TPP would let America, not China, lead the way on global trade', *The Washington Post*, 2 May.

Olney, R 1895. 'Richard Olney to Thomas F. Bayard', Papers Relating to the Foreign Relations of the United States, with the Annual Message of the President, Transmitted to Congress, Washington Government Printing Office, 2 December.

Orbán, V 2014. 'Full text of Viktor Orbán's speech at Băile Tuşnad (Tusnádfürdő) of 26 July 2014', *The Budapest Beacon*, 26 July.

Padoa-Schioppa, T 2004. *The Euro and Its Central Bank: Getting United After the Union*, MIT Press, Cambridge.

Page, SE 2008. *The difference: How the power of diversity creates better groups, firms, schools, and societies*, Princeton University Press. Princeton.

Paravicini, G 2017. 'Angela Merkel: Europe must take "our fate" into own hands', *Politico*, 28 May.

Patterson, HO 1993. 'The Nature, Causes, and Implications of Ethnic Identification' in M Walzer, and C Fried, C (eds.), *Minorities: Community and Identity*, Springer, Berlin.

Peterson, JB 2007. 'A Psycho-ontological Analysis of Genesis 2–6', *Archive for the Psychology of Religion*, Vol.29, No.1, pp.87–2007.

Peterson, JB 2018. *12 Rules for Life: An Antidote to Chaos*, Penguin Random House, Toronto.

Plato 2016, *The Republic*, translated by Benjamin Jowett, Devoted Publishing, Ontario.

Polanyi, K 1957. *The great transformation*, Beacon Press, Boston.

Polyakova, A 2014. 'Strange Bedfellows: Putin and Europe's Far Right', *World Affairs*, September/October.

Posen, B 1993. 'The Security Dilemma and Ethnic Conflict', *Survival*, Vol.35, No.1, pp.27–47.

Putin, V 2005. 'State of the Nation Address', *Government of the Russian Federation*, 25 April.

Putin, V 2011. Prime Minister Vladimir Putin chairs a meeting of the organising committee for the celebration of Pyotr Stolypin's 150th birthday anniversary, *Government of the Russian Federation*, 13 July.

Putin, V 2012, 'Russia and the Changing World', *RT*, 27 February.

Putin, V 2013a. Meeting of the Valdai International Discussion Club, *Government of the Russian Federation*, 19 September. Available at http://en.kremlin.ru/events/president/news/19243 [accessed 12 December 2017].

Putin, V 2013b. Presidential Address to the Federal Assembly, President of Russia, 12 December. Available at http://en.kremlin.ru/events/president/news/19825 [accessed 17 December 2017].

Putnam, RD 1995. 'Bowling alone: America's declining social capital', *Journal of Democracy*, Vol.6, No.1, pp.65–78.

Putnam, RD 2007. 'E pluribus unum: Diversity and community in the twenty-first century the 2006 Johan Skytte Prize Lecture', *Scandinavian Political Studies*, Vol.30, No.2, pp.137–174.

Putnam, RD and Campbell, DE 2010. *American grace: How religion divides and unites us*, Simon and Schuster, New York.

Quigley, C 1961. *The Evolution of Civilisations: A Historical Analysis*, Liberty Press, Indianapolis.

Quigley, C 1966. *Tragedy and Hope*, Macmillan, New York.

Ravven, HM 2013. *The Self Beyond Itself: An Alternative History of Ethics, the New Brain Sciences, and the Myth of Free Will*, The New Press, New York.

Raza, W 2007. 'European Union Trade Politics: Pursuit of Neo-Mercantilism in Different Flora', in W Blaas and J Becker (eds.), *Strategic Arena Switching in International Trade Negotiations,* Ashgate, Hampshire, pp. 67–96.

RBK 2013, Expert: Vladimit Putin became the leader of world conservativism [Ekspert: Vladimir Putin stal liderom mirovovo konservatizma], *RBK*, 10 December.

Reagan, R 1984. 'Remarks at an Ecumenical Prayer Breakfast in Dallas, Texas', *Reagan Library*, 23 August.

Reich, RB 1991. *The Work of Nations: Preparing ourselves for 21st Century Capitalism*, Knopf, New York.

Reilly, B 2007. 'Democratization and Electoral Reform in the Asia-Pacific Region Is There an "Asian Model" of Democracy?', *Comparative Political Studies*, Vol.40, No.11, pp.1350–1371.

Richardson, B 2016. 'Christmas vacation, "round of golf" are microaggressions at UNC', *The Washington Times*, 26 June.

Robertson, R 2012. 'Globalisation or glocalisation?', *The Journal of International Communication*, Vol.18, No.2, pp.191–208.

Rodrik, D 1997. 'Has globalization gone too far?', *California Management Review*, Vol.39, No.3, pp.29–53.

Rodrik, D 2012. *The globalization paradox: why global markets, states, and democracy can't coexist*, Oxford University Press, Oxford.

Roe, P 2004. *Ethnic violence and the societal security dilemma*, Routledge, London.

Rorty, R 1998. *Achieving our country: Leftist thought in twentieth-century America*, Harvard University Press.

Rorty, R 1999. *Philosophy and social hope*, Penguin Books, London.

Russian Federation 2015, Plenary session of the 19th St Petersburg International Economic Forum, 19 June.

Rustow, DA 1970. 'Transitions to democracy: Toward a dynamic model', *Comparative politics*, Vol.2, No.3, pp.337–363.

Rutland, P and Kazantsev, A 2016. 'The limits of Russia's "soft power"', *Journal of Political Power*, Vol.9, No.3, pp.395–413.

Sagan, C 1996. *Demon-Haunted World: Science as a Candle in the Dark*, Ballantine Books, New York.

Sakwa, R 2010a. 'The dual state in Russia', *Post-Soviet Affairs*, Vol.26, No.3, pp. 185–206.

Sakwa, R 2010b. *The crisis of Russian democracy: the dual state, factionalism and the Medvedev succession*, Cambridge University Press, Cambridge.

Sander, TH and Putnam, RD 2010. 'Still Bowling Alone? The Post–9/11 Split', *Journal of Democracy*, Vol.21, No.1, pp.9–16.

Saramago, J 2005. *The Double*, Vintage, London.

Saul, S 2016. 'Campuses Cautiously Train Freshmen Against Subtle Insults', *The New York Times*, 6 September.

Schmitt, C 2008[1932]. *The Concept of the Political*, University of Chicago Press. Chicago.

Schmoller, G 1897. *The Mercantile System and its Historical Significance*, Macmillan, London.

Schrag, P 1971. *Decline of the WASP*, Simon and Schuster, New York.

Schweitzer, A 1949. *The philosophy of civilization*, Prometheus Books, New York.

Shorten, R 2012. *Modernism and totalitarianism: rethinking the intellectual sources of Nazism and Stalinism, 1945 to the present*, Palgrave Macmillan, London.

Shulevitz, J 2015. 'In College and Hiding From Scary Ideas', *The New York Times*, 21 March.

Simmel, G 1971[1903]. *The Metropolis and Mental Life*, University of Chicago Press.

Smith, RM 1997. *Civic Ideals: Conflicting Visions of Citizenship in U.S. History*, Yale University Press, New Haven.

Sokal, A and Bricmont, J 1998. *Intellectual Impostures: Postmodern Philosophers' Abuse of Science*, Profile Books, London.

Solzhenitsyn, A 1978. 'The Exhausted West', *Harvard Magazine*, July–August.

Solzhenitsyn, A 1986. *Warning to the West*, Macmillan, London.

Sorokin, PA 1941. *The Crisis of Our Age*, E.P. Dutton, New York.

Sorokin, PA 1964. *The Basic Trends of Our Time*, Rowman & Littlefield, Maryland.

Sowell, T 1995. *The Vision of the Anointed. Self-Congratulation as a Basis for Social Policy*, Basic Books, New York.

Sowell, T 2002. *A Conflict of Visions: Ideological Origins of Political Struggles*, Basic Books, New York.

Spengler, O 1991[1922]. 'The Two Faces of Russia and Germany's Eastern Problems', *Politische Schriften*, Munich, 14 February.

Spengler, O 1991. *The decline of the West*, Oxford Paperbacks, Oxford.

Spolaore, E 2013. *What is European integration really about? A political guide for economists*, no.w19122, National Bureau of Economic Research.

Stalenheim, P, Perdomo, C, and Skons, E 2008. 'Military Expenditure', *SIPRI Yearbook*.

Stenhouse, L 1971. 'The humanities curriculum project: The rationale', *Theory into Practice*, Vol.10, No.3, pp.154–162.

Stenner, K 2005. *The authoritarian dynamic*, Cambridge University Press, Cambridge.

Stevenson RL 2004[1886]. *The Strange Case of Dr. Jekyll and Mr. Hyde*, The Collector's Library, London.

Steuart J 1770. *An Inquiry into the Principles of Political Economy*, J.J. Tourneisen, Dublin.

Stiglitz, J 2016. *The Euro: And its Threat to the Future of Europe*, Penguin Books, London.

Stockhammer, E 2014. 'The Euro crisis and contradictions of neoliberalism in Europe', *Post Keynesian Economics Study Group*, Working Paper 1401, pp.1–18.

Summers, L 2016. 'How to embrace nationalism responsibly', *The Washington Post*, 10 July.

Szabo, SF 2015. *Germany, Russia, and the rise of Geo-Economics*, Bloomsbury Publishing, London.

Szlajfer A 2012. *Economic Nationalism and Globalization: Lessons from Latin America and Central Europe*, Brill, Leiden.

Tainter, J 1990. *The Collapse of Complex Societies*, Cambridge University Press, Cambridge.

Tanji, M and Lawson, S 1997. ' "Democratic Peace" and "Asian Democracy": A Universalist-Particularist Tension', *Alternatives: Global, Local, Political*, Vol.22, No.1, pp.135–155.

Taylor, S 2009. 'Klaus Provokes walk-out in the Parliament', *Politico*, 19 February.

Thompson, WR 1992. 'Dehio, Long Cycles, and the Geohistorical Context of Structural Transition', *World Politics*, Vol.45, No.1, pp.127–152.

Thornton, BS 2008. *Decline and Fall: Europe's Slow-Motion Suicide*, Encounter Books, New York.

Tocqueville, A 1945[1839]. *Democracy in America*, Knopf, New York.

Todd, J 2016. 'Safer to stand alone once more?', in GE Barstad, A Hjelde, S Kvam, A Parianou, and J Todd (eds.), *Language and Nation: Crossroads and Connections*, Waxmann, Munster, pp.83–104.

Tönnies, F 1957[1887]. *Community and society*, Dover Publications, New York.

Toynbee, JA 1946. *Study of history*, Oxford University Press, Oxford.

Tsymbursky, V 1993. 'Ostrov Rossiya: Perspektivy rossiyskoy geopolitiki' (Island Russia: Perspectives on Russian geopolitics, *Polis*, Issue 5, pp.11–17.

Tucker, RW and Hendrickson, DC 1992. *Empire of liberty: the statecraft of Thomas Jefferson*, Oxford University Press, Cambridge.

Turner, FJ 2008[1893]. *The significance of the frontier in American history*, Penguin Books, London.

Tusk, D 2016. Speech by President Donald Turk at the event marking the 40th anniversary of European People Party (EEP), *European Council*, 30 May.

US Treasury 2013. 'Report to Congress on International Economic and Exchange Rate Policies', *US Department of the Treasury Office of International Affairs*, 30 October.

Van Tyne, CH 1927. *England and America*, Cambridge University Press, New York.

Vico, G 2002[1725]. *Scienza nuova, The First New Science*, translated by Leon Pompa, Cambridge University Press, Cambridge.

Villasenor, J 2017. 'Views among college students regarding the First Amendment: Results from a new survey', *Brooking Institute*, 18 September.

Voegelin, E 1974. 'Reason: The classic experience', *The Southern Review*, Vol.10, No.2, p.237–264.

Wæver, O 1993. *Identity, migration and the new security agenda in Europe*, Pinter, London.

Waltz, K 1979. *Theory of International Politics*, Waveland Press, Illinois.

Wax, A and Alexander, L 2017. 'Paying the price for breakdown of the country's bourgeois culture', *The Inquirer*, 9 August.

Weber, M 1924a. *Economy and society: An outline of interpretive sociology*, University of California Press, California.

Weber, M 1924b. *Gesammelte Aufsditze zur Soziologie und Sozialpolitik*, Mohr, Tübingen.

Weber, M 1950. 'The Social Causes of the Decay of Ancient Civilization', *The Journal of General Education,* Vol.5, No.1, pp.75–88.

Weber, M 1958. *The Protestant Ethic and the Spirit of Capitalism*, Scribner, New York.

Welk, W 1938. *Fascist Economic Policy*, Harvard University Press, Cambridge.

Werner, RA 2015, 'Are sanctions making Russia stronger?', *The Japan Times*, 21 October.

Whitman, A 1969. 'Lindbergh Traveling Widely as Conservationist', *The New York Times*, 23 June.

Wiebe, RH 1967. *The search for order, 1877–1920*, Hill and Wang, New York.

Wilcox, AB and Menon, V 2017. 'No, Republicans Aren't Hypocrites on Family Values', *Politico*, 28 November.

Williams, WA 2011. *The contours of American history*, Verso Books, New York.

Williams, WE 2015. 'The True Black Tragedy: Illegitimacy Rate of Nearly 75%', *CNS News*, 19 May.

Wolters, E 2013. 'Noam Chomsky calls Jacques Lacan a "charlatan" ', *Critical Theory*, 28 February.

Wood, N 1991. *Cicero's Social and Political Thought*, University of California Press, Berkeley.

Yack, B 1996. 'The myth of the civic nation', *Critical Review*, Vol.10, No.2, pp.193–211.

Yong, E 2012. 'The Where of What: How Brains Represent Thousands of Objects', *National Geographic*, 19 December.

Zakaria, F 1997. 'The rise of illiberal democracy', *Foreign Affairs*, Vol.76, No.6, pp.22–43.

Index

neorealism, 19
the Netherlands, 180–1
New Romanticism, 172–4
Nietzsche, Friedrich, 22–3, 42, 83
nihilism: and the decline of civilisations,
    22–3, 43, 48, 169; of postmodernism,
    75–6
North American Free Trade Agreement
    (NAFTA), 123
Nowicki, Andy, 26–7

Obama, Barack, 6, 84, 170, 179
Olney, Richard, 44
Orbán, Victor, 181
O'Sullivan, John L., 44
the Other: in Ancient Greece, 166; and
    ethno-cultural identities, 56; in fascism,
    25; and identity politics, 81, 82;
    normative threat from, 172; and the
    order/chaos struggle, 35; political
    differentiation of, 57, 60; in relation to
    patriotism, 60; in the Roman Empire,
    166–7; Russia as, 174–6

patriotism, 60
peripheral gemeinschaft-based civilisation,
    164
Pettit, P, 28
Plato, 15, 17, 20, 29, 76, 137
Poland, 181
Polanyi, Karl, 30–1
political liberalism, 29–30
political pluralism, 53
politics: classical realism and, 18–19;
    disillusionment with liberalism, 1, 2;
    identity politics, 80–3, 139, 171;
    political communities, 59–60; political
    radicalism, 173, 174; secessionist
    movements, 4; virtue signalling, 84–5
populism: and the detached establishment,
    173–4; in Europe, 179–82; rise of, 2,
    184–5; and support for Russian
    conservatism, 4–5, 180; in the United
    States, 176–9
postmodernism: in American university
    campuses, 86–8; concept of, 73, 74–5;
    criticism of, 76; deconstruction of the
    international system, 88–90;
    deconstruction of metanarratives, 75;
    hostility towards Western civilisation,
    75; and identity groups, 82;
    intersectionality, 84; neomodernism as
    answer to, 148; as nihilistic, 75–6;
    oppressor-victim dichotomy, 75, 83–5,

87; Russian opposition to, 150–1; slave
    morality, 83; tolerance and mini-
    narratives, 75, 76–8
premodernism, 73
proletariat: elites/internal proletariat rift in
    the US, 176–7; external proletariat, 164;
    internal proletariat, 164; schism from
    the elite, 42–3, 48–9, 116
Putin, Vladimir: definition of soft power,
    144; dictatorship of law, 157; on
    economic determinism, 162; Island
    Russia theory, 140–1; on liberalism,
    153; on the new Russia, 139–40;
    opposition to postmodernism, 150–1;
    protectionism, 160; Russian
    conservatism, 176, 178–9, 185
Putnam, RD, 67

Quigley, Carroll, 39, 47, 48
Qutb, Sayyid, 25–6

rationalism, 80, 131, 148, 155, 165, 175,
    183–4
Reagan, Ronald, 114, 179
reason: culture/rational society conflict,
    39–40; dialectical relationship with
    chaos, 47–8; imagination/reason cycle
    of civilisations, 37–8; rational/irrational
    desires of Man, 6, 16–17, 20–5
Reich, RB, 118
religion: absence of and moral decline, 22–3,
    24, 25–7, 154; absence of civilisational
    collapse, 66; Christian values in American
    society, 62, 65–6; Christianity after the
    Roman Empire, 167; Christianity in
    China, 68–9; during the communist era,
    138–9; as defence against gesellschaft,
    169; and the emerging nation-state, 59;
    and the fear of chaos, 40–1; genesis
    stories, 35–6; Islam, 69–70, 165, 169; and
    national identity formation, 59, 68–70;
    nature vs. society struggle, 35–6; political
    Islam, 69–70; role in community, 21–2;
    the Russian Orthodox Church, 59, 153–4,
    175; secularisation during the
    Enlightenment, 21
Rodrik, D, 117, 120
Roman Empire, 166–7
romantic nationalism: in America, 176–9;
    concept of, 24, 60; within Eurasianism,
    152–4; and populist movements, 184–5;
    re-emergence of, 171–4
Romanticism, 24, 174–5
Roosevelt, Theodore, 44, 106

Made in the USA
Columbia, SC
21 June 2021